Voice of a *Voyage*

Rediscovering the World
During a Ten-year Circumnavigation

Voice of a Voyage

Rediscovering the World
During a Ten-year Circumnavigation

For Betsy,
friend, sailor, chauffeur,
bit back to the first—Forward!
Thank you!
Fair winds (from the right direction),
Doann
April 2015

Doann Houghton-Alico

SUNSTONE
PRESS

SANTA FE

Sunstone books may be purchased for educational, business, or sales promotional use.
For information please write: Special Markets Department, Sunstone Press,
P.O. Box 2321, Santa Fe, New Mexico 87504-2321.

Book and Cover design › Vicki Ahl
Body typeface › Adobe Caslon Pro
Printed on acid-free paper
∞
eBook 978-1-61139-276-0

Library of Congress Cataloging-in-Publication Data

Houghton-Alico, Doann.
    Voice of a voyage : rediscovering the world during a ten-year circumnavigation / by Doann Houghton-Alico.
        pages cm
    Includes bibliographical references.
    ISBN 978-0-86534-990-2 (softcover : alk. paper)
    1. Houghton-Alico, Doann--Travel. 2. Voyages around the world. 3. Sailors--United States--Biography.
    4. Women sailors--United States--Biography. I. Title.
    GV810.92.H68A3 2014
    797.1092--dc23
    [B]
                                    2014011480

WWW.SUNSTONEPRESS.COM
SUNSTONE PRESS / POST OFFICE BOX 2321 / SANTA FE, NM 87504-2321 /USA
(505) 988-4418 / ORDERS ONLY (800) 243-5644 / FAX (505) 988-1025

Dedicated to the oceans and seas of the world

Contents

Acknowledgments

*A*lthough this is my story, and I am totally responsible for its contents, it could not be told nor could it have happened without the assistance of many people. I am eternally grateful to my husband, Wayne Edgar, for introducing me to the undersea world that can only be witnessed when scuba diving. Also, I could not possibly have done this voyage without him and our special yacht, S/V *Bali Ha'i III*. My thanks to him for sharing my love of adventure and sailing.

My deepest thanks to my sister Rosalie, who has always been my closest friend and has continued to support me emotionally through all the vicissitudes of my life and has been a stalwart fan of my writing. To Elizabeth Aharonian Moon, roommate in college and friend since then, I owe a special debt of gratitude. She was my final reader, critiquer, and editor, which allowed me to improve the manuscript and save the reader from too many pedantic tangents that I was so eager to explore and many other potential problems. Her dedication and assistance was above and beyond the "call of duty." My deep-felt thanks to my "Jiminy Cricket," Elaine Long, who kept me true to my goals. I want to also extend my thanks to Jennifer Bosveld, former publisher of Pudding House Publications, for her immediate acceptance and wholehearted support for my chapbook, *Dancing Fish*, based on early excerpts from this book, and her love of my writing. My appreciation also to Eduardo Rey Brummel and Suzy Patterson for their editing of earlier versions of this book.

A special thank you and wish for continued fair winds to those of the cruising community of which we were a part. It truly is a community in the finest sense of the word. You all know who you are. I am including this special remembrance from my poem *An Elegy for a Time at Sea* for our close friend, Captain Steven Reinken, S/V *Ariel*, (1952–2014): *He was a thoughtful man who loved the sea, fair winds, dear friend, on this your last journey.*

To all the local people we met, my deepest thanks and tears of joy when I think of you, who so generously welcomed us into your homes, your communities, your hearts. Those shared experiences are part of the fabric of my soul.

I also want to thank the many experts in oceanography, whales, birds, marine biology, history, and so many other topics who generously shared their knowledge and expertise with me.

To my final readers including Patricia Clark, Marge Dorfmeister, Alexander Drummond, Anita Jepson-Gilbert, and Medley Strickland; to Dan Downing and Ken Brandon for help on the itinerary maps; to my brother, John H. Alico, and to Mark Wiard for their help with the photos; and to the special people at Sunstone Press, thank you!

Photos not attributed to another person were taken by my husband or me or taken of us at our request with our cameras.

The following poems were previously published in my chapbook, *Dancing Fish*, published by Pudding House Publications in 2011, although some have been slightly revised for this book: "Antonio of the Rio Dulce," "Dancing Fish," "Death Sidles Up Through the Trees," "Encountering Grace in Granada," "Light Travel," "Mayan Time," "Massawa, Eritrea: A Prose Poem Portrait," "Night Watch," "Polynesian Geometry," "Tea in a Bombed-out Alley," "The Calligraphy Lesson," "The Length of Fingers," "What I Have Learned," and "Where Blue Meets Blue." "Death Sidles Up Through the Trees," "Fragments," and "I Hear the Ants Breathing" were published in the anthology, *Parade of Poets*, Shavano Poets Society, 2012. An earlier version of "Dancing Fish" titled "The Dance of the Silver Fishes" was published in the anthology *30 Years or 30 Miles From Here*, Riverstone Press of the Foothills, 2008.

Author's Notes

*T*his narrative is true, however I have changed the names of many of the people encountered during this voyage to protect their privacy. Where I used actual names, it was with the permission of those people or to support a local business or organization.

Although the chapter titles relate to regions of the world as we sailed west, this is not a chronological account. Rather as themes and issues suggested themselves to me as a result of where in the world I was, I move back and forth to tie experiences together, so that the voyage as a whole becomes one tapestry. I have tried to make these jumps not too abrupt and to provide context so the reader doesn't have to work too hard to figure out just where in the world I was.

The names of places, people, and even items, such as qat (aka khat, gat, ghat, and probably more), often have various spellings when translated into English. I have used the English spelling most common in the area about which I was writing.

Much of the historical and cultural information about the countries we visited is from a variety of sources including my visits to specific sites; local museums; conversations with local people; publications by the country's historical, cultural, and tourist departments; local newspapers; and various history and guide books. It is not possible to cite them all, or even to sort out who told me what, but when relating unusual, not commonly known stories, I have tried to provide a corroborating source—often from the Internet—even if that was not my original source.

When referring to statute miles, I use the single term *miles*; when referring to nautical miles, I use both words. A nautical mile is 1.15 greater than a statute mile, and is used for measuring distance at sea. The itinerary maps are sketches and not meant to be exact replications of island dimensions or positions.

I have only scratched the surface of the stories and adventures I experienced during the ten years of this voyage, which took place from 2001–2010, so not even all the countries we visited are included. All together we checked in to forty-one countries in S/V *Bali Ha'i III* and visited four others by plane or land and sailed over 43,000 nautical miles.

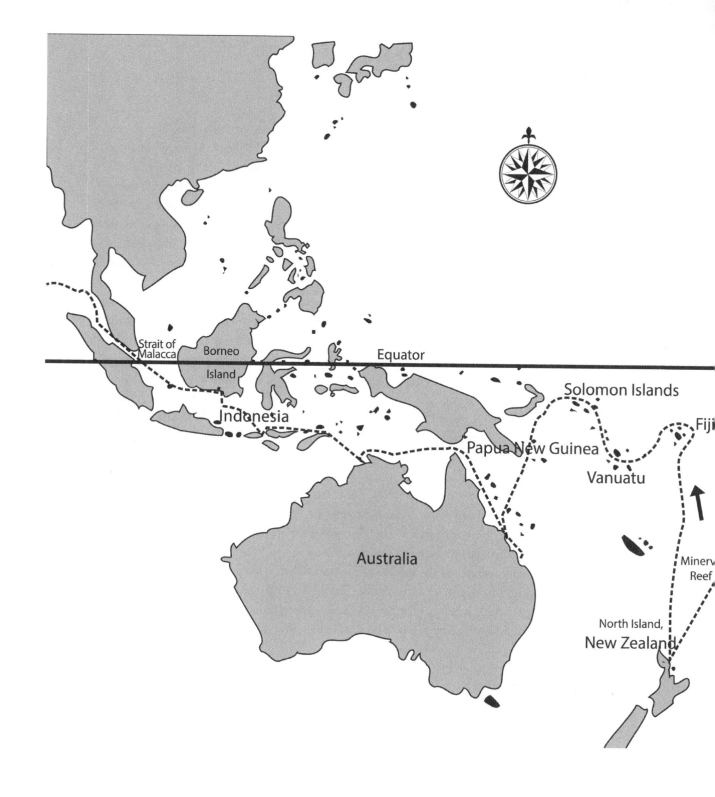

Strait of Malacca

Borneo Island

Equator

Indonesia

Solomon Islands

Papua New Guinea

Fiji

Vanuatu

Australia

Minerva Reef

North Island, New Zealand

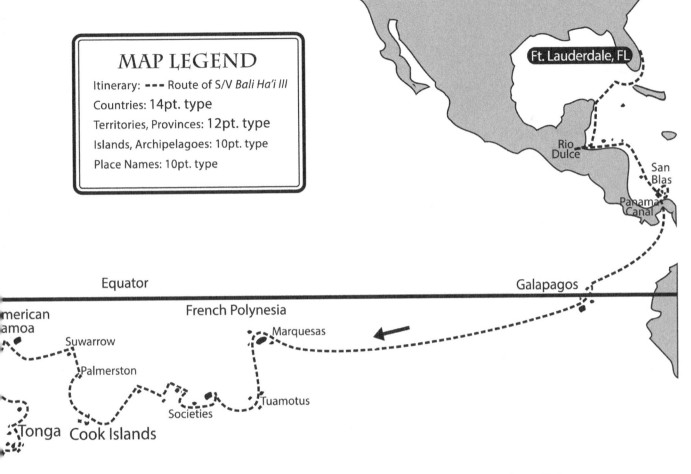

MAP LEGEND

Itinerary: - - - Route of S/V *Bali Ha'i III*

Countries: 14pt. type

Territories, Provinces: 12pt. type

Islands, Archipelagoes: 10pt. type

Place Names: 10pt. type

Ft. Lauderdale, FL

Rio Dulce

San Blas

Panama Canal

Equator

Galapagos

French Polynesia

American Samoa

Suwarrow

Palmerston

Marquesas

Tuamotus

Societies

Tonga Cook Islands

Rapa Nui
(Easter Island)

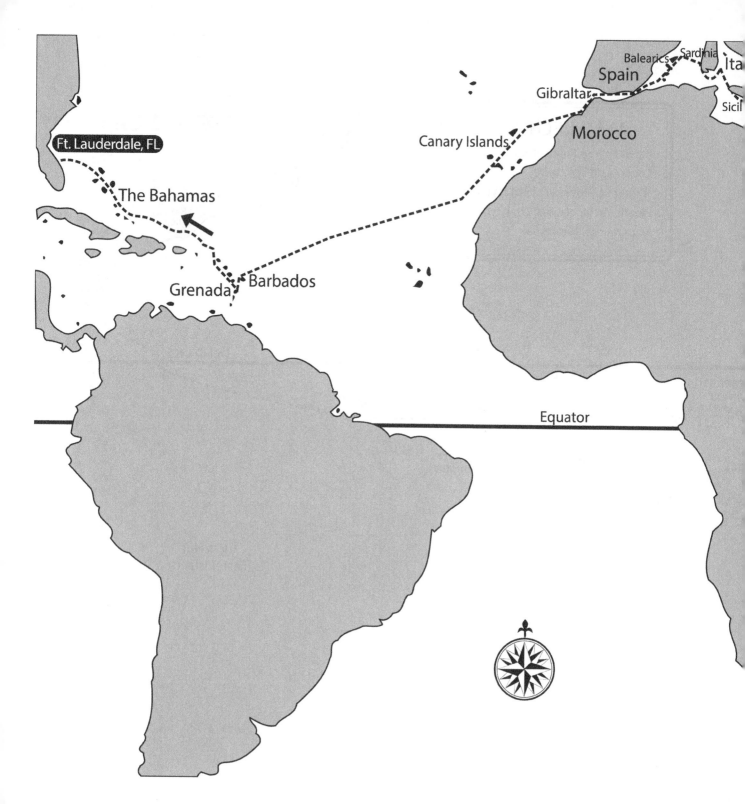

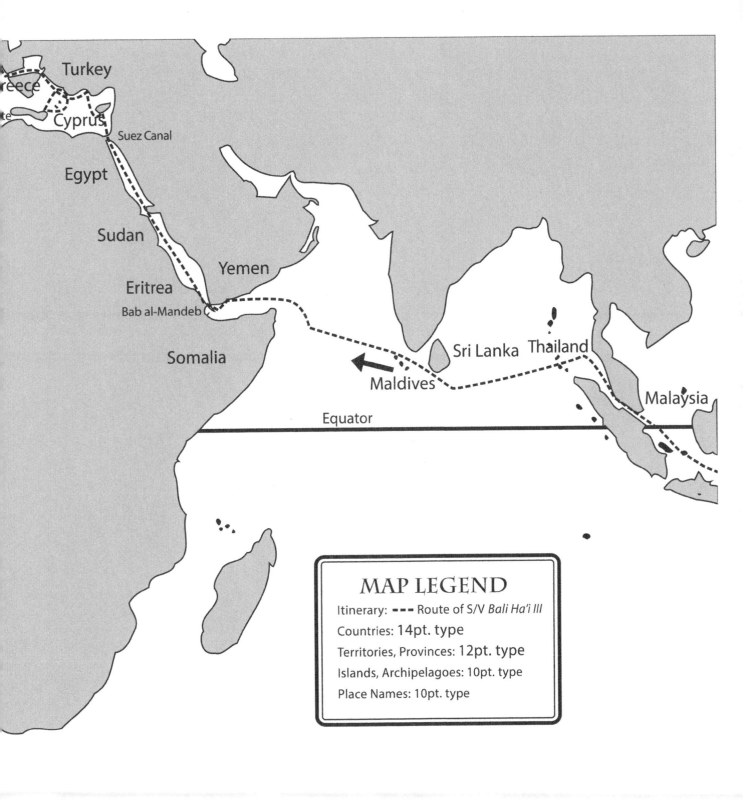

Turkey

Greece

Cyprus

Crete

Suez Canal

Egypt

Sudan

Yemen

Eritrea

Bab al-Mandeb

Somalia

Sri Lanka

Thailand

Maldives

Malaysia

Equator

MAP LEGEND

Itinerary: ▪▪▪ Route of S/V *Bali Ha'i III*

Countries: 14pt. type

Territories, Provinces: 12pt. type

Islands, Archipelagoes: 10pt. type

Place Names: 10pt. type

1

Reflections on the Prelude

We shall not cease from exploration
And the end of all our exploring
Will be to arrive where we started
And know the place for the first time.
—T. S. Eliot, "Little Gidding," *Four Quartets IV*

Knowing Fear

Roooll, tharump, roooll, tharump: spice jars, plates, CDs, and everything else slides back and forth in harsh dissonance. Our boat slashes through whale-sized waves. Sounds mix discordantly: the swirling violent wind; waves crashing on deck as if we are slamming into a brick wall; all our possessions skidding back and forth in their lockers; metal against metal as the mainsail boom, although sheeted in, swings just violently enough for the mandrel to break, adding that jarring pattern to this frightening cacophony.

This storm wants us out of its way. If it has to smash us to pieces to get on, that's what will happen. I watch our mainsail immediately torn to shreds. In this, our ultimate storm, there isn't time to get it down. Pieces fly by, some catch in the wind generator. It jams, blades broken, metal stand akimbo.

I am wedged in the navigation station seat in the pilothouse. Although here I'm protected from the main force of the storm, I cower as a wave towers over us and crashes down on the roof, green water splaying over the cockpit and aft deck. My husband, Wayne, is now in the cockpit hand-steering. We're literally between a rock and a hard place. The rocks are about one hundred yards behind us and the solid coast of an Australian island about one-third of a mile ahead. No room to maneuver away from the wind. We can't turn and head downwind because of the land configuration. We have no choice but to turn directly into the wind and take it head on.

Wayne starts the engine at full cruise power, but we're making no progress away from the rocks. He revs up to full throttle, which is barely keeping us away. I look back to see if Wayne is still there, wondering how I can possibly save him if he isn't, yet knowing that would be impossible. I try to yell against the wind, "The anemometer's pegged out at 60 knots." He can't hear me. It makes no difference; it doesn't read any higher. This wind is much faster than that.

It is a freak storm. For the first time when sailing I know fear, yet I'm not frightened in an adrenaline-rush sense. Between wave and wind karate chops, I wonder,

Why not? Shouldn't I be scared to death? There is time to think as there isn't anything I can really do about my situation. Besides, I can't move without being knocked about. My eyes are locked on these vicious, furious dark green-black waves trying with all their natural might to knock us over. My brain is split. Half is aware of the need to react to what will happen. Half is floating somewhere above all this madness. Knowing fear and being terrified aren't the same. What is it that I really fear? Being out of control? Of having no choices? Of being a puppet in a play that I not only didn't write, but couldn't even imagine? Somehow I don't think it is death.

It was unpredicted, and no weather patterns have shown it as a possibility. It comes up so quickly, Wayne is wearing only shorts and soon gets hypothermia. I go out and steer, while he warms up in the pilot house. I block myself on the side of the wheel leveraged against the cockpit seat—it's the only way I can get enough strength to turn the wheel, otherwise, the force of the waves is too great, and I'll be knocked overboard. No more thinking. I become some sort of physical machine wrenching the wheel this way, then afraid I've over-steered, tugging it back. The bow plunges down; I hold my breath a moment until I can sense it coming up again. I feel the pattern, but I'm not fitting into it, so I work harder. Suddenly I am no longer afraid—only because machines don't have feelings.

The storm lasts a little over two hours, but it is a time not told by clocks. My life did not flash before my eyes, but much else did.

≈≈≈

When this storm hit, we were six years into our circumnavigation with over 18,000 nautical miles under our keel from this voyage alone, and many more from

sails on our previous boats. So I knew that it would be just the two of us out there on our boat with wind and waves that do not always lend themselves to forecasting. We had to react to what was happening each moment, and if we made the wrong choice, we paid for it. But this storm was different. It hit us so suddenly and so violently that we had no time to prepare and no choices. We had to go with it and wait for what would happen.

Before, I hadn't thought I could drown because I'm an excellent swimmer and love the water, but I had never seen the ocean so angry, so inhospitable, so chaotic. It was not as if we hadn't been in storms before, but later we both agreed—Wayne who had been sailing for over thirty-five years, and I for twenty at that time—that we had never experienced a storm of this magnitude. We heard later that the wind had been clocked nearby at 84 knots, the equivalent of 96 miles per hour.

I thought again about my fear. Was it about dying, could that really be true? At the time of the storm, I was sixty-five and felt that I had lived an interesting and often lovely life. I had to laugh at myself at that thought. Years ago, I was bragging about all I had accomplished (I'm embarrassed now, but *bragging* is definitely the correct verb) when someone smiled enigmatically at me and said, "You know that's a Chinese curse, 'May you have an interesting life.'" That cured me. Now when people occasionally say to me what an interesting life I have, I am the one who smiles enigmatically.

I was looking for many encounters during this circumnavigation and expected to know much more when it was over, but knowing fear and seeing the reflection of death in life's mirror weren't among them.

After the storm: *Bali Ha'i's* torn main sail caught in the wind generator.

After the storm: *Bali Ha'i's* broken mandrel.

Departure

It is the little side streets and alleys of life that bring us to major events. We turn the corner and we're sailing around the world. Retirement—it conjures up different feelings for those of us in the developed world in which it is a reality, so unlike many of those I met on this voyage, who must work until death.

Many of my retired American friends find their lives so busy and full they wonder how they ever had time for work. My husband, on the other hand, never wanted to stop working. He had been a United Airlines pilot for thirty-seven years and a Captain for twenty-four of those years. It was not work, nor an occupation, not even a career—it was his identity, his life. He had even turned down a management position because it would have meant less flying time. At that time (2000) an FAA regulation required U.S. commercial airline pilots to retire at age sixty. Wayne intentionally flew until ten minutes before his forced retirement. I was with him as a passenger on that flight from Hong Kong to Singapore and told him later of the loud applause he received when, as he brought that 747-400 down for his umpteenth perfect landing, the purser announced this Captain's retirement, a sound Wayne couldn't hear in the cockpit.

Although Wayne was engaged in the design and building of our sailing yacht, S/V *Bali Ha'i III*, and the planning of our cruise, he found retirement a bitter pill. I think his goal for the cruise was to forget how much he had loved flying and that he couldn't do it anymore. For him, it was a journey into oblivion, a time to dream of what had been and was no longer. I hadn't understood.

For many reasons, I was ready to retire from my position as CEO/president of a technical writing company that I had started in 1980. I had been an inconsistent manager of people—sometimes inspirational, sometimes dictatorial. I was learning to be better at that, but something negative happened to the work ethic in the United States in the 1990s. I had multiple benefits not required by a small company: health insurance; paid vacations; matching pension contributions; and not only maternity, but paternity leave. I gave these in an effort to forge a bond of respect, loyalty, and responsibility with my employees. With the exception of a few long-time employees, I felt I had a revolving door for workers with no sense of loyalty, accountability, or skills. I just wanted to be rid of this new breed of incompetent, disaffected employee. I had lost my drive. For me, it was clearly time for a different venue.

Many in my generation of American women (I was born in 1940) had struggled for independence, respect, and equal rights in the workplace. Our trials were similar to those of our grandmothers who fought for voting rights. But it was done. Our daughters could choose, could succeed in their own right. I was tired; and I, personally, was finished with that battle.

So it was that Wayne and I departed much of our known life, not just places and people. Departure is not just leaving. In one literal sense it is to die—that was how Wayne departed from his career as an airline captain. Another meaning is to turn aside, to deviate. That was what it meant for me. I moved away from an established course. And so in 2001, we departed and sailed around the world.

I remember the preparation: provisioning; ordering spare parts; endless lists of what we needed to have and to do; my computer tables listing canned goods, dried foods, toiletries, cleaning supplies, passage meals, medical supplies, and their storage location; canned goods labeled with permanent marker in case the labels soaked off as can happen at sea, which had been advice from somewhere. It never happened. Like the disappearing labels, many situations we prepared for didn't happen, while many others that we never dreamed of, read about, or imagined, did.

One of those was the storms. We had to leave Florida as hurricane season approached because of the late delivery of our boat and the fact that the truck driver had backed into something, breaking the rudder on his trip down from Canada, where the boat had been built, to Florida. We spent the first three weeks after delivery of S/V *Bali Ha'i III* waiting for a new rudder to be built and shipped to us. Technically, *Bali Ha'i* is a cutter rig because she has an inner forestay (basically the rigging for the headsail), but Wayne designed it for quick release, so for those who know sailing we generally sailed her as a sloop.

She was our third sailboat, all named *Bali Ha'i* from the song in *South Pacific* because of these lines:

> *Bali Ha'i may call you...come away, come away;*
> *Bali Ha'i will whisper on the wind of the sea,*
> *here am I your special island, come to me, come to me...*
> *you'll find me where the sky meets the sea.*

Wayne had assured me that she was fast, and he was right about that. *Bali Ha'i's* speed was based on her design and the materials used. Although 63 feet in length, her beam was only 15.5 feet. Built of aluminum with a carbon-fiber mast reduced the weight considerably. I believe our average cruising speed for the entire circumnavigation was over 8.5 knots, and with good winds, we often sailed over 9 knots and frequently sailed over 200 nautical miles in a twenty-four-hour period. She was also a comfortable boat to sail. Wayne had designed our fresh-water tanks high and outboard behind the settees in the main saloon to serve as ballast with a high-speed pump that could transfer two hundred and fifty gallons of water from one side to the other in two and one-half minutes. This position of the tanks cut down the heel angle (amount of tilt of the boat in the water) and gave us a better sailing position, and also made moving around on board a lot easier. She was easy to sail and very responsive. She had a well-equipped nav station, where we spent much of our time when underway, if not in the cockpit.

Cruising Life: *Bali Ha'i* at anchor in Fiji.

She was (and still is) a beautiful boat. I had insisted we not have another white hull like the majority of sailboats, and found a color called teal that corresponded to beautiful tropical turquoise water. At first, Wayne was hesitant, but after he saw her painted, he loved it too. Plus, we discovered later, it was easy to find her in crowded anchorages when returning from trips ashore, not just because of the 87-foot mast, but the hull color. We never did see another yacht the same color.

He had also assured me that with weather information we could avoid big storms (turned out he was wrong about that). In fact, on June 4, 2001 on our first passage from the Dry Tortugas, Florida to Isla Mujeres, Mexico, we hit the edge of a tropical storm about midnight off the coast of Cuba—my watch, of course—a storm that somehow never made it into Wayne's weather data. But it was really nothing compared to storms we would experience later. I was able to reef the sails, and with the winds, we just went faster. In fact as I reviewed our log, I read that the seas were from eight to twelve feet and occasionally higher and the winds ranged from 18 to 55 knots, giving us an average speed just over 9 knots—pretty fast for a cruising sailboat. As Wayne wrote in the log on June 6, 2001, "A rough and wet ride through the Yucatan Straits to Isla Mujeres, [where] we dropped anchor at the harbor entrance at 01:45 and waited for the sun to come up before entering." We were on our way!

I recall the moment in time after leaving the

Dry Tortugas, the southwestern-most group of islands off Florida, when I looked back and the United States was out of sight. That, for me, was the actual moment of leaving. We were finally offshore heading west, not returning the same way, but actually sailing all the way around the world. Before, we had always turned around, returned, when our time was up out there. Now, there was no turning back, except to look and reflect. It seemed like a time of innocence. I was sixty-years old, but in some ways, I was a naïve child. I couldn't have even dreamed then what I would learn, what I would experience, how this might change me.

Where Blue Meets Blue

Farewells, whispered fears,
smiles and tears,
hands hover to hold
for a moment.

Small photos, dishes
stowed; dead
flowers, old letters discarded.

What does it mean to leave,
to finally say
good-bye?

Are there clues in the drifting leaf
detached from the tree,
the Green turtle exhausted
slipping into the sea?

We ignore these lessons of leaves, forgotten progeny,
sail on to open sea

until blue meets blue; only then,
turn to see we
are alone,
where the sky
meets the sea.

What did it mean to leave? What will it mean to return? What place will I know then?

Learning, Knowing, Feeling

In the calm of my night watch during a passage, a wave towered over the stern and lifted us toward the sky as it calmly curled underneath our keel. My hands on the wheel, I swayed with the curve of the waves. The moon was visible, an intimate shimmering silken thread that connected me, the boat, the sea, the night. The waves and I danced in our private ballet. In this tall, curving sea, my thoughts were stripped bare, no nonsense, no peripheral issues, nothing in sight except water and sky. It made it so easy to contemplate, to remember, to dream, to wish, to hope, to ponder—a slow, languid way to think there in the dark, with only the surrounding sea.

Standing at the wheel, I considered my goals. My first was to learn. In my organized fashion, I took courses in marine biology and bird biology, and I did learn from those courses. But to learn, I needed to see in specialized ways. So learning to see became a second goal.

Years later, I remember thinking at one anchorage, as two colorful parrots squawked by, what I didn't know when I left—not just that those birds were female Rainbow Lorikeets *(Trichoglossus haematodus)*, or what to do with a large stalk of quickly ripening bananas, or how to take down a ripped sail in the dark of night with waves sloshing across the deck—but what I could see and feel out there; what I could learn from people, the natural environment, cultures, myself.

I often stopped by the school if there was one in our various anchorages. In my rediscovery of this world, I found the children ingenious and creatively perceptive in their comments and questions. Usually I would be asked to teach an English class, which was always fun for both the students and for me. The schools ranged from a one-room thatched hut to a modern, well-equipped school building. No matter what type of building, it was clear that education was valued throughout the countries we visited by students and their families.

Like so many cruisers, we provided much else—boxes of school books, exercise books for schoolwork, pens, pencils, medicines, clothes, kilo bags of rice, tinned meat and vegetables—whatever we had room for. Once it was cartons of diapers, toilet paper, and a crucial medicine that had to be refrigerated for a sick infant many nautical miles away.

Cruising Life: The author with students during an English lesson in Sri Lanka.

≈≈≈

There was yet more to understand and assimilate—something elusive. I needed time and experience to frame and formulate my perceptions about this world I was rediscovering. It appeared and dissolved like the horizon through clouds. Seeing is not believing; seeing is only one step on the path. I realized, as Rachel Carson wrote, "It is more important to feel than to know." She didn't mean we don't also need to know, but that knowledge without compassion is meaningless. I hoped to learn, to see, to feel, to give back, and in this process to know the place of self, my own geography, the map of my own mind, and what it took to nourish my soul: this was an offering to be taken from the sea.

2

Central America: The Multifarious Nature of Seeing

We knew that what seemed to us true could be only relatively true anyway. There is no other kind of observation.

—John Steinbeck, *The Log from the Sea of Cortez*

Seeing the Past

Perhaps randomly, perhaps not, a line of Mayan women each spaced about thirty yards apart wove through white, pink, red, and tan bodies haphazardly scattered along the beach. The bodies belonged to sun lovers, mostly from Europe. I heard shouts for drinks, whispered propositions, sighs in French, German, English, Italian, and, of course, Spanish. The dozen or so Mayan women were barefoot and wore semitraditional dress—much black cloth, headscarves, and trim in the Yucatan-Mayan style of classic geometric and animal patterns in bright red, yellow, green, and blue, which decorated their fringes, sleeves, and belts. The sharp juxtaposition of colors and cultures was as blatant as the sun. The Mayan women plodded through in a serpentine line selling the same trinkets: small woven bracelets and beaded necklaces. Did it take this many *vendedoras* for at least one to be seen?

Mayan Time

You emerge from a shimmering mirage haze,
bodies swathed in black, sparks of scarlet,
yellow, aqua braided through hems and sashes,
brown, hardened feet walking the hot sand,
forearms and hands entwined with trinkets.

The planes of your faces are Mayan,
their lines map the way you have come,
eyes look into yesterday,
rigid bodies mirror a past.

You offer ornaments to pink ankles and wrists
lying spread on the sand connected to bodies
with no ideas, no visible planes,
eyes seeing only today.
You weave through; one,
then another, moments later another.

The pattern of movement is the feathered serpent,
that creased, shadowy being of unknown age
now only glimpsed among glittery moments
caught in grains of time
from eyes that look past.

We were anchored at Isla Mujeres, a small island off Mexico's Yucatan coast, our first landfall. It was an agreeable place geared to tourists-for-a-day, who came over from Cancun on ferries to snorkel, walk the cobble streets, and look for bargains. They left before the sun set, so evenings had a somewhat dishabille, after-the-party look with a quiet remembrance of more festive times about them.

On the northwest end of the island was one of those quintessential Caribbean beaches with coco palms and shimmery turquoise shoal water that suddenly dropped off to that cold cobalt blue signifying deep ocean.

Before heading south, we sailed to the National Park around Isla Contoy. It was nesting season for thousands of Magnificent Frigatebirds and Double-crested Cormorants. Brown Pelicans and Least Terns also nested there at different times. I spotted one Greater Flamingo, which was stopping for R&R on its flight from its nesting site near Merida to somewhere in the Caribbean. I saw White Ibises, black iguanas, and lots of reef fish—especially diverse species of angelfish, butterflyfish, parrotfish, and damselfish colored in multiple shades of red, yellow, purple, blue, green, brown, as well as silver, black, and white; some with stripes, dots, dashes, or squiggly lines. These were patterns for camouflage, gender, mating—a bouquet of evolutionary diversity.

According to the ranger four species of sea turtles laid eggs on this island: Green, Hawksbill, Leatherback, and Loggerhead. As we picked our way out of the Isla Contoy anchorage in *Bali Ha'i* through shallow areas and coral heads, we watched two Green turtles mating—a rare sighting. (Years later, on a long dinghy ride from our anchorage to a blue grotto in Kastellorizon, one of my favorite Greek islands, we saw two loggerhead turtles mating.) A large Manta ray jumped completely out of the water just in front of us. Since it's a plankton eater, what was the reason for the jump? Escaping sharks? Shaking off parasites? Sending a message to compatriots? Just plain fun? The nesting, the mating, these cycles of life have been happening for eons longer than the Mayans have been around. Here in this small protected space, the thread of time carried me back beyond centuries.

For me, this voyage was about learning to see in a specialized way. I wanted to see beyond sights, into meaning. In the Yucatan, I saw an invisible people, the Mayan, wavering in their precarious present. What a people do with their past is as important as their future vision, but I saw their past only as a shimmery haze floating through time and no dreams for the future in their eyes.

There was also a thread of the natural world carrying my thoughts to a past we, as humans, did not experience. The sea turtles and Manta rays with their ancient histories provided another link to a time so far beyond human memory that only paleontologists and five-year-old, dinosaur-mad kids can imagine it.

Evolutionarily, both the sea turtles and the Manta rays have been inordinately successful—until now. I was taking a Marine Biology course from the University of

Southern California as throughout our voyage, we sailed over, and I scuba dove under exactly what I was studying. In my course work, I discovered that in the case of the sea turtles, both taxonomic families that exist today were neighbors of the dinosaurs. Manta rays are related to sharks, and that entire family also has had a successful evolutionary history. If not the exact same family of today, they had close ancestors that made it through the Age of Reptiles into the Age of Mammals. Unlike the dinosaurs, sharks and their relatives survived the mass extinction that did in so many other life forms at the end of the Mesozoic era, the K-T (Cretaceous-Tertiary) event.

My learning took many forms ranging from formalized course taking, reading, observing, talking to experts, and listening to the whispered stories of children.

I read about the major meteor that hit near the Yucatan about sixty-five million years ago, creating the Chicxulub crater, measuring 105 miles wide. Such a gigantic impact resulted in tidal waves, earthquakes, and firestorms recorded in the rocks of the area that are the same age as the impact. The earthquakes and firestorms would have created major particulate matter in the air, with the domino effect of blocking sunlight impacting plant growth. This would have starved out the vegetarians in the crowd, and subsequently the carnivores. That's what happens when one messes with the sun. Whether K-T was one major impact or a series is debated, but the result is uncontestable: extinction of approximately 70 percent of the existing species of life.

Clearly the Manta rays and the sea turtles had the persistence, adaptations, and drive for survival that worked in the past—but will it carry them into the future, for now they are endangered? This change in their ability to survive is laid clearly at our feet. Here, to my eyes, the Mayans were experiencing their own K-T event. Their dissolution was not the result of one catastrophic event. It has been occurring over time at the hands of the Spanish conquerors, the Mexican and Guatemalan governments and citizens (who, in fact, owe some of their ancestry to the Mayan people), the tourists, and the Mayans themselves.

≈≈≈

From Isla Mujeres, we sailed down the Yucatan peninsula, stopping first at Playa del Carmen, a place both my husband and I each had visited at different times, but more than twenty years ago. The metamorphosis of Playa del Carmen to the tourist town of T-shirt and souvenir shops and hawkers for the multitude of cafes and American fast-food eateries is all too common in many places around the world and devastating to the culture and stories that once resided there.

Farther down the coast squats Tulum, originally called *Zama* meaning "to dawn" by the Mayan, and the only known major ancient Mayan city on the coast, where much of their sea trade took place. Its earth-hugging presence is broken by the Castillo, an incongruous Spanish name for the tallest structure among the ruins. Here is found the feathered serpent motif, possibly called Kukulcan or Kukulkna by the early Mayan, and a god of the ruling class, which I learned from reading about Mayan culture.

Today, Kukulcan has joined the Catholicism imposed by Spanish colonialism and lives on in the minds of some Mayan worshippers and on tacky tourist refrigerator magnets. For the Mayans, presumably, he has evolved from a god of the ruling class to a god of the people. The name Quetzalcoatl, in the Nahuatl language of the Aztecs, is more familiar to Caucasians. The Quetzal Norteño (*Pharomachrus mocinno*) is a bird, commonly known in English as the Resplendent Quetzal. The Quetzalcoatl deity is allegorically translated as a serpent with the feathers of the quetzal and had been known for two thousand years in ancient Mesoamerica before the Spanish arrived.

Outside the Tulum ruins, we had a simple lunch of tortillas and beans at a thatch-roofed, open-air palapa with a sand floor and resident iguana. Small pole shanties for hanging a hammock were for rent to the young backpacker crowd. Outside the ruins, few clues to the Classic Maya were in evidence.

The Mayan held sway in the Yucatan with their well-established city-states, particularly in the Classic Mayan period from about 250 to 900 CE. Interestingly, not one of the remaining written records of this period mentions the common people. The records are all about kings and high priests, often one and the same, and their accomplishments, mainly in battle. There are also pyramids and temples built for these rulers' aggrandizement—their grandeur known from extant examples at Tikal, Chichen Itza, Copan, and so many other sites. This mentality of egocentric rulers and high priests was reflected again when we visited Rapa Nui (Easter Island). Their megalomania and disregard of the common people brought both societies to their knees.

Like the early people of Rapa Nui, the Mayans of that time had no draft animals, so the pyramids in the Yucatan and the monstrous moai on Rapa Nui were built on the backs of human labor. Strong backs may well be the genetic inheritance of the common people of both societies, but what happened to their spirit?

Yasmin Saikia, PhD, authored a scholarly, but very readable book, *Fragmented Memories*. In it she writes of a people in Assam, India who have constructed an identity that is, in fact, not historically documented, which exists somewhere "between history and memory,"[1] yet these people have the historical and memorial trappings of this identity. I think of the Mayans, who have a history and a collective memory that has been diluted, dissolved, and separated from their realistic past, preventing a dreamed future.

≈≈≈

From Tulum, we sailed south stopping at various anchorages. At Bahia Ascension while snorkeling some distance from the boat, I was surprised by an overly curious Lemon shark whose yellow eyes I will always remember; perhaps so yellow because of the way the sun hit them as the shark neared the surface. This image remains unfaded.

From there, we sailed to Bahia del Espiritu Santo, followed by Cayo Norte, a small cay off the coast in the Chinchorro Bank. It was an odd sight sticking up in the western Caribbean, almost like an atoll with a fringing reef, small cay in the center, clumps of coral scattered about, and home to numerous shipwrecks, old and new. There was a lighthouse on the cay and a small Mexican Navy garrison to prevent drug trafficking and poaching. They came to inspect us after we anchored, giving my Spanish a workout. Extremely polite, they gave us permission to fish there. From Playa del Carmen through Cayo Norte, we were the only cruising boat, which along with my perception of Mayan history and the historical context of the natural world, gave me a sense of suspended time.

After Cayo Norte we sailed to Xcalak, our last port in Mexico. Xcalak (pronounced like "shall-ack") was the quintessential Mexican fishing village, literally and figuratively at the end of a long sandy road. This place hadn't changed in forty years; I would bet on it. There was a chipped concrete building labeled Harbor Master, with cobwebs under the eaves and an office that was always empty. A series of large wind generators had only one that spun at all in the wind and none that worked—the result of a misguided foreign aid program. Children fished and swam from the town pier just as their parents and grandparents had in their day. The fishermen left early to go out in boats named *Angel, Theresa, Maria Ana*, all wooden, white paint peeling, but with huge, paradoxical outboards on back. One person ran the boat, one or two others dove for conch or lobster and checked fish traps, returning by mid-afternoon.

The streets were quiet from late morning to late afternoon; then in the evening everyone was out, sitting on their steps, eating, drinking, gossiping, admonishing their children, riding bicycles on some errand of importance. This was how they carried on the business of life, a comfortable pattern day after day. These were the Mexicans of the country, but they were not Mayan.

With the end of the day in Xcalak, the people seemed to come like Kukulcan to rest in the sandy incongruity of the Yucatan. Xcalak was the antithesis of Playa del Carmen. Yet I wondered if the tourists—with their noise, their need for trinkets, and their hunger for the fast food of the United States—could be erased, would not the Carmenites be spending their evenings as wisely as the citizens of Xcalak? The Mayans—invisible.

Seeing the Future in the Past: Burning Bridges

We followed the *sweet river*, the Rio Dulce in Guatemala, as it wound up through a canyon of white limestone cliffs covered with vines and tropical growth, broadened out into a large bay, narrowed again about forty miles upstream where the only bridge crossed the river and the town of Fronteras was located, then opened up again into a large lake, Lago Izabel. It was the bridge that created Fronteras—without it, the town would have no purpose. As we motored up the river I spotted innumerable white Great Egrets, Brown Pelicans, black Double-crested Cormorants, and always Black Vultures. Creating color were Green Herons, the bright yellow breast of the Tropical Kingbird, multihued parrots, and occasionally a stab of neon blue or green as a Belted or Green Kingfisher swooped down along the murky green of a tributary.

In some seemingly random way, the brown stick-and-mud homes of the Mayan clung to a small rock ledge, a piece of muddy shoreline, the damp mouth of a creek, or the uneven hillside along the river. A few small brown-skinned men were out in their hollowed out *cayucos* throwing nets for what fish survived the constant overfishing, or squatted by their homes watching the river with black eyes reflecting the shadows of their lives. The women were doing everything else. At night the howler monkeys with their eerie cries created the appropriate spine-tingling backdrop.

The Rio was hot and humid, and Fronteras had the feel and taste of dust before we got there. It was not just on the deck and cockpit settees, but in our eyes and on our tongues where it clung like the vines on the limestone cliffs coming up the river. The river wasn't really swimmable, at least below the bridge; presumably the crocodiles had been hunted out, their place now fouled by garbage and sewage.

Antonio came to us in his cayuco as we lay at anchor partway up the Rio waiting for other cruising friends with whom we were planning to explore some of the tributaries. He offered us gifts and to show us around on shore. With my hesitant Spanish, we more or less communicated. After our friends Steve and Gayla arrived on S/V *Ariel*, we followed Antonio to shore for a tour of his land, which technically belonged to a rich fellow who lived in Guatemala City, but who hadn't been to the Rio for a few years. Although Antonio expressed loyalty to him, it seemed this landowner no longer supported his caretaker. But Antonio wasn't merely the caretaker of this land, he was its lover.

Antonio of the Rio Dulce

He paddles to us in his mahogany cayuco,
water the color of the burnt sienna land
spilling into its rough hollow core,
created by fire and hands that match the wood
thick, scarred, umber.

He is Antonio, the caretaker.
His black eyes reflect the river, welcome us.
He points to his wife
and many children on the red clay bank.
Mud crabs crawl over banana stalks piled at his feet,
gifts we don't know how to accept.

His landlord is absent;
our gain, as ashore he leads us
on a snaking path through land this river has made.
He drifts barefoot over twisted vines and roots.
We are amazed: his stubby rooted feet have wings.
We clump through, trespassers behind him.

In Mayan, he softly speaks the names of trees,
shows us their fruit, whispers their praises.
His body blends into the lower trunks,
thick, brown, straight;
black hair so dark it hurts the backs of our eyes.
We can't get our mouths around his Mayan words.

Next his secret cave,
muddy slide down prickly rope, our hands
spotted with blood,
grim-looking bats stream about our heads,
gray stalactites bend crooked arms
to the thigh-deep water.
He smiles and his pride ricochets
off damp, slimy walls.
One of us complains out of fear.

He comes by his links to life
from centuries-old blood lines
beyond a time we know.
We are not of this melting climate that breeds
epiphytes, orchids, crocodiles, fer de lances,
and a land that coalesces into a river.
Leaving, we drift past giant snowflake egrets
perched in palms and pines.
Faster, we pass his cayuco as he throws
his dream-like spinning net.

30

We wave and receive his blessed smile.
In the heavy, humid silence, we hear the river
whispering,
Antonio, Antonio, Antonio

In Guatemala at least 80 percent of the population is indigenous—basically Mayan, even after the civil war in which the powers-that-be tried to kill them off. Their population is increasing rapidly due to lack of access to and knowledge of birth control methods; the entrenched teachings of Catholicism; and the cultural pattern of having many children, which previously helped to combat the heavy infant mortality, although that is much lower now. I watched as day to day, the women and older children—older starting at five or six—trudged up the hillsides, farther and farther each day collecting what wood they could for cooking and heating. There was a school, but few children seemed to attend. How could they? They were collecting wood. Families worked hard using slash-and-burn techniques for planting so that the mountainsides were being denuded, resulting in severe erosion. We saw the fallout of this increasing population, deforestation, and lack of education among the Mayan and others that are considered indigenous as a common spiral of poverty and hopelessness in Central America as well as other parts of the world. This was their contribution to their own K-T event that I wrote of previously.

Analytically it would seem that an expanding population is contrary to dissolution, but because of their lifestyle, it will implode. This already happens when the rains come and the deforestation results in massive mud slides decimating villages, homes, people, crops, and

animals in its path, leaving behind raw scars that cannot be healed in a lifetime on either the land or in the souls of those remaining.

Patterns repeat. Historically it's difficult to put an end-date on the collapse of the Mayan civilization. The Spanish conquered the last of the Mayan-controlled land in 1697, but in reality, the concept of Mayan civilization died prior to that. For comparison with the present, I looked at Jared Diamond's book, *Collapse*, and the causes of the death of the greatness that was Mayan culture: (1) Their damage to their environment, especially by deforestation and erosion; (2) climate changes, specifically drought that occurred, probably repeatedly; and (3) political and cultural factors, especially the competition among kings and nobles that led to a chronic emphasis on war and erecting monuments rather than on solving underlying problems.[2] Today, it is not so much wars and public monuments, but corruption and accumulation of wealth by a few—not Mayan—with the same results.

In front of my eyes, I saw much of this happening again. What I didn't see, I read about in newspapers soon after we left this part of Central America, as recurring hurricanes with strong rains caused mud slides, death, and major devastation.

Guatemala is extremely agricultural, growing everything from bananas and other tropical fruit to apples, pears, onions, and potatoes. How much longer can that last? The Mayans aren't the only ones destroying the land. Dole, the monopolistic purveyor of fruit and vegetables, owns much of western Guatemala. Their monocrop approach with heavy pesticide and herbicide use is at least as destructive as the denuding of the mountainsides by the poverty-stricken Mayans.

How do we define the collapse of a civilization? Southern Mexico, Honduras, Nicaragua all have governments and are recognized by various regional and global organizations. But are they effective? Is there a social identity? Are basic human needs met? Is there a growing economy? Is there a shared memory, or as Saikia wrote, is there "identity construction," are they, too, "between history and memory"?[3] What is real and what is fabricated? Along the Rio there was a disconnect, a disassociation from the concept of belonging, a sense of timelessness that carried with it a sluggish tiredness to being in the present.

Some argue that the Earth's population is not the problem, and there are indications its rate of increase is slowing down, although by 2050, the UN Population Fund (UNFPA) forecasts a population between 8.3 to 10.9 billion using a range of variables. In 2013 as I completed the writing of this book, long after my visit to Central America, the population was a little over 7.1 billion. More tragic is:

> Growth is expected to be particularly dramatic in the least developed countries of the world, which are projected to double in size from 898 million inhabitants in 2013 to 1.8 billion in 2050 and to 2.9 billion in 2100. High population growth rates prevail in many developing countries, most of which are on the UN's list of 49 least developed countries. Between 2013 and 2100, the populations of 35 countries could triple or more. Among them, the populations of Burundi, Malawi, Mali, Niger, Nigeria, Somalia, Uganda, United Republic of Tanzania and Zambia are projected to increase at least five-fold by 2100.[4]

Without some kind of global economic parity there will always be instability. The unbelievable rapid burgeoning of communication technology has made the *have-nots* quite aware of what it is the *haves* have. They want it too. Instead I watched them walking miles to cut wood to cook a simple meal, and this singular act of cutting wood decreases their chance of ever having a sustainable life. Yet if they don't, what choice do they have? More than twigs for a cook fire were being burned; the bridge to the future was burning also.

Antonio, tell me, where is your tomorrow?

Seeing Color

Swatches of color appear in my memory: a sunset-pink cloud of flamingos taking off then banking in the mid-day sun at Anegada in the British Virgin Islands; a cluster of azure butterflies at our ankles as if trying to guide my son and me so many years ago on a Colorado trail; the varying ocean blues hinting at their depth; the forty or so greens boasted of by Ireland and seen through raindrops, which painted those greens; the giant aquamarine gems of ice found within the glacier at Rhone and again in Alaska; the triple rainbows that I've seen outside Taos, in New Zealand, and from my home in Colorado; and, of course, those yellow shark eyes. My color images glow in quilt-like patterns prompted by some memory, some clue linking the past to what I see now.

In Copan, the red earth mixed with water and flowed as blood down the mountainside. This earth should be causing motes of dust, like the sand-colored dirt of Fronteras, landing on white shirts, macaw feathers, signs telling of ruins, even the ruins themselves. Instead it turned from its home, this earth, to brown the sea, for in this place the primaries of red from the soil and blue from the ocean form brown, not purple as we were taught as children: brown that settles on the violet, pink, and yellow coral and sponges, suffocating, stagnating, bringing death.

Las Montañas de Copan

The blood of *las montañas*
flows like all fluids—down.
Trickles into creeks, pulsates into rivers,
spreads out, funnels into rapids, serpentines down,
always down,
down to the sea.

Encarnado, colorado, tinto, rojo:
the many names for red your language holds.
The life seeps out of you,
as it has always done, *por muchos siglos*.
Rise, fall; as the breath of Olmecs, Mayans,
others before and after,
too many people, parasitical, on your breast.

It happens again,
this time
I am watching.

Color patterns frustrated me as I tried to remember a specific fish: was it blue then yellow with white or was the yellow line first? And on that bird, was there a white eye ring? Sometimes memory fails rather than creating a picture, a quilt, a pattern. How much we depend on color to shape our images. Yet some of those old black-and-white films were all the more dramatic without the added shades: *High Noon* is the quintessential example. Then there is the child's red coat in *Schindler's List*, the one color in that remarkable, dark movie. I remember those scenes better than the fish I was trying to identify last week.

Patterns of color reminded me of the Red-footed and Blue-footed Boobies, two species so similar, but with this brightly colored difference. How in the world did they end up with blue and red? It seems reasonable that they might have evolved as mating attractions, although both males and females have the same color feet, so that doesn't make sense. The colors, I suppose, developed from some random mutation that worked. But I wonder, Why? Why not green or yellow, or even pink, but bright blue and bright red? What an interesting quirk of mutation to end up with these colors. What strange path did they follow to get to this conclusion? It might have been the males who started this fashion fad to attract the females—the opposite pattern of the human world. Tracing back the evolutionary "where are you from" path of many of these tropical birds and sea life is a fascinating journey. With the discovery of DNA, uncovering family relationships is easier, but there is still no definitive answer as to why the red and blue of the boobies' feet.

Camouflage is another set of color patterns that fascinates. In the Colorado mountains where I live when on shore, we have herds of mountain sheep. Unless they move they are difficult to see against the rocky slopes. Here at sea along the reefs, I have searched in vain for tunicates—although common marine invertebrates, they are often mistaken for sponges—on a sponge-encrusted coral only to have one suddenly pop into view that was there all the time. I had thought anything that was prey to a predator would wear camouflage, but it certainly isn't always true. The undersea world shows us there are many ways of tricking the eye of the hunter. Several species of butterflyfish are perfect examples, with a large black eye-like spot near their caudal fin or the posterior part of their dorsal fin so it's hard to tell if they're coming or going.

In Panama, under the care of two wonderful, expert-eyed women from the country's Audubon Society, I learned to better see the sometimes resplendent, sometimes camouflaged, myriad species of birds in the rainforest chaos of branches. Everywhere I looked there was growth: leaves the size of elephant ears, tiny lavender orchids, lianas like extended boa constrictors wound around skyscraping tree trunks. Surrounding us was a symphony of monkey chatter, insect buzz, and bizarre (to me) bird calls.

Panama sits in a unique geographical ornithological space. It is at once a Lego-like connector between the North and South Americas, a melting pot for Aves, and a migratory flyway from northward and southward for many species to spend a season in this small land bridge. My *Guide to the Birds of Panama* says there are 929 species identified in the country.[5] I subtracted the long-distance migrants just passing through quickly, the rarities, and the pelagics, and still ended up with 732 species, and this for a country a little larger than Ireland and a little smaller than the state of South Carolina.

After my special rainforest tour with my outstanding Audubon birders, Wayne and I visited an odd cylindrical tower formerly a lookout post for Panama Canal security and now a peculiar B&B where we could see various levels of the rainforest canopy and the birds that inhabit each particular layer of space. My newly gained knowledge enabled me to see and name various species of birds for him including a Golden-collared Manakin (*Manacus vitellinus*), with its bright sunshine-yellow neck ring and throat set off by a black cap and back. I also identified a Lovely Cotinga (*Cotinga amabilis*), which I imagined as a brilliant Mountain Bluebird-blue that had spilled deep red burgundy on neck and belly.

But color in Panama is not confined to its birds. In the San Blas, a group of islands off Panama's east coast, live the Kuna Indians, famous for their layered fabric embroidery work, *molas*. Ironically when we were there, the best mola creator was Lisa, an apparently very gay guy, who was as colorful as his handiwork with long very brightly painted fingernails, several gold rings, a handsome, finely chiseled face, and the classic Kuna black-as-night hair and eyes.

Panama: One of the author's molas made by Lisa.

Panama's radiant birds notwithstanding, nothing I have seen on land or sea comes close to the mesmerizing impact of a healthy, live coral reef with its diversity of life and color. Uninhabited, remote islands of the South Pacific and areas of the Red Sea have the best examples, but the atolls off Belize were a fitting introduction for what was to come. While all these atolls were at least partially protected, the difference between the one where the Belize National Park employees were in charge and Lighthouse Reef, where the Audubon Society employed the rangers, was extreme. Under our boat at Lighthouse were so many Caribbean spiny lobsters that there weren't enough hidey holes for them all, and a few got chased around from one place to another by the lobsters that already had a place to hide. It was interesting behavior to watch. At the other park, we saw local fishermen within the No Fishing Area signs, while park employees sat on the beach and watched or slept.

At Glover's Reef, the Guggenheim Foundation managed a marine research station, and the field scientists there welcomed our assistance with observations measuring salinity and water temperature, part of the monitoring for coral bleaching. In other parts of the ocean world, researchers quickly accepted my offer to lend a hand with their labor-intensive field work. These opportunities prepared me to see in different ways. In Moorea, I helped with a few different projects. One was to see what it was that motivated the sharks to come to the shark-feeding tour boats: was it the sound of the boat, the time of day, the smell of food? The field biologist and I were snorkeling at the time the boat normally came, but without the boat or the food. No sharks showed up. Time could be crossed off the list.

Other research required more intense examination, not just being on the lookout for sharks. This kind of seeing was so specialized that, unless we forced ourselves, we missed the bigger picture. We were looking for one type of relationship, one type of behavior, one type of species. To find this focus in the underwater environment and to see how it fits into the larger picture was a lesson in life. It was bi-tasking sight, seeing two things at once and integrating them, a type of layering. This is something we do many times a day unconsciously, but it was interesting to separate the layers consciously, filter them, and reassemble what we had seen—especially underwater.

Belize: Young lobsters looking for a place to hide.

The Language of Seeing

There is another side to seeing that I discovered in Belize while free-diving. I came upon a juvenile Magnificent urchin, which enabled me to see in ways that differ from being in a known place, where the familiar surrounds. Usually these urchins are found at much deeper depths; even scuba divers rarely see them. There is always a context for extrapolating something new from something known. Underwater, the rules change. As many hours as we spend down there, it is never ours. Finding something totally out of the ordinary and unexpected requires more than a surprised reaction.

This animal's common name is young (or juvenile) Magnificent urchin; scientifically it's known as *Astropyga magnifica*. I could hardly believe the design of this creature.

Who Could Dream You?

Who would believe you?
Your rococo ornateness,
shocking among the pedestrian turtle grass,
the wavering peacock spines,
the stabbing blue neon lights,
the five red-lipped lobes
curling to reveal creamy yellow,
your central translucent globe
topped with a tiny blood-red tear.
You take my breath away,
I must go up for air.
I dive back,
you're still there—
I didn't dream you.

But who
could dream you
into being?

Language evolves and steals and imitates and sometimes dances around a meaning. Could the words of my native language possibly come close to a picture of that creature? Does English have the stabbing jolt of color, let alone the nuance of that being? Is our original landscape made up of too many hedgerows and rolling green hills to accommodate such vivacity, such a shocking collection of forms, such incongruity of life?

I understand that the Marshall Islanders have 170 words related to coconuts.[6] Likewise, our sailing environment forces a preciseness of thought and thus words. For example the use of port and starboard resulted from this need for exactitude. If one just said right or left, whose right: the speaker, the boat, the person at the wheel? Sailors, for example, rarely speak of just wind. Usually its speed is attached, such as wind of 20 to 25 knots or it's a Force 5 (ideal at 17 to 21 knots) or worse a Force 10 (at 48 to 55 knots), a shortcut means of describing wind speed using the Beaufort Wind Scale. Or it can be identified by its position: on the nose (not good), on the beam (great), or downwind (not great, but OK depending on your rig and sail configuration). Don't ever call what landlubbers refer to as rope as such on a boat. It can be a dingy painter, a main sheet, a furling line, or multiple other names all referring to use, but never a rope.

My musings on language reminded me that our American society fails us linguistically in another way, generally protecting us from being educated in other languages except on an individual choice basis. Is it because we are a nation of immigrants and the goal of those earlier immigrants was to become American? What a gift to be multilingual! To think, joke, and sing love songs in another language is truly to understand the people who speak that language from birth. The depth and breadth of a culture could be measured by the richness of its language. The corollary being that to understand a culture, one must know its language. This may be one reason why, as a nation, we Americans fumble so much in our interactions with the rest of the world, since we have become so bereft of language skills.

In Belize, we returned to an English-speaking country, inheriting that with their former British colonial history. What a loss it would be if we all spoke the same. Yet, I was relieved to have a break from working with words whenever I spoke. Just before leaving Mexico, we had dinner with a Frenchman in Xcalak. He spoke Spanish better than I do, but only a smattering of English. He could not understand Wayne's English very well, but managed with my English, Spanish, French blend. A few days later in another port, I saw him from a distance after I had spent a hot and sticky day doing errands on land, and I shamefully chose to avoid him because I didn't have the energy to work at speaking.

So I was learning to see, but was I learning to speak the language of those sights? I could recognize a Storm Petrel, could differentiate a Masked Booby from a Brown, discern different mushroom corals, glimpse a yellow shark's eyes. I saw patterns: the cleaning stations of cleaner wrasse and gobies picking off parasites from larger grouper and parrotfish, the march of the Mayan trinket sellers, the similarities of echinoderms from the urchins to the sea cucumbers, the public evening lives of

Xcalak's citizens. But I was still learning the language of my rediscovered world.

The Panama Canal: Seeing Plus Everything Else

There are three locks to go up then across the lake, then down two locks to the Pacific. But this place, this canal, this path between the seas was as full of tragedy, bravery, brilliance, stupidity, hopelessness, courage, drudgery, persistence, drama, and vision as any human endeavor could be.[7] To fully appreciate our canal transit, Wayne and I learned its history. I could not have seen it for what it was without that background.

The U.S. completion of the canal was a historic pivot point. The personal failure of Ferdinand De Lesseps, renowned builder of the Suez Canal, reflected not only France's failure at a Central American canal, but symbolized an end to global European domination. America's success reflected a president's vision (Teddy Roosevelt) and commitment and the grit and spirit that would be shown again and again by the United States in the two world wars. It also marked the beginning of U.S. domination in the global playing field. But the success of building the Panama Canal was so much more than one of the playing fields for world events. The medical history alone is fascinating. More people died of malaria than yellow fever with the battle against those two diseases a microcosm of the Canal story: stubbornness, antiquated notions, and stupidity versus perseverance, scientific study, and the hard-headed commitment of specific individuals.

Going through The Canal on our own yacht, and

this was *The* Canal, was an experience filled with sights, sounds, procedures, and emotions. First, there was the flurry of logistics: a meeting with the Canal Authority, now under the Panamanian government, to pay—it is expensive—to arrange the date, time, and yachts we would be side-tied to, and to determine our staging area. We were assigned to be in the staging area at 6:45 a.m. on December 8, 2001. We expected to be in the middle as the longest yacht is positioned there (S/V *Bali Ha'i III* is 63 feet), but we were coupled with a 70-foot motor yacht and their buddies on a smaller trawler. Wayne approached the two owner/captains of the motor yachts that would be our rafting partners to discuss the logistics a few days before, but they waved him off. Then we had to complete the acquisition of line handlers, followed by the boat preparation with fenders, lines, and engine check.

The day dawned, or almost—it was still dark as we slowly motored our way into the staging area and positioned ourselves on the starboard side of the motor yacht. A large container ship was in front of us. Wayne, the other yacht owners, and the line handlers tied the three yachts together side-by-side. The arrogant owner/captain of the center motor yacht refused to trust our cleats (*Bali Ha'i* was new and built of aluminum—there was no way those cleats were going to come out), so our lines were cross tied. The pilot boat brought each of us our pilots, which we were required to have and pay for. Ours deftly jumped aboard, but that was the most activity we saw from him.

Finally it was our turn; we slowly followed the container ship into the first lock. I watched fascinated as the original gates slowly swung closed behind us; the ends of our lines were monkey fists and were thrown by our line handlers up to the canal tenders on the ramparts. Then the water started gushing in at a furious rate, and we rose. Once level with the next lock, those gates opened and when the container ship started to move, we three yachts were hard-pressed to maintain our positions with the huge backwash. In fact, our supercilious center motor yacht couldn't, and his friend in the smaller trawler was about to be crushed into the wall. Our experienced and extremely competent head line-handler, who was a taxi driver when not handling lines, quickly worked with Wayne to maneuver them out of trouble, much to the chagrin of the other two yachts, although they should have been thankful.

Once through the locks and into Lake Gatun, our pilot told us that if we could get across quickly we could go down the other side right away; otherwise we would have to wait a long time as our container ship couldn't transit until another ship got through. Wayne put it on full throttle, and we beat the motor yachts across the lake, much to Wayne's satisfaction, and they were left behind to wait.

We transited down one lock only as we were going to spend time at the Pedro Miguel Yacht Club, located in a small side lagoon and which, from the look of it, had fallen on hard times (it closed a few years later). It was here that our first year ended. We kept *Bali Ha'i* there for a little over three months to wait for anticipated good winds, currents, and conditions to start our Pacific crossing. We took a trip back to the States to visit family and friends for the holidays, but while at Pedro Miguel we made many lasting friendships with other cruisers, some of whom we would see in various anchorages here and there around the world and even long after the completion of our circumnavigation. Those friendships were just one part of the supportive, friendly, multinational, constantly moving—expanding and shrinking, depending on the anchorage—cruising community. The extensive camaraderie and helpfulness among those of us who lived on our boats and sailed the world made the relationships exceptional.

Panama: Cruisers provisioning for South Pacific passage. Photograph by Gayla Morkel Phelps, S/V _Ariel_.

Cruising Life: Dinghies tied to the stern of _Ariel_ indicating some socializing going on. Photograph by Gayla Morkel Phelps, S/V _Ariel_.

≈≈≈

We left Pedro Miguel on March 18, 2002 under sunny skies and pleasant temperatures to transit the remaining locks, crossed under the Pan-American Bridge and officially entered the Pacific, with some fellow cruisers as line handlers. We appeased the appropriate gods, especially Jupiter, with a few coins and some whiskey poured into the sea.

Later, alone, on our way to the Galápagos, on March 26 at 9:41 p.m. we crossed the equator. Wayne instigated our equator-crossing ceremony to emulate naval ritual. First, we had to dress appropriately: Wayne wearing a tie, but no shirt (it was hot), and I sporting a flashy, sequined top. We again ceremoniously appeased the gods and announced ourselves official *shellbacks*. Although Wayne had flown across the equator many times and I had a few times, sailing across it was quite another matter, and the old rites must be observed, which would bring sailors favorable winds and not too many storms.

Passages: Wayne dressed for the equator crossing ritual.

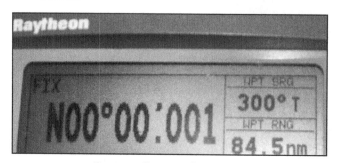

Passages: Crossing the equator.

Seeing People: Where Are You From?

There were eight of us plus our guide. We were on Isabella Island in the Galápagos on our way to see a large caldera, beyond which was a strikingly inhospitable landscape of still smoking, gurgling, spitting volcanic openings in the gray and *colorado*-colored place. *Colorado,* the Spanish word for a stone-soil-red color, has no clear translation into English. It is a reflection of different landscapes—Iberia, Mexico, the U.S. Southwest, places where the land is a sere reddish brown that seems to absorb and then give back a spectrum of sunrise and sunset so that land reflects sky in shades of blended pink, orange, magenta. How could English with all its shades of green understand and speak of such a color.

My horse was mottled brown with what appeared to be a once-brown mane now tinged with gray, like me, I suppose. Her ribs showed and her step was unsure. That combined with the crudely woven rope reins and wooden frame saddle covered with burlap and rags that rocked slightly from side to side made me watch the so-called trail with its mud holes and slippery rocks as if I were the one putting one foot in front of the other, willing her with all my concentration not to slip.

We arrived and dismounted. To call this place *land* seemed a misnomer. Yet this process we were witnessing was how much of our land was formed. Volcanic eruptions are still creating new land in the Pacific; but that's another story. Isabella Island is the largest of the Galápagos, also known as the Archipelago de Colón and the Islas Encantadas (Bewitched Islands), a historic name derived from the fact that the strong currents affected early ships and confounded navigators so that the islands came and went, so to speak.

Before our horseback ride to this seemingly unearthly place, we had all sailed our own sailboats to the Galápagos arriving there from various ports and previous landfalls: three of us from the United States, one from Germany, two from Sweden, and two from Norway. We had established our nationalities early on,

but there was little talk as we concentrated on getting to our destination. Near the caldera, the wife in the Swedish couple spoke loudly to me, probably to make sure she got through my grim concentration on my mare's footing.

"I am pleased to hear you speak that you are from the U.S., and not say you are American. I cannot tolerate people from your country who say they are Americans. Everyone from those continents over there is an American."

I grimaced at her through gritted teeth, but were they clamped shut due to my horse or her comments? What were we supposed to call ourselves? There are Canadians, Spanish, Chinese, French, Mexicans, but what works for the United States of America? Why didn't our country's forebears think about this problem? What's in the name? United States of America: a reflection of our early independent spirit, the individuality of each state, the rights of the smaller unit versus the rights of the totality. Concepts we still harbor, often to the detriment of the whole. But what about our name as a people?

Wherever we sailed, we would be asked "What is your name?" "Where are you from?" "How long did it take you to sail here from America?" "How old are you?" "How many children do you have?" Sometimes we would say we were from the United States, sometimes America, but either way, they responded, "Oh, American." So we are American, and the earliest immigrants to our country are called Native Americans, although my understanding is that most would rather be called by their tribal name, such as Navajo, Apache, Inuit; but if one doesn't know the tribe, then Indians, and, finally, Americans. We acknowledge that everyone from our continent is a North (or *Nord* or *Norte*) American (*Américain, Americano*), but few, if any, Canadians would ever label themselves as Americans, and Mexicans might say "*Yo también soy Americano*," but they would proudly announce their Mexican heritage first. Central Americans, a sort of no-man's-land in terms of continents, seem to prefer their country appellations. South Americans, like Mexicans, while preferring first their specific country, understandably also identify themselves as Americans.

These labels are of interest only because of what they indicate about a person. It is a shortcut, of sorts, to know something about each other. There are the usual stereotypes that accompany each label, then we spend the rest of the time getting to know each other, only to realize our stereotypes are wrong—not that we drop them, of course. Perhaps, after all, they help us to see only what is relatively true.

3

The Longest Passage: What It Means to Travel

To live is to see, and traveling sometimes speeds up the process.
—Edward Hoagland, "Heading Out from Home,"
The Tugman's Passage

Underway: Limbo or a Place of Its Own?

Squid flying at night off waves, looking for a meal, avoiding predators, having a grand time. And then suddenly ending up on our deck. I could almost hear them screaming, "Lord Poseidon, what in the depths is this? Where am I?" Young ones crying; older ones stoically meeting their fate. The first four days out of the Galápagos we averaged about fifteen dead squid a night. During the day we saw schools of them near the surface. "Hey guys," I yelled. "Stay away, we're dangerous." Gradually they seemingly learned their lesson—in reality, we moved out of squid-filled waters, only to go through the same experience with flying fish. We would have liked to have eaten a few since they were dead anyway, but their condition after who knows how many hours on our deck didn't encourage our gastronomic desires.

Our longest passage in distance was from the Galápagos to the Marquesas, French Polynesia—3,673 statute miles and took us fifteen days with an average speed of 8.78 knots. We made the fastest passage of the approximately forty cruising boats to leave the Galápagos for the Marquesas that season. Even though, as our log noted, the clew (bottom) of our mainsail blew out in 40-knot winds when at 11:15 p.m. on day eleven a rascally wave swept over the deck and filled the bottom of the sail tearing it as the boat righted itself after suddenly being pushed abeam of the wind. It wouldn't be the last time we had to take the mainsail down in the dead of night in rolling seas and wrestle that massive, blowing sail into a tied-up lump of wet, white fabric on the slippery, salty deck. On to the Marquesas we sailed with headsail alone.

Dolphins came and played in our bow wake acknowledging our presence, and we saw a Humpback whale from a distance. We caught a beautiful multicolored Mahi-mahi, depleting that species by one, but filling our bellies with the succulent fresh meat, feeding some leftovers of the skeleton to the sharks, the remainder sinking for the bottom feeders: worms, crabs, and crawlers at whatever depth that might be.

Always there was the excitement of moving on. I wondered what the next landfall would be like for me; would I see old friends, make new ones, understand enough of the language, find provisions we needed or wanted, be able to get ashore easily? In some places that was its own challenge.

In one anchorage at Ua Pou, Marquesas, the surge was so strong it washed us right up on top of the rocks, and I literally had to jump out at just the right moment. Our one-year-old dinghy motor had died, much to our annoyance. Perhaps fortunately, however, because we were using my inflatable sea kayak, which made the ride over the rocks a little easier. Some places I have fallen in. Once somewhere in Central America at night as I climbed up a series of old tires to reach the pier, I slipped, ending up in an oil- and refuse-polluted harbor—as if the fall wasn't bad enough. Wayne grabbed my hand and pulled me up, and I climbed again, successfully this time, and we proceeded on to a small restaurant for the usual fare of chicken, rice, and beans. In the heat, my clothes quickly dried.

≈≈≈

The movement under sail from one landfall to another brought up a myriad of feelings and thoughts. There was the logical work to be done of charting a course, checking the weather, calibrating distances, provisioning, accruing knowledge of the next destination that beckoned us on, and, of course, once underway, keeping watch. There were also the niggling questions of what would the passage really be like: would we have severe winds, would we have enough wind, would there be sudden squalls, what about system failures, and in some places concern about pirates. There was always some

ceremony and ritual to leaving, even if it was only asking a stranger to cast off our lines or the signal from Wayne to me at the wheel that the anchor was up and to head on, but often there were some good-byes, last-minute pictures, waving to someone.

There is the transitory nature of travel from one point to another, but there is also the aspect of the actual journey being an entity in and of itself. Going from one place to another has its own magic, its own life, its own meaning. The metaphor for life itself is a journey from birth to death. There is something both physical and metaphysical in a journey. This process, this time, this movable space we took up as we sailed on became for me a place of its own.

This time on a sailboat alone at sea, out of sight of land for days on end—I wondered how it would shape me and the space through which I traveled? What path can endure when all that is left is the yacht's wake melting into the waves and the swell of the ocean behind?

≈≈≈

After the routine briefing to me on our position, the current trim of the sails, the weather, and traffic (ships in the area), Wayne would go below for his five- to six-hour sleep. It would be about 10:00 p.m. somewhere first in the Caribbean, then the Pacific, followed by the Coral Sea and others like the Gulf of Carpentaria, the Strait of Malacca, the Andaman Sea, other oceans.

Night Watch

Waves crest, hiss, whisper,
ask the unanswerable, question the reason,
even hold cryptic hushed conversations

as if in a closet hung with long velvet dresses,
or behind closed French doors
shrouded in golden satin drapes.

Songlines run from past to future,
memories, dreams, the wished for sonatas
playing the scale of one's life.

The watch searches the waning horizon
for the true words, the real meaning—
they fade into reminiscence just as the wake
becomes a memory
on the surface of the sea.

Usually when I started my night watch there was only blackness, then the awakening of my brain synapses that translated sight into meaning would come into play as I sipped a cup of hot tea or coffee. We always had our nav lights on, as prescribed by law, but large ships today don't see or even look for small craft, so it is up to us to stay vigilant. On these same 360-degree scans of the horizon, I would notice the moon's status, as it waxed and waned with the passing nights—one way I measured the transit of time on a passage.

For me there was a sublime pleasure in my watch from about 10:00 p.m. to 3:00 a.m. or later. I was alone in this world, but connected through wind, waves, stars, the bioluminescence of algae and other oceanic life forms, the moon when it was out. In all these primordial ways I was just another strand of this life. The senses I used the most were listening as well as seeing.

Night watches for me were a time of alchemy

Passages: S/V *Bali Ha'i III* underway with only our wake to show our passage. Photograph by crew of S/V *Reflections*.

when the simple task of keeping watch was transformed into a mystical and inscrutable time. When the wind was steady and the sails were set, I often sat in the back of the cockpit, the autopilot on, checking for traffic every ten minutes or less by standing up to take a thorough scrutiny of the dark. I belonged to that space and time.

It was a time of being present in a way that I have never experienced anywhere else: not the stillness of our cabin in a remote area of the Colorado mountains, meditation, nor the most sacred places I have visited. Nothing came close to this dimension of life for me.

I've always been fascinated by the Southern Cross, probably because I didn't grow up with it outside my bedroom window. Ironically, considering its importance in the Southern Hemisphere, it's the smallest of the eighty-eight constellations in our galaxy.

Light Travel

The Southern Cross lies on its side
anchoring the Milky Way,
nonchalantly playing across the sky
with a careless leap above the sea
introducing one shore to the other.

In our wake, planktonic starbursts streak by,
in company with comical light balloons
puffed up to speak,
but collapsing without a squeak.

Where are they going,
these lights of sea and sky?
What space and time serve them
that we never quite grasp,
never quite fathom?

If I slip down and join
this phosphorescent stream,
will I discover boundless time
that dwells beyond our certainty?

As the days and nights of a passage mounted, our sleep patterns were established, albeit shortened, creating some effects of sleep deprivation. I felt this especially as I had shorter sleep periods than Wayne, who had trouble napping during the day, thus needed more sleep at night. Gradually a sense of displacement crept in, a disconnect from the normal routines of life on land or at anchor. We ate, slept, kept watch, read, checked charts, calculated distances, talked on the Single Side Band (High Frequency) radio net to report our position and hear from our fellow cruisers making the same passage, if there were any. We needed sharpened senses, but the longer the passage, the more attention that took. It felt natural, yet in a disembodied way. Maybe it was the isolation, having only ourselves to depend on, and being disconnected from a known world, but each passage created a life of its own.

We were out of touch with the daily horrors of war, poverty, crime, and the bizarre irrelevancies that the media, particularly those in the United States, love to report. We did not hear mobile phones, TV, horns honking, auto antitheft devices bleating away. Although no Circe, no Cyclops, no Lotus-Eaters, we had our little adventures: a whale, a pod of dolphins, a torn sail, and, of course, mourning all the squid and flying fish we unintentionally killed. And we had our pleasures: for me, a well-written book, Billy Collins's or Mary Oliver's poetry, Yo-Yo Ma's magic playing through my headphones, and, of course, my night watches. Occasionally we would have an unexpected visitor, such as a Brown Booby landing on our deck for a respite.

Passages: A Brown Booby visits.

The disengagement from anything outside the
life of the passage itself forged a space/time continuum
that could not happen on land. Here, we did not belong
to land patterns. It was this disconnection that enabled
the passage to become its own place, and for me to be
connected to it in a metaphysical manner. I cannot fill a
full glass; first I must empty it. That's what happens on a
passage, I emptied myself of land-based life, then filled
up on the sea. Because the sea is not the normal home of
humans, it created this unexpected and engaging open
space within me, like one of the colorful sponges seen on
coral reefs, or an anemone taking in what passes by.

  When spoken aloud as a chant, the following poem
gives a sense of the floating timeframe of a passage.

Time shows up
on watch hands
as it passes
knot by knot.

Knots measure
days passing.

White pelagic terns quiver,
painted blue breasts;
reflections up,
shadows down.

Knots measure
days passing.

Blue is the color
of distance, of depth,
of jack lines flat on the white deck,
of remembered eels' eyes.

Knots measure
days passing.

One drifts
as wind,
rises and falls
as the swell.

Slowly in measured beats,
time floats past
on a piece of sargassum weed,
then caught in the wake.

Knots measure
days passing.

Knots measure
days passing.

Dispersal: Cattle Egrets, Crocodiles, and Polynesians

In one last beat of her wings, a starving Cattle Egret fell below a foamy wave crest. We never saw her again. Did she land to float until death took her or did she dive head first into the wave and sink below looking death straight in the eye? All was lost, she knew, there was no turning back. She had left her home area, driven out by cousins, aunts, uncles, even siblings. It wasn't personal; it was survival—there simply wasn't enough food to go around. She was bound and determined to live so she could pass down her collection of genes to the next generation; that's what life had meant for her.

How did she get to this end? She had flown away from her birthplace alone. Nothing looked suitable to her below—buildings, pavement, cars. She didn't know the names of these things, but she was experienced enough to know she could not find the insects that gave her the strength in her wings, the feeling of life. Then, something got her attention below. She wheeled around and came down for a landing—grass, trees, a pond, and a large heron. She would stay out of its way, but, yes, she could find food here. In a patch of hibiscus bushes she found several grasshoppers. Just as she thought she might settle down, a large dog raced toward her. She moved quickly out of the bushes and lifted off again.

Was this to be her life, always moving, a nomad? Soon she came to the end of land, and saw a huge pond, more water than she could imagine, but across it, there seemed to be land; she would head there. That night she spent on one of the small islands just west of Key West—insects to eat, no people, but a resident osprey who didn't care for company. She tried staying out of its way, but after a few days of dodging, she gave up and took to the air.

She landed again on one of the Dry Tortugas. Now she was tired and hungry, but this was windswept sand. She half-heartedly tried a small ghost crab. There was nothing for her here. It was the wrong environment. She settled down behind some driftwood to await the discovery of the next leg of her journey. Others, like her, had come here; their bones testament to the inappropriateness of this place for them. She would keep going, but this night, she slept.

The next morning she watched as something moved away from the island. She may have wondered in her own way, "Was this a large animal I could follow that will churn up insects for me?" Follow she did.

≈≈≈

The incident that prompted this imagined story of the Cattle Egret occurred early on in our voyage when we set sail from the Dry Tortugas southwest of Key West, for Isla Mujeres, Mexico, a trip of approximately 310 nautical miles. I noticed a Cattle Egret following us and thought she might land on the spreaders as we got farther offshore, but she didn't. After a few hours, a deep-sea fishing boat motored by about two miles off our beam. She left us to follow that boat, but she never made it.

From my bird biology course, I learned that Cattle Egrets (*Bubulcus ibis*) have an amazing dispersal record. Native to Africa their expanding range is well documented. In the late 1800s, they apparently left West Africa and crossed the southern Atlantic to settle on the northeast coast of South America. In 1933, they were in southern Australia; in the 1950s, southern France, the Volga Delta, Mexico, Belize, Honduras, Guatemala, Newfoundland, Hawaii, New Jersey, Massachusetts. By 1977, they had spread all the way down to Tierra del Fuego, and their range continues to expand.[1]

Since this species was so adept at scattering to the winds, I wondered why it didn't happen sooner. A partial answer may be found in the availability of their feeding environment. Generally, they forage in flocks intermixed with large grazing animals in herds, such as cattle and elephants. They actually eat the insects stirred up by the grazers and do not eat ticks and the like off the animals themselves. In the North and South American continents, it has only been since the late 1800s that large areas were cleared for grazing. While they probably would have loved the Great Plains of North America when bison herds were still there, they would have had to get past a large forested area to even find the plains. That was too big an obstacle. They also forage along shorelines. The problem in the Dry Tortugas was there just wasn't enough food.

These birds have always been travelers with a purpose. Juveniles commonly disperse after breeding season. These characteristics were helpful for this later extreme dispersal. One of the interesting aspects of their dispersal is that it was done in big chunks, not a short trip here followed by another jump a little farther. These birds were on a mission. For them, it related to survival of their species.

This concept of dispersal led me to the Saltwater crocodiles (*Crocodylus porosus*) of the Solomon Islands, which have been dispersing for the same reason: survival, but from quite different causes. The relatively recent rapacious logging of many of the Solomon islands—much of it sent to China for making plywood—carries silt into the estuaries, creeks, and edges of the sea that are the habitats of the salties. To collect these logs, ships and boats churn up the waters that used to be wild. And so the crocs move on a little, but people get in their way.

These are the same aggressive crocs found in Australia and mainly live in brackish water, although they can be found in fresh water rivers too. The young are born in nests on land but always near the water and are first raised in fresh water. As they get older they move to saltier environments. This is our planet's largest reptile with females up to about ten feet and males up to about twenty feet, although a few have been measured even longer. Interestingly, like the Cattle Egrets, the young often disperse to new territories; but in the salties' case, it is because they are territorial and only so many crocs can stand to be near each other.

Their bodies are an engineering marvel and another splendid evolutionary phenomenon. Their air-based senses—eyes, ears, noses—are on the top of their head so they can be submerged and easily see, hear, breathe, and smell with just a flat piece of hide with a few bumps on it barely above the water's surface. Even when they were lying still on a log, I found it sometimes difficult to distinguish them.

Interestingly it is the temperature of the nest that makes a difference in whether or not the eggs are hatched as males or females. For males, the nest needs to be about 88.8° F; higher or lower and they will be female. The eggs and juveniles are eaten by many other animals including snakes, birds, goannas, wild pigs, even turtles. Like sea turtles, it's estimated that 1 percent or less of the hatchlings will mature enough to mate and reproduce.[2]

Crocs are definitely carnivores and will eat almost anything from snakes and birds to people and water buffalo. As with the mountain lions in Colorado, tigers in India, wild elephants in Thailand, the salties' dispersal from their normal homeland is caused by intervention into their space by humans. No, it is more than intervention, it is our possession of their space. So the animals move and adapt to sharing space with these two-legged creatures who in a few cases become a new food source. Of course, this creates dramatic headlines and calls for death to the killers; the four-legged killers, that is. And all this for plywood.

Who are we to think we are the only species worth saving?

≈≈≈

Cattle Egrets and salties are not the only species that use dispersal to survive. The Polynesians knew not only how to save themselves, but to increase their territory and their peoples via dispersal. Polynesian culture has been called "a culture of mobility" in academic papers.[3] Polynesia means *many islands*, and the Polynesians were able to inhabit a large area of the South Pacific because of their extraordinary long-distance, open-water sailing and navigation skills.

The early Polynesians used stars, wind, the sun and moon, clouds, wave shape, sea birds, and seaweed as tools for navigation. Although they had no written language, they did have elaborate ocean charts made of wood, shells, stones, and other natural objects. They sailed huge double-hulled canoes, carrying plants, animals, and people. Their reasons are believed to have been overpopulation and/or power competitions among chiefs, which forced groups to leave their initial island and move on. Added to that could just as easily have been a sense of adventure and the visceral drive to explore. Many traditional legends tell of competing chiefs, usually related to each other, in power struggles and, if the loser wasn't killed, he could take his people and move on. In Raiatea near Tahiti, the story is that brothers—Pa'ao and Lonopele—feuded and killed each other's sons at which time Pa'ao left to settle Hawai'i. Such stories dramatize a core cultural tenet—in this case, dispersal.

I knew from having visited the three corners that the vast Polynesian Triangle stretches from Hawai'i in the north, Aotearoa (New Zealand) in the southwest, and Rapa Nui (Easter Island) in the southeast. It covers an area of roughly 10 to 12 million square miles. Including the three triangle points of land, plus the Cook Islands, Fiji, French Polynesia, both Samoas, and Tonga, the total land area is only a little over 119,000 square miles—in other words, a lot of water. The people who managed this amazing dispersal became known as Polynesians. There is considerable debate about the actual timeframe, particularly as new tools become available to date artifacts. It is generally agreed that they started their migration from Southeast Asia via New Guinea to Fiji, Tonga, and Samoa, possibly about 900 BCE. From Tonga and Samoa, the Polynesian culture differentiated itself from Melanesian and moved on to settle the Cook Islands, Tahiti, Tuamotus, and Hiva Oa in the Marquesas, reaching Rapa Nui, the Hawaiian Islands, and Aotearoa probably by 1000 CE. Who knows how many cousins, brothers, and uncles fought to cause this dispersal or how many dreamers, like us, wondered what was past the next wave?

The various Polynesian cultures have related

languages and similar cultural organization. In fact, in Hawaiian and the southern Marquesan languages there are many of the same words, such as *mano* for shark. The Polynesian society was highly structured, based on hereditary chiefdoms and a cadre of priests to manage conduct based on a set of *tabus*, from which comes our word *taboo*. During our cruising the South Pacific islands, we would occasionally see a *tabu sign*, which usually meant *do not enter*, but also *do not do* something, although it is difficult to know what has become taboo because of the influence of the missionaries (that is another story) and what is from the old culture.[4]

I learned much of Polynesian history not just by reading about it, but mostly by visiting small museums throughout Polynesia and talking to Polynesians, many of whom have become more involved in learning and spreading information about their history in recent times. In the 1970s, along with all the other movements of that decade, a few Hawaiians became more interested in their heritage, particularly the sailing and navigational abilities of their ancestors, and formed the Polynesian Voyaging Society. Ironically, the only known person to still have those skills was a Micronesian, Mau Piailug, from Satawal Island in the Carolines. His education was from his grandfather. The Society's founders convinced him to come to Hawai'i and hand down his skills. His knowledge is documented by the successful voyages that followed. The first was in 1976 in a replica of an ancient canoe, Hōkūle'a, sailing approximately 2,400 miles from Hawai'i arriving in Tahiti exactly where and when Piailug intended to make landfall, although he had never sailed that area before. There have been many other voyages since then to the far-flung reaches of the Polynesian

Triangle, a testament to the perseverance and vision of the Society's members and supporters.[5]

Hawaiian Nainoa Thompson, an avid and successful student of Piailug's, later suggested using traditional materials to build an historically accurate canoe. Ironically just as there was no traditional knowledge in Hawai'i, neither were there trees, often koa, of the right size and shape. These trees had been decimated by centuries of logging, certainly not just by the Polynesians, but mainly by the exploitative colonials that came later. Other native people came to the rescue, and a northwestern North American tribe sent two immense Sitka spruce logs for the canoe. With this realization of the destruction of Hawai'i's environment, the Society worked with other organizations and created Mālama Hawai'i (to care for and protect Hawai'i). The purpose was to take "responsibility to strengthen what we value about Hawai'i: its beauty, its mana, its unique environment and native culture, its multi-ethnic community."[6]

Other knowledge was lacking also; for example, how to create the sennit, the coconut husk fiber rope used for lashing the outrigger to the spars and thus to the canoe, among other uses. Sennit was so important in the seaworthiness of a canoe that prayers were given to the overseeing god—Tangaroa in Samoa and Tonga; Tane in Tahiti and other central Polynesian islands including Hawai'i. Having been taught how to make a simple coconut fiber broom on Suwarrow in the Cook Islands, clearly a much cruder type of work, I can appreciate the skill required for sennit. Even for the broom, it required stripping down multiple strands of fiber in a painstaking way. The following by the exceptionally skilled and talented Te Rangi Hīroa (Sir Peter Henry Buck), a Polynesian poet, medical doctor, and anthropologist, expresses the importance of sennit.

> What have I, O Tane,
> Tane, god of beauty!
> 'Tis sennit.
> 'Tis sennit from the host of heaven,
> 'Tis sennit of thine, O Tane!
> Thread it from the inside, it comes outside
> —Te Rangi Hīroa (Sir Peter Henry Buck),
> *Vikings of the Sunrise*

The Polynesians were quite organized about their dispersal. As mentioned previously, they carried plants, which included breadfruit, paper mulberry, taro, and yam; animals including chickens, dogs, and pigs. The paper mulberry (*Broussonetia papyrifera)* originally from East Asia and called *wauke* in Hawaiian, is used to make tapa cloth. In modern times, the ability to make tapa was starting to die out along with navigational skills and the building of traditional canoes.

The importance of tapa was brought home to us when we visited Ua Pou in the Marquesas where Richard, the curator of the museum, had brought in a high-school class to see how the old women, whom he had caringly gathered, made tapa from the inner bark of the paper mulberry tree. I enjoyed observing the amazement on the faces of the young students as they watched women who could be their grandmothers, sitting on the floor on tapa mats they had probably made, pounding away on the fibrous material for more tapa cloth. Today tapa is mostly used for decoration and to sell to tourists, but originally it was used for clothing, bedding, funeral coverings, various ceremonial uses—anything where fabric was needed.

French Polynesia, Marquesas: The dramatic island of Ua Pou.

French Polynesia, Marquesas: One of the author's tapa paintings purchased in the Marquesas.

at local bakeries, it is its own world, dominated in the Polynesian style by chiefs, as we quickly found out.

Fifteen or so sailing yachts lay at anchor off the rocky shore in an indentation along the leeward coast. By now, used to this influx of boats headed for the South Pacific at this time of year thanks to winds and currents, a few of the villagers exercised their entrepreneurial skills, as well as the traditional Polynesian welcoming of strangers, by arranging a pig roast with a small charge. It was the host family's daughter's birthday, and we all sang Happy Birthday to her in our native languages, which included: English, German, French, Spanish, Catalan, Portuguese, Danish, Swedish, and Finnish. We were rewarded with a night of Marquesan music on guitar and native drums and

Extinction, I could see, doesn't only happen to species. Richard, like the members of the Polynesian Voyaging Society, recognized that ancient traditions are not only worth saving, but give substance to their culture and validate its history.

Landfall

Our voyage was made up of passages and landfalls. As diverse as they may be, they both created the journey. The landfall at Fatu Hiva in the Marquesas, although not the first, was significant, not only because of completing the longest passage, but for the dramatic landscape of towering spires of rock and greenness of the mountainous volcanic remains and the foreignness of the culture. Although the Marquesas are the easternmost ramparts of French Polynesia, with baguettes available

French Polynesia, Marquesas: Dramatic anchorage at Fatu Hiva, our first landfall in the South Pacific.
Photograph by Gayla Morkel Phelps, S/V *Ariel*.

a flavorful meal. There was *poisson cru*, the deliciously ubiquitous French Polynesian marinated fish in lime with coconut milk; cabbage salad; various root vegetables including taro and manioc, with which we would become all too familiar; taro greens; and shredded, barbecued pig—that is, they said it was pig. It certainly wasn't pig; Wayne thought it was goat as there are feral goats there. Whatever it was, it was tasty, and both Wayne and I had seconds. Two days later (fortunately there was a gap between the eating and this knowledge), we learned we had eaten barbecued dog.

One of the Brit cruisers gave a bottle of rum to two young village men who had paddled to his boat to check out the foreign visitors. The young Marquesans got noticeably drunk and continued around the anchorage pestering other cruisers for more booze, which, thankfully, they weren't given. The next day, the chief called all of us in and angrily told us if that happened again, we would all have to leave.

A few years later, we had to get special written permission from a chief to visit the Lau group of islands in Fiji, where cruising boats hadn't been allowed for years because of two incidents instigated by thoughtless cruisers. One involved having a local young woman stay overnight on board a yacht of young men, and the other involved alcohol. As cruisers, we were guests not only in their waters, but in their culture. We brought our homes with us and established ourselves, in a sense, in the local community when we anchored. We were more than tourists, less than members of that community. As such, we walked a fine line between intimacy and separateness, and it was critical that we observed and respected local cultural mores.

Becoming a Wanderer

This voyage at sea: had I constructed my own diaspora or had I become a nomad? Rather, I thought I was becoming a wanderer, a voyager meandering around the world. A traveler seemed too separate from the places traveled to. Generally we were heading west, and we had set courses that we followed on passages—there were certain harbors we were aiming for. Yet, it was all changeable depending on wind and whims. Yes, I wished to be a wanderer.

I didn't have a safe childhood. My father was a complex and tormented man. During the time of our circumnavigation when he was in his mid-nineties in an assisted-living complex, he was sent to a psychiatric hospital for evaluation after a violent episode with another resident. He was diagnosed as having severe narcissistic personality disorder. This isn't an illness, like bipolarity or even schizophrenia, which can be, at least partially, controlled with meds. At that point the diagnosis only helped me to understand a little better his abusive behavior.

We had traveled extensively in the United States when I was a child, although we always kept our house in New York. In retrospect, I realize it was because my father couldn't keep a steady job with his personality, although he was bright and competent in his field of metallurgy and mechanical engineering. After my mother's death, I learned that it was her trust fund that paid for our lives then. There were two advantages when we traveled. First, there was less chance for abuse. Second, he was always interested in seeing the odd off-the-road places, like the

Petrified Forest, or made a point of going to the various capitols of those states we passed through for us to see.

By the time I was twelve in 1952, I had been in over thirty states and lived in six; driven across the country about five times and flown coast to coast once—this in a time when such travel wasn't that common. In fact, the flight was prejet and took all day with a stop in Chicago. We dressed up then for plane travel: shiny black patent leather shoes that we called Mary Janes, white socks with lace at the top, little dresses. In the car, we were more casual, and in the West my mother often had us in blue jeans and our cowgirl boots so when we stopped, we could clamber about.

My sister, who was my main companion, and then, as now, my best friend, was thirteen months younger. We both had matching beige tweed Samsonite suitcases, which we covered with decals as we traveled through states and places: New Mexico and its Zia sign, the Grand Canyon, Niagara Falls, Illinois birthplace of Lincoln, and so many others. Funky as it might be, I would love to have that suitcase now. It was thrown away by my father and first stepmother (we refer to her as the wicked one), when my sister and I were in college and they moved from the house we had always kept in New York. Thrown away along with our bicycles, my diary, my sister's cherished horse collection, all the bits and pieces of our childhood lost to us.

Travel may have meant a modicum of safety to me, and perhaps that is what I was looking for on this voyage too. That sounds odd: to look for safety sailing around the world in a small (relatively speaking) sailboat. It could have been the sense of being unreachable, not that my father could literally have caught up with me. In fact,

he died, finally, at age ninety-seven, while we were still sailing.

≈≈≈

Dispersal involves movement from one point to another of several of the same organisms: dandelion seeds, Cattle Egrets, crocodiles, Polynesians. These were travelers with a purpose: survival. Perhaps I was traveling too with the same purpose: survival. Yet, mine was a wandering sort of travel. I needed to step away; I needed to see for myself. Yes, I had survived abuse—now I wanted to rediscover my own world.

One of the advantages of GPS is always knowing where one is, but what does that mean? We have our latitude and longitude, but then we relate that to a chart (called a map on land). Sometimes when clearly we were at sea, it showed us on land. Charts are not always correct, and more often than I would have thought there are large hatch-marked areas—uncharted. I think most of my life has been sailed in uncharted waters.

Travel, wandering, dispersal; they add up to moving on for different reasons, different causes. But it is all of these that have created this beautifully diverse planet we inhabit, that we need to preserve, that we need to see, that we need to understand, that we need to save. Species, cultures, traditional knowledge, diversity—it is all worth saving. It is through travel that, as Hoagland wrote in the epigraph for this chapter, the process of seeing, of living speeds up. I would add that it also enables us to understand the need for survival, not just of ourselves.

4

South Pacific: The Dichotomy of Gift-Giving

The sea does not reward those who are too anxious, too greedy, or too impatient. To dig for treasures shows not only impatience and greed, but lack of faith. Patience, patience, patience, is what the sea teaches. Patience and faith. One should lie empty, open, choiceless as a beach— waiting for a gift from the sea.

— Anne Morrow Lindbergh, *Gift from the Sea*

We make a living by what we get, we make a life by what we give.

— Sir Winston Churchill

Polynesia: Establishing Yourself with Gifts

Gifts sailed through our stay in Polynesia just as comfortably as we sailed through the pass on the western side of Raroia, a large coral atoll, where we anchored off the small village. This was our first stop in the Tuamotus, also known as the Dangerous Isles because they are reef-strewn, low-lying atolls—hungry traps for unwary ships.

Stepping ashore on the white sand beach sprinkled with seashells, we were immediately greeted by Thomas, "*Bon jour*, wellcomb, I speak leettle inglish."

As he bedecked us with cowrie shell necklaces, I answered, "*C'est bon. Je parle un peu de français.*"

"OK, we will be well." He smiled with teeth as white as the sand beneath his large brown feet. In the Polynesian style, he was dark-haired and dark-eyed with

creamy brown skin, and, although of medium height, hefty, without being actually fat. He was quite effeminate; in a western country he would have been taken for gay. In Polynesia, however, if there aren't enough girls in the family, one of the boys may be treated this way to help with those chores considered women's work, but it isn't related to their sexuality. "*Maintenant*, I show you my village."

The homes, like the village, were small; the sandy paths and most yards carefully outlined with shells in some places, vibrant hibiscus shrubs in others. Everyone we saw greeted us enthusiastically, but without a great deal of curiosity, although few cruising boats anchor here. The next day was Father's Day, and Thomas invited us to the feast he was preparing for his father. Later a young

Swedish couple and their two lovely, young, flaxen-haired daughters anchored, came ashore, and were invited also.

On the fête day, we assembled our gifts and dressed festively for the celebration. Ashore Thomas greeted us again as we pulled the dinghies up on the beach. He brought to mind a mother cat as he fussed over us, but his means of making us presentable was to drape more cowrie shell necklaces around our necks. He gently nudged us along with a somewhat proprietary manner. We were definitely *his*. As part of the Father's Day festivities he had made a lovely, intricate flower headdress for his father and presented Wayne with a large shark jaw and the Swedish papa with a gift also.

French Polynesia, Tuamotus: Father's Day fête.

Thomas's parents spoke only French, but with Thomas's "leetle inglish" and my *"peu de français"* we were able to communicate reasonably well. He told us proudly, "I am the only person on my island to go away from here. Le Marine de Guerre du France sent me à *France apprendre médecine. Je suis un medique.*" He blushed, a little abashed at what to him sounded almost boastful.

The feast was a great success. Papa's best gift may have been stroking the blonde heads of the little Swedish girls. Their mother cut their hair the next day and brought him a lock of their white-blonde hair, so unusual to him.

We were hard pressed to keep up with Thomas's gifts to us, never wanting to outdo him, but reciprocating in a way that showed our appreciation of his gifts to us and our respect for him. Gift-giving in Polynesia was not only a core cultural behavior, but an art form. As an outsider, trying to get it right required quivering antennae, imagination, a loss of ethnocentrism, and a stock of T-shirts, tapes, CDs, rice, and whatever we could think of. One of the gifts I often gave was to take pictures of the family, then print them copies.

Polynesia is about now; there is no past or future tense in most (if not all) of the local languages. "Thomas, what was life like *quand votre papa* was *un jeune fils*?"

"*Je ne sais pas.* Heyerdahl wrecked here. They almost dead."

Thomas's father was a young boy then, but he remembers that night. Thor Heyerdahl crashed Kon Tiki on the far eastern side of Raroia atoll and was only saved from death by those from this village across the ten-or-so-mile lagoon, who saw the signal fire that Heyerdahl and his sick and wounded crew had built. Continued life was the gift the villagers gave Heyerdahl and his crew along with food, cowrie necklaces, maybe even some black pearls. It isn't known what Heyerdahl gave back. His theory of these Polynesians originating from South America holds little water today. On the other hand, trade with South America from the early navigationally savvy Polynesians was certainly possible.

This was probably the most exciting event to have happened there in any living person's memory, but what is more important to the Polynesians is today. Thomas knew little of this event from his father.

One reason traditional Polynesians often make poor business people in the Western model is not only the immediacy of their lives without future planning, but the gift-giving aspect of their culture. It isn't right to have too much of anything if someone else is in need, especially someone from an extended family. It doesn't matter if it is money, pigs, fish, tinned food, or even children. It is a communal approach, but with clearly understood mores and implications. This was our lesson from Raroia.

Polynesian Geometry

The triangle runs from Hawai'i
to Rapa Nui to Māori land.

The circle meanders from my *fale*
around to auntie's, to mama's,
to the chief's, then his sister's,
to the pastor's, then the school,
and back to me.

Auntie wants my youngest son,
mama wants my last tin of corned beef,
the chief wants my new mat,
his sister wants my best *sulu*,
the pastor wants my red pen,
the school wants me to cook my own taro for all.

Down at the beach,
the round fat eels are waiting
to be caught.

Note: in Samoa, a *fale* (pronounced fah' lāy) is a thatch-roofed, open-sided house; a *sulu* is like a sarong.

Child-giving sounds extreme to Westerners: pangs of guilt, lawsuits later, desperate searches for birth parents. No such problem in Polynesia. If someone can't take care of the child they have or needs a child, they find a relative or someone in their clannish circle to give or take. We know of two such incidents of child-giving on Ua Pou in the Marquesas.

In Robert's case, a friend of his father's, who lived several kilometers away on the other side of the island's dramatic pinnacles, was visiting. The friend and his wife had no children and were saddened by that. Robert's father and his wife had just had their fourth child, a son, so Papa gave the new-born Robert to the friend, who dutifully trudged home at night over rock-strewn trails and presented his wife with a new son. They raised him until he was school age and then presented him to his second adopted family, that of a Scotch merchant in Taioha'e, a major town of the Marquesas on another island, so Robert could be educated. There he had to learn a new English word each day and complete his school lessons, then he would be rewarded with a treat. When he finished school, he returned to the village of his first adopted parents.

"I was not discarded; I was a gift first, and then second it was for me to learn, so you see, it was all a good thing."

When we met him, Robert was a beefy fellow in his fifties and had two teen-age sons of his own, whom he wanted us to adopt and take sailing with us to educate them. We passed on that opportunity. He enjoyed arranging local meals for the cruisers who visited there and telling us his people's creation story. Although we paid for the meal and brought some small gifts, as his voice blended with the firelight, that entrancing evening was his lovely gift to us.

Richard, an intelligent, articulate, young man deeply dedicated to maintaining the singular aspects of Marquesan culture, had also been a gift as a child. When we met him, he was the curator of the growing museum on Ua Pou. At the time we visited, he was explaining to a group of local high-school students the art of tapa-cloth making as they watched the women pounding out the bark. Richard's parents had given him to a French gendarme and his wife, who promised to educate him, which they did in France. Upon graduation, Richard returned to his birth village and soon took over the museum, which is his passion. He has built it up to become a major resource for tradition on the island and a fascinating place to visit.

Such child-giving is not like adoption in the Western world. It has nothing to do with the birth parents not wanting or being able to keep the child. It has to do with their relationship with the recipient parents and their need. Neither Robert nor Richard felt in any way abandoned or rejected by their birth parents. Rather they saw that they had been honored. It was true that sometimes what we call illegitimate children were given away, but again it had to do with the child being a gift or that it was better for the child.

≈≈≈

In the Marquesas, one of the islands we sailed to was Ua Huta, infrequently visited by yachts. The setting is like a Norwegian fjord built in Southwestern U.S. geology, and the anchorage is rather difficult with the tide and some swell rushing in and out. We went ashore in the dinghy and were walking up the only road we saw when the local policeman picked us up to offer a ride. He drove us to the local museum, which he unlocked specifically for us, and then to the botanic gardens, only about two miles away, but over a very high hill. I was glad for the ride as it was hot and humid. There I actually got to see a Pihiti (*Vini ultramarina*) in the wild, its blue color flashing brightly against the green shrubbery. This is an endemic lorikeet that only lives on this island, although has been reintroduced on a few other Marquesan islands.

The surge created constant motion, and we lost a stern anchor when the line above the chain was sawed off by a rock, but fortunately we had another anchor out that kept us off the rocky fjord-like walls. After that, we decided it was time to get out of there. We had to wait, however, as a ferry-type boat had come in to pick up all the school-age children heading back to boarding school after their holiday (there were no schools on this island as it was too small). Our next anchorage at Ua Huta was in an even more remote bay with wild horses and goats on the hillsides, and literally thousands of Sooty Terns soaring above the hills and out over the ocean with a few Great Frigatebirds (*Fregata minor*) thrown in. These experiences—from locals helping us unasked to rapid changes due to conditions—were typical of so many of the places we anchored.

≈≈≈

My voyage was filled with gift stories, but a few particularly precious ones stand out. Two of those survive only in my memory and photos as they were not objects, but actions. The first was given not only to me, but to a small handful of cruisers in the Marquesas. Because several of us had wanted to attend a local pig roast, I had tried to organize one at an island where we had arrived ahead of the others. All was set until the day before, when it turned out the family couldn't really get a pig. Several of the other cruisers dropped out, to their loss as it turned out. I think there were four couples, our friends Steve and Gayla from S/V *Ariel* with their crew of another couple, and our new friends from Great Britain on S/V *Amoenitas*, who would become long-time pals.

The dinner was served in a kitchen of sorts with tables pushed together and an odd assortment of plates and silverware. The meal was filling and flavorful with many courses, including *poisson cru*, fresh grilled fish, chicken in tomato sauce, local greens that seemed like a cross between spinach and chard, salad, corn, fresh papaya and mangoes, drinking nuts (green coconuts cut open at the end and served with a straw for their fresh sweet watery milk, then the best part, broken open for the coconut custard on the inside), fresh lemonade, and coconut cake.

At the end of the meal, our hosts had their young granddaughter perform a few traditional Polynesian dances for us. She was about eight, and rather shy, but sweet and charming in her childish innocence. Then we all sang songs together, some in English, some in French. It was an evening of camaraderie that cannot be planned, but happened in a magical way.

The second gift in memory and video only was for my birthday in a remote Tuamotu island. Another large atoll, this island had just two families on it who were related: easy-going—one could almost say lazy—tubby Tupo and his wife, Lana, their several kids, Tupo's sister, Iris, and her hard-working husband, who had one grown daughter away in Tahiti. We became quite close to them and participated in their everyday lives.

Mapo, the oldest son, was the glue for Tupo's family. He organized the work, put the little girls to bed, and did whatever was needed. Later we heard the girls had contracted dengue fever, a devastating mosquito-borne illness something like malaria, while at school in Tahiti, and it was Mapo they wanted to come and care for them, which he did. He was a huge fellow physically, about eighteen years old when we were there, and the gentlest, most thoughtful, hard-working son one could want—the perfect counterpart to his dad.

We became involved in island life in a variety of ways: we took Mapo diving with us using our equipment as he had none, Wayne helped the men in the family with the fish drive when they knew the supply ship was coming, we ate our meals ashore taking some tinned and dried food supplies. It could possibly be said that we helped with the copra collection. I write *possibly* because our contribution was quite minimal: I was inept at scraping the coconut meat out, and Wayne couldn't split coconuts fast enough to be an asset. But they enjoyed watching us struggle as they sped through the process, and we all laughed our way through the work.

French Polynesia, Tuamotus: The kids.

Copra is dried coconut meat from which the oil is extracted and used for many goods, including cosmetics. France subsidizes copra production, the French form of welfare. Families had to perform work to earn money. Even though what the French government paid was well over the market price, it's a much better system than the

U.S. welfare we saw in American Samoa, which is just a handout for nothing.

The fish drive was interesting, although what we would consider an environmental disaster. It didn't happen frequently, so it is hoped that life would be sustainable there for some time. The men of the family plus Wayne went out in one small boat to the reef. They walked along the top of the reef with long sticks in their hands toward a three-sided, closely woven wire enclosure beating their sticks on the reef, which drove the fish toward the enclosure. Once they had driven the fish in, they closed the fourth side with Mapo inside. Using a dip net, he scooped the fish up and passed the net outside to another person who dumped the fish into the small boat.

Back at their rickety wooden pier, the boys brought the fish ashore in old baskets. There under a thatched roof over a sand floor, Tupo's wife, Lana, sorted the fish by species and strung about ten or twelve on a piece of line through their gills and hung them in the water. The inedible fish she just threw back in the water, but most of those were already dead. The accountant from the supply boat came ashore, set up his little table and chair on the wet sand, and marked down each line of fish as it was thrown into the supply boat's tender. At the end of the accounting process, Lana identified what she needed in the way of rice, salt, sugar, petrol, and flour. The accountant tallied up both sides and paid Lana the remainder of their fish and copra credit.

I thought about those little dead fish that no one would eat, their bright reef colors draining out of their small bodies lying in the shallows. That was probably why the eels were so fat that young, chubby, tomboy Lucie tried to catch. In the life of the sea, nothing is wasted. It's just when we enter into it that the normal routine is changed. I should mourn as much for the coral squashed by the men and boys that morning as for the little yellow and white butterflyfish with the black teardrop spot seeming to drip off its side, the small-fry Lemonpeel angelfish still in its infancy with its juvenile marking of a blue ringed tear on its side, and the petite damselfishes, including my favorite, the Humbug dascyllus. I'm not sure it was a favorite for its name or its tiny pouty black and white striped shape like a miniature flattened soccer ball.

For my birthday, Lana and her sister-in-law, Pearl, conspired to bake me a birthday cake beautifully decorated with fresh, bright red hibiscus blossoms. Louis Jean, Tupo and Lana's sixteen-year-old son, played music on his homemade ukulele, and Rose, then eleven, danced and sang with the quintessential coconut palms, turquoise water, and soft breeze adding to the perfect ambiance. At first, her smile was embarrassed, then more confident, as she sang and swayed in traditional Polynesian dances, her small, graceful hands weaving the fabric of the story. As I

get older and forget more and more, some memories will stay with me forever and that evening is one of them.

One of the "gifts" of spending time in the Tuamotus was getting to know the black pearl farmers, sorting through their pearls, and buying what we wanted. Occasionally a local person who befriended us would give us one or two as a gift.

French Polynesia, Tuamotus: A friend and the author sort through imperfect black pearls.

One meaningful gift that I have is a lovely fan woven onto a pearl oyster shell made by the grandmother of our adopted family on Palmerston Island in the Cook Islands. This is an odd sort of place: a particularly remote atoll with no pass into the lagoon, so yachts and the supply ship have to anchor outside the reef. When the wind changes, they had better be ready to leave instantly, which is what happened to us.

Palmerston was settled by a British trader, William Marsters, who took at least two Polynesian wives there in 1863 and set up separate encampments for each one and their children on the main island of the atoll. He added a third wife shortly thereafter and another one later, although the last one didn't seem to have her own island section. One descendent described her family's section as the one "where the sun rises." Few yachts visit there, but when they are spotted in the distance, the young men from the three families compete to meet the yacht and adopt them for their family. Joseph and his brother were the ones who reached us first. They helped us anchor outside the reef.

Every morning they would come out to where we were anchored and take us ashore, or we would go in our dinghy. We had our main meals with that family, and they helped us with whatever we wanted to do such as fishing or bird watching. The protocol was if we wanted to visit another family, we needed to get our family's permission first. The first day, we participated in a three-times-around-the-island (it's a tiny island) run-walk race that the grandfather of our family had organized. He was in charge of the little clinic, and keeping fit was important to the health of all the families.

The original Marsters patriarch had a few rules, including that one couldn't marry within their own matriarchal family. In 1888, the British barque, *Queen's Island*, stopped at Palmerston and reported that there were thirty-three people on the island, who all spoke fluent English, and that "the family appear to live on the happiest terms." They noted only one wife, "a half-caste *kanaka*," eleven sons, and four daughters. A British missionary, William Wyatt Gill, who met Marsters, thought him "one of those waifs so common in the Pacific." It turns out he was a bit more than a waif, as he left a wife and two children in England, and there was a report that he carried a loaded gun with him all the time as allegedly the women (his Polynesian wives) had a plot against him.[1]

Cook Islands, Palmerston: The grandmother's gift to the author.

There are numerous Marsters on the island now and some in Rarotonga, the main island of the Cooks, and even New Zealand, along with a few in the United States and Europe no doubt. We had heard there was a contact person in Rarotonga to speak to in case the Palmerston islanders needed anything as the supply ship only came every few months and not always then. After locating the contact, she told me, "Yes, the islanders need many things. How soon are you going? I will find out exactly what and get these things, then you will come and store them on your boat, yes?"

"Yes," I responded, not that I felt there was a choice, nor did we mean for there to be. A few days later, she contacted me. It happened that some medicine was needed quickly requiring refrigeration for a sick baby; there were also numerous packages of diapers and toilet paper, canned food, and more. Fortunately we had refrigeration (not all sailboats do because of the energy required). Also, *Bali Ha'i,* as I've noted before, is fast for a sailboat, which would be critical in getting the medicine to Palmerston. We set sail late in the afternoon after we dutifully loaded the supplies on board *Bali Ha'i.* We sailed 330 nautical miles, having to make large tacks downwind due to the high swell. It took us a little less than two days. During the night we heard a whale blow nearby, but couldn't see it.

We also had aboard exercise notebooks and pencils for the Lucky School, which the Palmerston islanders had built a few years before, so named because they felt most lucky to have their own building for their few students from grades one through six. Unfortunately the young Brit fellow they had hired as a teacher for a year quit after six months. A woman from the village was coordinating the students' studies, but they were desperate for someone to teach. I made sure they understood I wasn't a teacher, but would do what I could and could teach a science class and writing.

During our first year, I had developed an ecology course to provide a free, self-contained, but customizable, educational program for nine- to twelve-year-olds. Because the lifestyle of the students in remote areas was one of subsistence and was environmentally dependent, these students already had a strong sense of their environment. Designed to provide enhanced perspectives of the students' sense of place, it was meant to provide an opportunity for discovering some different ways of looking at what they already knew and to strengthen a sense of stewardship for their area. The basis of the course was to map out a small study site and observe it, identifying what lived there and the food chains, then imagining what would happen if certain aspects were changed, such as one species disappearing.

I sought the advice of many professionals in developing it and appreciated their giving of their expertise. But it was only once that I actually taught the course myself, and that was at the Lucky School. I had donated the course to many individuals, schools, and organizations throughout our circumnavigation.

The first day ashore on Palmerston, I met the woman who had become in charge of the school by default; she was excited that I could teach writing. My idea was to get the kids to write short stories about their lives and the island. She announced they really needed help with cursive. Oh no! I went to four different elementary schools and blame my horrendous handwriting on that. Whatever my excuse, my writing is hardly cursive and not terribly legible, even to me at times.

I cautiously asked if she had a paper with the proper shape of the letters. "No," she replied, "we have nothing." That night on the boat, Wayne and I tried to come up with appropriate cursive letters. What was I to do? I ended up writing a Dr. Seuss-like poem and printed it from my computer in a script font. At the school the following day, I attempted to write some of the poem's made-up words in cursive for them; and together we created a story, which I wrote down on their blackboard more or less in cursive, I think. Here's part of the silliness I used to cover up my inability with cursive:

> I've been secretly told
> by a fellow quite bold
> that on Pammotu Isle,
> Not far from here—only one mile,
> They have a gargary game
> that brings the winners
> fantabulous fame.
>
> Now here's how it's played.
> (But I wouldn't play even if paid!)
> The players line up,
> the chief yells 'Zup!'
> Then they run for a coconut tree.
> The pivoty point is to see
> who climbs to the tiptapity top.
> But no, not here does it stop!
> This isn't the absterist end,
> for now they must bend,
> plait and weave the palm fronds

> into mercury, magical wands
> that are used to slingshot
> not one, but the whole lot
> of nuts to a bolicky box
> made of dead coral and rollicky rocks.

Both the students and I had great fun with the environmental science course! My students were captivated and thoroughly engaged even to the youngest, who was a little rascal, always climbing about and making funny faces trying to capture the interest of his older classmates. We happily left the classroom and dashed off to measure out an area of trees and brush, sandy beach, and lagoon in which we would make our observations. We made an inventory of what was living there, although I was hard pressed to keep the younger boys from crushing the snails. The ability of all of them to find eels

Cook Islands, Palmerston: My class at the Lucky School.

was impressive although not surprising given that eels were a food source for them. The older students became very thoughtful at the idea that perhaps all the eels could be eaten and what the consequences might be. The little rascal only thought it would be a disaster if there were none for him to catch.

The wind changed rapidly in the early morning of our fifth day at anchor there, and we had to leave suddenly. As soon as they saw the wind change, Joseph and his brother and cousins from our family came out quickly in their boat to help us. He leaned up to the rail in the worsening sea and handed me the fan his grandmother had made for me. Now it hangs on the wall above my bed. I hated leaving the children without even a good-bye, but we had to get off quickly or we would end up on the reef. The tears in my eyes as I steered away were not from the wind.

What I took away from Polynesia besides these gifts was the freedom of giving. We were given so much—both objects and gifts of self—not because the person wanted or expected something in return, but for their joy in giving and what it said about them. Giving between cultures stripped of the underpinnings of binding custom becomes a butterfly on wing, flying freely from one person to the other. It may only be in our Western culture that giving creates a spidery silken thread between the giver and the receiver forging some sort of entanglement. In Polynesia, for me, there was freedom and joy in both the giving and receiving.

American Samoa: The Descent of the Receiver

The difference between American Samoa and independent Samoa (previously called Western Samoa) is not measured in distance, which is a little over sixty-two miles. It is measured in values and attitudes, although both peoples come from the same Polynesian background and were a single political unit at one time.

The two Samoas have been separated politically since 1899 as a result of the Tripartite Treaty, when, as so often happened in the colonial period, blocks of land were established by foreign powers into territories, states, even countries, regardless of peoples, customs, and language. Eastern Samoa was given to the United States, and western Samoa was given to Germany, later governed by New Zealand at the beginning of World War I, and then given its independence in 1962—the first Pacific colony to achieve this.[2]

They share the tradition of *fa'asamoa*, the Samoan Way, much of which we learned about and witnessed while there. *Fa'asamoa* controls their internal political structure, legal system, and cultural behavior; dictates day-to-day behavior; and impacts many aspects of their culture such as respect for elders, including *matais* (literally translated as *chiefs*), teachers, doctors, and others in similar positions. So how can their values be so different? There is still the system of *matai* (chiefdom) governing the welfare and structure of each village in both Samoas. The honor of being a *matai*, however, is much more complex than just the chief designation. *Sa*, a time for prayer, is observed by both even in Pago Pago.

If we were out on an errand in Pago Pago and heard the bell-like sound made by the banging of a hammer on one of the large, ratty-looking, rusty, old scuba tanks with the bottoms cut out hanging conveniently from trees around the harbor, we would have to stop and observe the prayer period. Yet, we had only to move from one Samoa to the other to feel and sense a great divide.

American Samoa, officially an unincorporated territory of the United States, is nothing more than a U.S. welfare state. It is a reflection of the ignominies of the U.S. welfare system today. This type of giving is no gift. American Samoans have bartered their souls for fatty, tinned corned beef, potato chips, beer, and indolence. Every time we went provisioning, we saw American Samoans using food stamps for cigarettes and alcohol.

In the mornings, we watched the ferries shuttling the workers from independent Samoa to the Pago Pago canneries. These canneries received U.S. tax credits for providing jobs, presumably, but not in reality, to the American Samoans. According to local sources, it was the independent Samoans—thankful for the jobs although reportedly, and quite probably, exploited and paid low wages—who made up 80 percent of the American Samoa workforce.

From the cruising community network, I learned it was inexpensive to have clothes made there. I wandered the filthy side streets looking at the various tailoring shops, and decided on one where a tiny Filipino woman doggedly and expressively herded me into the equally tiny little room. Inside three other tiny little women sat at sewing machines. The rapid clicking and humming of the machines; the women's small heads bending over those machines, raising quickly to give me a brief smile; their petite hands flicking large mounds of colorful fabric this way and that created an impression of grinding labor. My little seamstress and I soon came to an agreement about the long skirt I wanted in the style of a sarong. As we chatted in pidgin English, I learned that the clothes the large American Samoans wear are made by these tiny Filipino seamstresses. These women sign a contract for a few years to live and work in these little shops and send their money home, sleeping on tables in their cramped workrooms wrapped in scanty sheets, when eyes and hands need a rest from the humming machines. A sailing friend suggested that it is the corpulent size of the American Samoans that requires these custom-made clothes and thus this modern version of a sweatshop.

Just before we arrived, heavy rains caused mudslides in the area; one person was killed, I believe, some houses were destroyed and a few more damaged. FEMA (the U.S. Federal Emergency Management Agency) jumped right in and set up a big tent with clerks to handle the claims. They expected about six hundred such claims, given the extended families that occupied the houses. Instead they got upward of six thousand! Of course most weren't legitimate. It was just one more indication of the corruption engendered by undeserved giving. In response to this shocking fraud, one letter to the editor from a local person stated (I'm paraphrasing, but this is quite close to the original sentiment), "How can we call ourselves Christians and have a church on every corner, when we steal, which these false claims are, and which the Bible forbids?"

The U.S. welfare system came out of the Depression, a time when extreme measures were needed. The Roosevelts—I use the plural because Eleanor was certainly involved with this—were brilliant in their solutions, one of which was the Civilian Conservation Corps (CCC). In a sense, it was government make-work, but projects that benefited the country. How did our welfare system evolve to simply handouts? While there have been some attempts to remedy the U.S. system, it certainly wasn't apparent in American Samoa.

I had to check out my perceptions, experiences, and the stories I had heard. Could righteous intentions have become so curdled and sour; handouts so poisonous to the soul?

The answer is yes. According to the U.S. General Accounting Office (GAO) in a 2006 report, there were significant weaknesses in American Samoa's fiscal reporting. For example, between the fiscal years 1997 through 2004, American Samoa was an average of over thirty-one months late with its audited financial reports and showed considerable internal control and compliance problems that "raise serious questions about the integrity and reliability" of these audits. In addition the GAO report expressed concern that the tracking of U.S. grant money "lacked effective internal controls to provide reasonable assurance that transactions are properly recorded; assets are safeguarded from fraud, waste, abuse, and mismanagement." Often, financial records appeared to have been "misplaced, lost, or destroyed without being detected."[3] I wondered if it was through lack of professional competence and documented procedures or by intent. Another report in 2010 confirmed that these issues continued.

The U.S. insular areas of American Samoa, the Commonwealth of the Northern Mariana Islands (CNMI), Guam, and the U.S. Virgin Islands (USVI) face serious economic and fiscal challenges and rely on federal funding to deliver critical services. The Department of the Interior, through its Office of Insular Affairs (OIA), provides roughly $70 million in grant funds annually to increase insular area self-sufficiency.

Internal control weaknesses previously reported by GAO and others continue to exist, and about 40 percent of grant projects funded through OIA have these weaknesses, which may increase their susceptibility to mismanagement.... Weaknesses associated with grant recipient activities were the most common issues GAO found, encompassing 62 percent of the weaknesses exhibited by OIA grant projects.[4]

In an act of charity, the state of Hawai'i had shipped cartons of old school books to the American Samoan school system, which didn't need them because the students had new books provided by U.S. taxpayers. We took several of those cartons and distributed the old books to other places in the South Pacific where they were needed, to people who were grateful and appreciative, and where education meant something.

Seeing American Samoa slammed the view home to me that no one benefits when benefits are given for nothing—when there is no sense of accountability, responsibility, liability, no sense of earning it. The dole takes away pride, and a people without pride have lost more than the value of what they have been given.

I thought of the French copra subsidy as a type of alternative even though their paternalistic colonialism seemed quite outdated. A society has a responsibility to care for those who really cannot care for themselves, but that concept and the U.S. welfare system have little in common today. There are innumerable ways to give people a helping hand out of poverty, illiteracy, devastating illness, substance abuse, even just plain bad luck and poor decisions—all of which a society and its government have a responsibility to do—without subjugating them to gifts that contaminate their sense of self.

The Rape of Rapa Nui: Losing What Was Given

Rapa Nui is the indigenous name for Easter Island. The island's giant *moai*, the world-famous, giant statues with their eyeless faces staring into the past, have much to answer for. Built as statuesque monuments to the spirit of specific chiefs, they represent not only male dominance, but the hierarchical dynasty of powerful chiefdoms, an egomaniacal system that has destroyed so many cultures, so many countries, so many people. The moai quarry brought home the anger and senselessness of it all. There were hundreds of partially completed moai abandoned at different stages of completion left willy-nilly in the caldera of reddish volcanic tuff that was so easy to carve. It looked like a burial ground for moai, but these were never fully born. It reminded me of archeological sites I have seen of dinosaur bones stripped of life: here a rib, there a partial skull, later a jawbone. If they are put together, they form a picture of the original. The moai all

together gave a picture of their time. The picture was of rapacious exploitation of resources from wood to people. An expression of my mother's came to mind: "Enough is enough, and too much is besides." The people, indeed, had had too much.

Chile, Rapa Nui: The author standing by an unfinished moai.

The eyes, with their large white irises and black stone pupils, of the standing moais were cut out of the stone faces during the revolt that occurred when, indeed, the people had had enough. One moai with eyes intact somehow survived. No longer could these chiefs-who-became-god-spirits watch over the people, ensuring their correct subservient behavior. The story unfolded for me in our wandering about the island of Rapa Nui, in legends and myths related to us while we were there, and in my remembrances of other places. This story was not just one of exploitation of people, but more dramatically the devastation of this small piece of land remotely stuck in the middle of a vast sea.

Chile, Rapa Nui: Moai with eyes intact.

Rapa Nui was settled by Polynesians between 700 and 1000 CE, who called it *Te-Pito-te-Henua*, land's end. According to legend, it was settled in the traditional Polynesian way of a chief—in this case, Hotu Matua—bringing his extended family, plants, and animals in large canoes searching for a new land. They found lush palm forests of a species now extinct and volcanic soil ready for their crops—clearly a gift. They prospered and the population grew, estimated at between seven thousand to nine thousand by 1550. As the population increased, distinct chiefdoms controlled different parts of the island. It isn't known with any certainty, but it may have been the competition for power that fueled the moai building. It's believed that giant wooden logs were used to roll the moai to their locations; that is, until the last tree was cut down.

At one specific moment in time, someone did cut down the very last tree on the island. Before the cutting began, did anyone draw it, memorize it, take some leaves to save? In whose memory did this tree survive? Who watched it burn or turn into timber with tears in their eyes and hearts of shame and loss? What did that man feel who chopped it down? He could see it was the last one; the island wasn't that big for him to not know. Was there a race to get to it? Was it the final prize—consolation for death to come? Did anyone mourn its loss?

The trees were just one of the losses: birds, wildlife, wildflowers, fish, mollusks—all such life was winnowed down to a few mostly inedible (to humans) species. This small, complete little island was a gift to the first arriving Polynesians; a place that could nurture them if they nurtured it. Somehow that didn't happen. This loss, this slipping away of what could have been, can be laid directly at the feet of leadership and religion. The chiefs, who chose petty rivalries over wisdom, who saw themselves as demigods, who greedily accumulated power with the help of priests (sometimes one and the same), sentenced Rapa Nui to death.

Erosion accompanied the deforestation, as it always does, resulting in decreased food supplies. The battle for survival was between chiefdoms, and then individuals.

According to local archeological studies, there is some evidence of cannibalism during this period. The trees were gone, the topsoil was gone, the crops were gone, the social structure was gone. Boats could not be built, thus fishing and harvesting food from the sea could only be done close to shore. This society imploded. It's estimated that less than eight hundred people were left in a social and environmental shambles.

So what did they do? Create a new religion, of course. We learned of the Birdman Cult while on a tour of some of the island's archeological sites. It may have been practiced somewhat during the reign of the moai—that is not clear—but it became the primary force. Special rights, possibly access to the scarce food, were given by the priests to the young man who could swim to one of the tiny, jagged, rock precipices jutting up out of the water across a rough, wave-battered, shark-patrolled channel and bring back a Sooty Tern egg unbroken. Could that have now become the main source of protein?

In 1862, the slave traders found what then was called Rapa Nui. They quickly decimated what young population there was, leaving the culture again in a shambles. But there's more. They were followed by the European missionaries who, according to current historical accounts in Rapa Nui itself, destroyed what remained of the Polynesian culture including the majority of the Rongorongo tablets, leaving a small shred of that culture's records. These tablets were the only written record of the entire Rapa Nui culture. The existing remnants of the Rongorongo tablets comprise about a score of fragments of wooden objects and a few petroglyphs that have, so far, proven indecipherable. Not only is there a mystery about the meaning of Rongorongo—is it a form of writing, a proto-writing, or what?—but who is actually responsible for their destruction? According to some records, the Catholic hierarchy tried to obtain these tablets when they discovered their existence, but were unable to do so because the natives had burned them or were using them for day-to-day tasks. It is true that the majority of the local people were most probably illiterate, so the tablets would have little meaning to them, once those who could read them had been decimated by disease and slavery. But it is also true that the Catholic Church does not have a good historical record for preserving anything it considered pagan.

Whatever the answers, the historical written record of this culture, their history, and this disaster-in-the-making is lost.[5] Nevertheless, the archeological record that has been, and continues to be, uncovered—albeit without a translation of the Rongorongo tablets—provides a historic parable for our times. Rapa Nui is a contained ecological system, but then, so is Earth.

Gift from the Deep: The Magic of Whales

Anchored off Kapa Island in the Vava'u group of the Kingdom of Tonga, I heard strange wailing sounds while below preparing dinner. I thought it was the lone whale we saw as we sailed down from Neiafu.

Wayne laughed at me, "No way." But then he heard it and reconsidered. "Maybe you're right," he conceded.

This haunting underwater sound vibrated through our hull. It was a male Humpback whale singing his come-hither mating song. It was a gift from the deep, a sound like no other; it penetrated my heart, my breath. I wanted to know this sound, to feel it vibrate on my skin, to sense it in my bones. I know I can never really understand what I call his language—linguistically it isn't even considered a language—but in my mind this system of communication speaks to both whale and human listeners. I was hooked; I wanted to learn what I could about Big Wing, the name I gave to the singer of this song. From the marine biology course that I was taking, interrogating (in a friendly way, I hoped) every marine biologist and whale researcher we met, and additional reading, I learned much more about this fascinating species. Some of that I relate here.

I made up his name from his scientific taxonomy: *Megaptera novaeangliae*. *Megaptera*, derived from Greek, *mega* meaning large, and *ptera* meaning wing, wing-like, or feather, presumably due to their large flippers, which can be one-third of their body length and do appear wing-like in the water. *Novaeanglinae* means New England, where they were numerous at one time, although hunted to near extinction there in the 1800s—to us the Humpback whale. This common name comes from the way they dive by curving their backs. Such an unfortunate name for such a splendid creature.

Big Wing did not eat while here in Tonga for two reasons: not only would his time be taken up with finding an appropriate mate and instinctively ensuring that his genes were represented in the next generation, but also because his food source wasn't here. He's a member of the Balaenopteridae family, named for their series of baleens, which are used in their unique way of feeding. They also have a series of pleats that stretch from their lower jaw part way down the underside of their body. It is through expanding these pleats that they are able to gulp huge amounts of water, literally tons.

In the Antarctic summer, Big Wing locates dense zooplankton patches or schools of anchovies, herring, or sardines; expands his pleats; opens his immense cavity; and takes a whale-sized gulp. Keeping the fish and krill inside with the baleen filters, he spits out the water, if one can call expelling that much water spitting. Sometimes either by himself or with a few comrades, he will approach a potential meal from below and slowly encircle it, constantly blowing bubbles through his blow hole, which forces the prey to concentrate inside a bubble net. He then lunges in for that whale-size mouthful.

Ironically, these great creatures evolved from land ancestors, which evolved from sea creatures. Evolutionarily, life started in the sea, some animals moved to land, then some, like these whales, returned to the sea. New fossil finds continue to change the evolutionary history of whales, but the interesting fact to me is the return to the sea. The general consensus is that this was due to waning food sources on land.[6]

The sea creates an odd mammal. Big Wing's forelimbs are flippers that move from the shoulders only; his nostrils become blowholes and are located oddly for a mammal, but efficiently, given his watery environment. His tail is a pair of paddles, which we call flukes. He moves his flukes up and down to swim, unlike fish, which move from muscle contractions and their fins move sideways. The underside of Big Wing's flukes are patterned uniquely in white and black and help in identifying him.

Like us, Big Wing has three layers of skin, but his

outer layer, or epidermis, is smooth and feels like the wet rubber pontoons on our inflatable dinghy. The inner layer, which we call blubber, is their hypodermis, which serves as a food resource during migration, provides insulation, and helps his streamlined shape, unlike *Homo sapiens*, who become less streamlined the more blubber we add.

As I am often cold (except in the hot, humid tropics), I was intrigued by how Big Wing, who is warm-blooded and has a body temperature about two degrees higher than mine, managed his body temperature, especially in the Antarctic. It works like a heating and air-conditioning system. In Big Wing, the arteries to his extremities—flukes, dorsal fin, and pectoral flippers, which don't have blubber—expand, allowing more blood to flow through and lose heat. But when he's cold, the blood is recirculated back to his body *before* it flows to his extremities, an efficient counter-current heat exchanger!

Like us, whales are vertebrates and have a skull housing a well-developed brain, lungs, and a respiratory system based on breathing air. Our two species also share a structured social order, although his is poorly understood by us, and relationships seem to be based mostly on capturing food and procreation and are short-lived—but then, so are some of ours.

Big Wing breathes through his blowhole, which is really his nose, not his mouth—as any proper yogi would tell me to do. The spout that usually gives a clue to his presence and others of his species is mostly steam from the warm, moist air expelled rapidly from his lungs when he comes to the surface.

Humpbacks are particularly acrobatic, and we were often entertained while sailing by their spyhopping, lobtailing, and breaching, which was impressive to see as they jump all the way out of the water, often spin sideways and crash down in a belly flop—and with all that blubber, it was quite a flop.

It is thought that humpbacks live about forty-five to fifty years, but this is not a fact really known. To reach old age, Big Wing must manage all of the following:

> Escape the whaling ships, particularly of Iceland, Japan, Norway, and Russia,
>
> Maintain a reasonable immune system to fend off infections from the multitude of parasites from minute algae to new viruses from human waste and increasing oceanic pollution to barnacles and shark suckers that find his body the perfect host,
>
> Protect his hearing and ability to communicate amid the increased sonic rumble permeating the sea from submarines, ships, offshore drilling, and military testing, and
>
> Avoid being poisoned by his food source as it becomes more polluted from dumping of industrial and other waste.[8]

In the early morning, I put my ear to the hull wall and heard Big Wing more clearly. This particular song was a haunting sound to my human ears. It sounded like a lonely call. He was searching now for companionship and warning other males to stay away, although the reason for the singing is only theorized and isn't known absolutely. It's believed that the longer the song, the more fit he demonstrates he is. It's as if holding his breath underwater is like how much weight a fellow can lift on

Tonga: Humpback whale spyhopping. Photograph copyright © 2013 Clinton Bauder.[7]

last year and the ones his father sang for many years before him. Each year, he makes minor changes, so that it is unique to him, but recognizable within the area he and the others habituate. Identifying the sonograms of these individual songs assists scientists to identify Big Wing and other individual males, although how reliable this may be is controversial.

In Tonga, we visited a pair of Kiwi field scientists anchored near us in their small, well-equipped research sailboat and were treated to their recordings of various whale songs they were studying. It was difficult for me to tell, but I thought I recognized the individual permutations of Big Wing as one of the soloists in this symphony resonating not only with the sound heard by human ears, but in the core of my soul.

Another day, I expected a different song from Big Wing, for I knew that he had found a partner. I was out in my sea kayak and saw the two of them: Big Wing and Angelina, I have named her. Next year, she will return here to give birth, nurse, and care for that calf for about one to seven years, then be ready to mate again. And the cycle continues, let us hope.

land. See my muscles! As one field biologist said, "A male singing a long song is probably worth waiting for!" This mating call is only one part of his complex vocabulary. Females vocalize also, but we can't hear them as they are out of our sound wave range, and are not thought to sing as the males do.

Big Wing's song is a sound that literally and figuratively comes from the depths. Before starting his song, Big Wing moves away from the other bachelor males that he travels with, and lowers his head. His complex song is almost the same as the one he sang

By the early 1900s, whaling in all the oceans decimated the humpbacks to about 10 percent of their original population worldwide. Today, in spite of the ban on all whale, dolphin, and porpoise products by the Convention on International Trade of Endangered Species (CITES) and the resolutions of the International Whaling Commission (IWC), established in 1946, there are thought to be only somewhere between thirty-five thousand and forty thousand left in a few separate populations—not enough to guarantee survival.[9]

The IWC allows limited whaling by indigenous people where the hunts are aspects of the culture of the people. These hunts usually involve few whales, and the communities make use of all of the whale. These are not threats to Big Wing's survival, except when they are abused, which happens occasionally.

Japan is a signatory to the IWC, and a flagrant nonobserver of its rules. DNA samples of whale meat sold in Japan prove that Humpback whale meat is sold there. In addition, Japan killed 330 Minke whales one season, claiming it was done for scientific purposes, selling the meat to "fund more dead-whale research," as Wesley Marx wrote in *The Frail Ocean*.[10] Russia manages its nonobservation differently: from 1948 to 1973 it reported a catch of 2,710 Humpback whales to the IWC; in reality, it was discovered they had killed 48,477.[11] Norway legally conducts its whale kills as it reserved its position on the IWC moratorium and thus is not bound by it—an indication of just how weak the IWC is. Iceland also continues hunting whales commercially.

The protections are failing.

≈≈≈

My gift, in addition to Big Wing's song and my kayaking not too far away when he came to the surface, was to swim with a mother and calf Humpback whale under careful conditions designed to protect the whales. Tonga and the Dominican Republic are the only two countries that allow this, as far as I know. In Tonga, we could surface snorkel in small groups of five with a guide, but only after it became clear that the mama whale was not intimidated by the nearby presence of the boat. No touching, no coming between the mother and calf, no close proximity.

The conditions were met, and I was in the water. I noted the barnacles on the mother whale's skin, the coloration pattern of her flukes, the number of shark suckers in the vicinity.

I had learned that a female doesn't reach maturity until between six- and fifteen-years old and then has a calf only every one to three years. It takes about one year for her pregnancy before the birth of the calf. Her mammary nipples are hidden in a slit, and the calf is fed not by suckling, but by a quick burst of potent mother's milk that she squirts down the calf's throat when it nudges her briefly exposed teat. I didn't have to read this, I saw it with my own eyes! I watched the calf nurse from his mother, a thin spiral of the thick viscous creamy milk swirled up to the surface near me, a vision I will carry in my archival memory forever. Finished feeding, the baby rested under his mother's head as she floated about twenty feet below the surface.

This calf was a curious little fellow. He slipped up to the surface frequently for air as he needed to breathe more often than his mother. When he came to the surface, he seemed to look around with wonder. Staying away from him became impossible as he swam up to me, and we swayed slowly in the water face to face, our eyes studying each other with curiosity, and, on my part, deep affection. I remained still, enchanted. His mom looked up at me, but stayed where she was, deeming me no threat to her baby. For an instant, I was part of their world.[12]

There are some events that seem so out of the realm of a land-based time/space plane that for a moment I am carried into eternity. Looking into the eye of a whale in her watery home can do that. This is not philosophical, not an affirmation of the unequivocal truth that we are all connected, not a liberal environmentalist expanding her horizons. This is palpable. This is knowing beyond intellect, even beyond compassion—more than my heart and soul are touched. This is, perhaps, enlightenment.

≈≈≈

A female Humpback whale struggling to stay afloat was spotted by a fisherman just east of the Farallon Islands outside the Golden Gate Bridge. She had become entangled in a spider web of crab traps and lines. He radioed an environmental group for help. She was weighted down by hundreds of pounds of traps that caused her to struggle to stay afloat. She also had hundreds of yards of line wrapped around her body, her tail, her torso, and a line tugging in her mouth.

Within a few hours, the rescue team arrived and determined that she was in critical condition and the only way to save her was to dive in and untangle her.

This is a very dangerous proposition. One slap of the tail could kill a rescuer.

They worked for hours with curved knives and eventually freed her.

After they freed her, the rescue divers reported that she swam in what to them seemed like "joyous circles." She then came back to each and every diver, one at a time, and nudged them and pushed each one very gently around. The divers considered it her thanks. One of the divers stated that it was "the most incredibly beautiful experience" of his life.

The rescuer who cut the rope out of her mouth says her eye was following him the whole time, "I will never be the same," he murmured with tears in his eyes.[13]

Gift from the Shallows: Coral Reefs

The gifts from the sea are innumerable, even as we blindly destroy them. None is quite so dazzlingly exquisite as a healthy coral reef. It transcends anything on land. As many as I have seen, I still find a healthy coral reef overwhelming. Where to look first; what to focus on? The colors, diversity of life forms, the myriad shapes, the movement of light and shadow were all mesmerizing to my eyes whether floating on the surface, free diving under mushroom shaped rocks or around huge circular brain corals, or scuba diving and enjoying the spectacle from within this magical space for an hour or however long my tank lasted.

So much of what I saw down there is hard to place in the real world. It's more than looking through water—it's something akin to Alice stepping through the looking-glass. It's more than not being in our air-filled surface existence; it's more than our not yet knowing everything about them. A coral reef is a miracle, a talisman for our times.

The colors change the deeper one goes, with the reds lost first. We found on a one thousand-foot dive in a submersible (a mini-submarine for three people) in the

Cayman Islands that even that far from the surface there is some ambient light and some slight differentiation in colors. Closer to the surface is where coral reefs really show their colors; like all objects on our planet, light gives them color. On a coral reef, it is the mind-numbing diversity of life that gives the breadth of color although it is often the small, negligible life forms—particularly microscopic algae—that add the richest color.

Under cloudy skies with a little rain, we motor-sailed to an out-of-the-way anchorage in Viani Bay, Fiji in August 2004. We had heard via the cruising community network that Jack Fisher, a local, would lead us to the best diving spots for a small fee. After anchoring, we dinghied over near to where he lived and wandered up the shell-lined path curving around an old breadfruit tree with the only makeshift object around, a wooden bench, where we had heard Jack could usually be found. He lived in a typical Fijian home: neatly woven palm-thatch roof, walls that in the southwest United States would be called a coyote fence, swept dirt floor, and everything neat and orderly. Even the brilliant red hibiscus bushes decorating his yard and the few banana trees in back all looked as if they should be exactly where they were.

The next several days were mostly sunny providing excellent light for our dives. The first few times, we went with him in our dinghy; he directed us where to anchor and where to dive while he pulled his hat over his eyes and sipped on the beer we had brought for him. Then some other cruisers showed up. Organizing cruisers is like the legendary herding of cats; nevertheless, the four boats in the anchorage managed a plan. We hired Jack and assembled on the largest catamaran, which had a great deck and perfect swim platforms to launch us all. Off we went with Jack steering and the owner/captain of the cat by his side. We got safely anchored in sand by the seawall, and after he instructed those of us who were scuba divers where to go, and likewise the snorkelers, Jack settled down with his supplied cold beer.

This reef wall was one of the most beautiful I have ever seen, interestingly not because of its diversity, but the opposite. It was almost entirely composed of tree corals. Imagine cauliflower—yes, that commonplace, insipid vegetable. Now shake it loose so one stalk holds several clusters of looser heads, and separately color each stalk and its heads magenta, burgundy, hot pink, violet, creamy yellow, and a few soft ivory, then place them so they cover the reef wall from just below sea level to about eighty feet down—a joyous hurrah of vibrancy and life. Then just off this resounding blaze of color in the cobalt blue of the sea, a black- and white-banded sea snake (a Yellow-lipped sea krait) sinuously, as only a snake in water could possible move, slowly spiraled down to disappear in the depths. I can recall this image where it shimmers behind my eyelids for minutes at a time.

Fiji: A sea snake exploring above the tide line. Photograph by Gayla Morkel Phelps, S/V *Ariel*.

Fiji: The author diving near staghorn coral.

I had learned about coral reefs from many sources including Darwin's *Voyage of the H.M.S. Beagle*, my marine biology course, my own observations, and information from the field marine biologists I visited and worked with throughout our voyage. Corals are animals and can be suffocated and beaten to death, just like us. Dive boats in many parts of the world contribute to killing reefs, which seems like self-sabotage. They often anchor on top of reefs, don't instruct their divers to not kick or touch the reefs, and throw trash and dump toilet waste overboard. In the past, divers and snorkelers were taught to maintain their position in the water using their fins and not their hands and arms, but we can't see our fins and too often we're kicking the little coral animals without being aware of it. Today, more attuned dive outfits request their experienced customers and teach their new ones to use their hands to paddle around the coral and keep their fins out of the way.

Healthy coral reefs have the largest diversity of life in the ocean. They provide protection for at least 25 percent of marine species identified to date, yet they are only .01 percent of the ocean floor. On one level this is ironic because they don't seem to have the required food supply; in fact, tropical seas, where coral reefs live, are frequently described as virtual deserts. So how can a desert sustain such immense life?

One reason for this great life diversity and the remarkable visual landscape is the number of microhabitats within a reef enabling such diverse creatures as elongated, fat moray eels; eight-armed, bulbous-headed octopuses; bullet-shaped wrasse; blown-up puffer fish; multi-branched, wavering feather stars; snails encased in shells of every shape, size, and color; and literally thousands more fish, worms, echinoderms, mollusks, and other species that make this their home.

The blue tropical waters are blue only because of the absence of phytoplankton and their process of photosynthesis that forms the basis of the oceanic food chain. Phytoplankton flourishes in the cold waters of the far north and south of our planet. One reason the whales don't eat on their migration to warmer waters to mate and calve is because there isn't anything to eat. So no phytoplankton, no photosynthesis; presumably no food. It wasn't until the year I graduated from high school in 1957 that this impossible puzzle was being solved. And the answer? *Symbiodinium microadriaticum* commonly called *Zooxanthellae*, a dinoflagellate algae that gives color to giant clam lips and feeds coral polyps, as well as many other activities.

Zooxanthellae live inside coral polyps and use the polyp's waste materials along with water and sunlight to complete photosynthesis and to produce the organic compounds that are the base of the complex reef feeding-web. This is what provides the coral polyp with the food it needs. It is a perfect mutualistic symbiotic relationship. The majority of the coral's food comes from this little algae food machine.

The large majority of corals are communal. One species of cactus coral, brain coral, lettuce coral, or any one of many other coral families are actually made up of hundreds, even thousands, of coral polyps, which are individual animals. Each polyp has a calcareous skeleton that includes both living and dead cells. Other species of algae grow on these skeletal structures. Together these algae make up the primary food producers of the reef food-chain.

All the giant clam species, including *Tridacna gigas* and *Tridacna maxima*, have individually colored mantles, or lips as I call them. I've seen them patterned in bright hues of blue, purple, turquoise, and green, as well as shades of brown and amber. This color comes from light diffracted from a skin-like layer of crystalline pigment under which lives the microscopic symbiotic algae *Zooxanthellae*. The algae use photosynthesis, just as its relatives in the coral polyps do, to provide the clam with much of its food. These mammoth clams are rapidly disappearing mainly due to poaching. Oriental fishing vessels, particularly Taiwanese and Chinese, often poaching in the territorial waters of other countries, hunt them for their adductor muscles—an Asian delicacy—that they cut out and leave the rest of the clam to die. In some areas where we have been scuba or free diving,

we have seen scores of empty shells, which look like headstones for these clams, the rotted bodies long since eaten by various detritus feeders.

Living coral reefs are disappearing fast. Finding a healthy coral reef is rare. Although I have seen many coral reefs around the world from the Caribbean to Australia, from Indonesia to the Red Sea, I have only seen healthy ones in any number in the Tuamotus of French Polynesia and the Red Sea below Egypt. This is probably because both areas are not heavily populated, and, at least for the Tuamotus, not easily visited. The threats are numerous and mostly of the human variety. Climate change is, of course, a, if not *the,* major problem, but also pollution and the proliferation of plastic especially bags and bottles, and the horrendous scouring of all the ocean's habitats by the voracious multinational fishing fleets that in the name of efficiency kill everything in their paths. In many parts of the western Pacific, particularly in Micronesia, including the Philippines, tropical fish for sale are obtained by poisoning the reef and capturing the spaced-out fish that float to the surface, many of which die before getting to market.

≈≈≈

The Tuamotus are coral atolls, many with quite large lagoons on the inside so that when the tide was running, it could be quite fast as it funneled in or out of the almost completely enclosed lagoon through the pass. There, pass diving was one of our favorite pastimes. We would coordinate with another boat or tow our dinghy on a long line. We would mark the time for the tide to be running in (that way at least if we got carried away we'd be inside the lagoon, rather than flung out into the ocean). While the center of a pass may be somewhat swept by the flood of water back and forth, the sides were infinitely interesting. Frequently we would see pelagic fish as we started the dive, or, depending on the depth, lying in wait in mid-channel for smaller fish to swim past. Often large sharks swam past: Lemon (which we tried to avoid), Gray reef, and others; sometimes even tuna and large jacks. As I sailed through underwater, depending on my speed I could see the full diversity of coral reef life. It was like watching a 3-D movie in living color, except I was the one moving. In one of the fastest passes, we were skimming by at a speed of at least 3 knots with no propulsion of our own.

On one dive I was with our friend Steve; Wayne was in the dinghy to pick us up. It was about our third or fourth dive, alternating the dinghy pick-up person. We had been coming up at about the same spot, but this time Steve and I went farther in; we just couldn't take our eyes off the multicolored world we were in. Finally we rose to the surface and could barely see Wayne. We shouted and waved, but he didn't see or hear us and was looking the wrong way toward where we all had been coming up before. After about twenty minutes as we were drifting farther away and starting to get a bit cold, Steve took off one of his fins and waved it around above his head. Finally Wayne saw us and came to pick us up. Since then, we bought position markers, attaching them to our BCs (buoyancy control vests that scuba divers wear), which could be inflated when we surfaced.

Some of my favorite coral reef inhabitants were the common, bright blue, skinny starfish (*Linckia laevigata*) and a funny looking sea cucumber (*Thelenota ananas*), which I nicknamed Prickly. I picked one up, and as I rubbed my palm along his back, I felt that the orange thorn-like papillae were soft and smooth-feeling, not really prickly as it had looked. His bottom, however, was rough, a little like Velcro. Sea cucumbers are efficient sand-making machines. What they take in one end—bits of coral, pebbles, whatever is lying on the bottom to which is attached what they really want, algae or waste material—comes out the other as sand.

Fiji: "Prickly" *(Thelenota ananas)*. **Photograph by Dave Jesinger, S/V** *Amoenitas.*

Like bees around pollen-laden blooms, the small coral reef fish, such as the Blue-green chromis and Humbug dascyllus, flittered around the various hard corals, especially the branched *Acroporas* often with pink, purple, or blue tips. When danger was perceived, these tiny dancing fish hid within the coral branches. They are about as big as a baby's hand. The dascyllus have wide black and white stripes, are somewhat flat rather than thick, and have a fin at the top of their back that makes them look like their head is lower as if they're pouting, but ready at any minute to break out in a smile. The Blue-green chromis are one of those special turquoisey colors in a large box of Crayola crayons—definitely not one of the standard colors—a color to be used only for a distinctive and favorite object in a drawing.

Coral reefs, like the oceans themselves, give so many gifts: patience, faith, the miracle of diversity, pure beauty. There are so many reasons to ensure these coral reefs survive—our planet will be bereft without them.

Suwarrow: The Gift of a Broom

Some gifts are not as conspicuous as the colorful coral reefs. They are gifts of time and sharing.

I met John in Suwarrow, a tiny atoll, all of it a nature reserve of the Cook Islands, about 220 miles from anything else and 500 miles from Rarotonga, the main Cook island. I was a sixty-something, Caucasian, college-educated Western woman, and John was a seventy-something, sinewy fellow of the black hair and eyes that are more Melanesian than Polynesian. He climbed sixty-foot coconut palms, saved his grandson from a shark attack, cooked coconut crabs to perfection, and patiently stripped palm fronds to make a broom. It was this that he taught me.

"No, no Missy, this way." He peeled off a strip in one neat piece; mine was raggedy. I tried again.

"Yes, yes, Missy. Slow to start, then." Zap, his came off in one neat sheath. I kept trying.

Finally we had a stack. Then we peeled them again, but this time some got discarded because they were not up to broom standards. We continued in companionable silence except for the "No, no, Missys," and an occasional "Yes, yes." Then John started humming something that sounded to me like a Gregorian chant with a South Pacific slant—his own creation. Finally we were ready to braid into the top a piece of black polypropylene line that conveniently had washed-up on shore a few days before. This was the broom's handle. Hours after we started, the brooms were done. His was neater of course, but they both looked like twiggy bunches of thick straw. Only I knew they were not.

I still have mine.

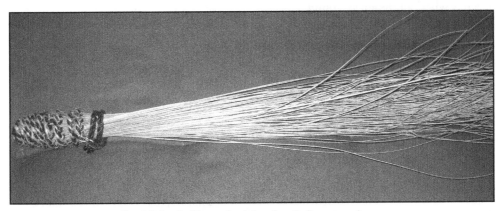

Cook Islands: The author's handmade Suwarrow broom.

5

Kiwi Land: The Lessons of Isolation

Come away, O human child!
To the waters and the wild
With a faery, hand in hand,
For the world's more full of weeping than you can understand.
—William Butler Yeats, *The Stolen Child*

Minerva Reef: The Beauty and Pain of Isolation

We left Tonga on November 27, 2003 for Minerva Reef—hoping the conditions would enable us to stop there—and then on to New Zealand. For me, there was something mystical and magical about sailing toward the Southern Ocean, although we never quite entered its realms as New Zealand was the farthest south we sailed. The Southern Ocean is where all the major round-the-world races are held because it has the winds—*the winds*—not to mention icebergs and other hazards. We were not in a hurry; not in any race to finish; we were only going to just north of Whangarei on the North Island of New Zealand, which is 37° south and not yet in the Southern Ocean, still the South Pacific. Tasmania, the southernmost part of Australia, isn't even that far south.

Both yachts and ships are lost in the Southern Ocean even today; dramatic rescues sometimes happen—sailors die, sailors are saved. It is one of those places on Earth where skill is not the only answer for survival; luck enters into it. But as it happens that is true for Minerva Reef too, named for a ship that wrecked there in 1829.

Sailing Toward the Southern Ocean

The southern swell remembers the cold
and races north
to meet the eastern wind waves.

Together, they hiss and whisper
the names of the dead
lying on the bottom somewhere near here.

It is my night watch; I am awake and listening.
Were you lost because someone fell asleep on watch,
a system failure, a storm?
I'm sorry, but what is it you want now?
Is it like this:

the body remembers past pain, which the mind forgot
and when you were touched you knew
with a flash of remembrance, yes, this happened?

Or is it like this:
a smile is the international code,
the laugh behind it
a thesaurus of synonyms,
but something was left out—a syllable perhaps?

You'll have to speak more clearly
if you want a tomb, a choir of angels,
a message sent home.

Oh, perhaps it's like this:
you forgot to tell something;
you're running up on deck to wave,
to yell, "I love you, take care,
remember…." then words were lost?

What whispered word
is carried on Southern Ocean waves?
What is it
to be remembered?

≈≈≈

Darwin learned about more than evolution and natural selection on his famous trip aboard the HMS *Beagle*. Among so many other facets of life on this planet, he discovered the primary development of coral reefs. And therein lies the story of Minerva Reef. Volcanoes rise; volcanoes sink. There are millions of years until the final subsidence, but it is this process that is responsible for the creation of most of the coral reefs of our planet. The first to form is the fringing reef, with free-swimming coral larvae settling on rocks adjacent to the shore of a volcanic mountain, but below the low-water mark.

Next in line of succession is the barrier reef. Still associated with land, it is separated by a lagoon from the shore, as now the volcano is sinking. Because the coral needs light to grow, it continues to build up, staying at its appropriate level below the sea surface. As the seaward side receives more nutrients, the landward side dies off and contributes to the lagoon. The Great Barrier Reef of Australia is the most famous and the biggest at about 1,615 miles long. It can be seen by astronauts in outer space. Its lagoon is called a channel since it is so large and ranges from approximately seven miles to forty miles wide. The second longest barrier reef is the Belize Barrier Reef in the western Caribbean, but it is only 185 miles long.[1]

The atoll is the crowning glory of reefs. The volcano is gone, sunk below the ocean's surface. What is left is a circular reef often with gaps, which become passes, some passable for yachts like ours. On many of the chunks of reef, sand has accumulated, as well as seeds and birds and land crabs and all kinds of fascinating creatures, plus the usual flies, ants, and cockroaches. Palm trees grow tall, grasses sprout, lantana blooms, bougainvillea gains a hold and showers its bounty of purple, magenta, and pink petals like a spread-out skirt around its slim waist. Inside is a lagoon protected now from the ocean's pounding, but with the flow of tides to keep it alive and moving, pulsing with life below the surface, sometimes in the form of coral pinnacles.

One pinnacle I saw in the Tuamotus was so full of coral, sponges, feather dusters, ascidians (also known by the silly, although accurate, name sea squirts—but I thought they were too pretty for that), mollusks, sea stars, and myriad fish. It was color, color, color, and I circled and circled and circled, spiraling up and down for over an hour. Such places with their diverse, spell-binding life were what I lived for.

It was within these lagoons that we often anchored, and such was Minerva Reef, except no sand had collected there, no petite islands formed, nothing grew above the water's surface. At high tide, nothing was visible, except water; at low tide there was just the barest top of the reef, mostly barren above the surface; below was another story. Around its edges lay various wrecks, some visible, others just noted on our charts, and, I'm sure, some that were known only to the sea and this reef. The wall on the outside of the reef extended over two thousand feet deep. The visibility seemed forever—in reality, it was about one hundred feet.

Minerva Reef: The reef top.

We scuba dove off the outside wall a few times and saw many coral reef fish along the upper part of the wall, and as we descended lower, schools of large pelagic fish, including tuna, and a large school of Gray reef sharks. Afterwards, I read about those sharks in my *Coral Reef Fishes*, which stated, "Among the most likely of sharks to attack divers, but generally gives a single nonfatal bite."

In that deep blue, I was mesmerized by space, color, and my floating weightlessness. I imagined that diving on a wall was like floating in space unconnected to the spaceship; or like freefalling with a parachute, but without the hard landing. The feeling for me was being a part of this space, this life; not just a visitor. I was confronting an impossible reality: mind succumbed, body not long after. I could be a piece of Sargassum weed, a pelagic tuna, a sinuous sea serpent—it didn't matter. I was there completely; there was no other possibility. Sometimes, I can dream myself back to that.

The underpinnings of a coral reef are its dead ancestors, as well as the calcium carbonate (limestone) skeletal remains of fish, sea stars, clams, bristle worms, and multitudes of other organisms. Like an ancient mausoleum in the sea, a coral reef is a Potter's Field, with no regard to social class or family, except in the taxonomic sense.

We were the only boat there for two days. Then a few other cruisers made their way through the pass, and one night there was a dramatic entrance that we facilitated. After sailing for two days and nights, Tommy, sailing alone on the yacht

Moondust, had arrived after dark from Tonga and radioed, "This is *Moondust* calling any yachts anchored in North Minerva lagoon. I'm single-handing and want to come in through the pass."

Wayne answered, "*Moondust*, this is *Bali Ha'i*. With no moon, we suggest you wait till morning. The pass is a bit tricky; even after you first get in there is a dogleg you need to make. Over."

"I know, I know. I see it on the chart, but I'm really tired, and I'm going to try it. Just give me coordinates, OK?"

We were the closest yacht to the pass and quickly talked it over. "*Moondust*, hang on a minute, we'll come out in our dinghy and position ourselves in the middle of the channel, then you can follow us in. We'll have our handheld VHF and spotlight. Over."

"OK, *Bali Ha'i*, will do."

Not long after, sitting in our dinghy, we flashed our light around and saw large waves breaking on either side of the pass. We positioned ourselves in the center of the entrance. Wayne maneuvered the dinghy; I handled the radio communications.

"*Moondust*, do you copy? We see your nav lights. Over."

"Roger, I copy and see your light. Over."

"*Moondust*, we're here and in the center of the pass." I paused a moment and another cruiser broke in from across the lagoon.

"*Moondust*, Tommy, you nervy devil, steer starboard. I'm looking at my radar and my GPS track coming in. Steer starboard a few degrees. This is *Lady J*."

"*Moondust*, this is *Bali Ha'i* mobile. If you steer starboard you'll end up on the reef. *Lady J*, we're here

in the pass; don't mislead him," I barked out. "Your info is wrong. *Moondust*, line yourself up with our light and you'll come straight in, then follow us through the channel to where you can anchor. Take your choice."

"I see you *Bali Ha'i* mobile; I'll follow you. I'm just tired and need to get anchored." His voice sounded as weary as his body must have been.

He came in through the center of the pass and followed our dinghy through the channel, the dogleg turn, and around a few coral heads to anchor safely in sand. The next morning he put his dinghy in the water and came by.

"I'll tell you," he said, taking a sip from the cup of hot coffee that I had put in his hand, "I'll never enter any lagoon again at night. Thanks for helping. I really appreciate it. You were there. *Lady J* wasn't. I'm not sure how he got mixed up, but thank God I followed your light." He shook his head in contemplation of what might have happened. His hair, eyes, and mustache were all in matching brown, but his eyes were tired and his mustache drooped as he told us about his wife leaving—not all partners share this dream. It sounded like a story he had repeated often, still surprised that it happened. He was in his early fifties, a slim fellow, with a dogged look, but that may have been the effect of the passage, rather than his life.

Tommy's decision to enter the lagoon was tough. Even with two of us, sometimes we were tired and just wanted to get there. We had other acquaintances who hove to (to stop one's yacht, but not anchor) off the entrance to Papeete, Tahiti because she was seasick and he was exhausted, but they hadn't factored in the current, and they ended up on the reef. They were able to get off without too much damage to their boat, but extensive damage to their pocketbooks.

A few days later, we celebrated Halloween on the reef with cruisers from various countries after discussing it via VHF radio. The north Minerva Reef lagoon is about six miles wide and about twelve miles long, and we were all anchored in different places. We picked a spot where the reef top was quite dead and the tide wouldn't come in too soon. *Lady J* had left by then, so I didn't have to meet them in person. The time was set for low tide so there would be some time to party before the reef was covered again. One of the dinghies was pulled up on to the reef and turned over to make a table for drinks and food. The party was great fun. Tommy founded the Minerva Reef Yacht Club that evening, and we all were given various titles. Mine was Mooring Officer! After a while, the water was lapping at our feet and about to float away our dinghy table and folding chairs, so we had to call it a night.

As much as this circumnavigation has allowed me to experience the interconnectedness of all life on this planet, so too has it taught me of our individual separateness and isolation. Tommy's entrance was like that: we could help, but he, alone, had to decide.

We may lead another into our hearts as we led the single-hander into the heart of the reef, its lagoon, but we maintain our separate selves and to do that, part of us is shrouded in secrecy and mystery, not unlike this reef in the middle of nowhere. We make the choice of who to lead in, but for us that's often more dangerous than who to follow.

Wayne and I had enjoyed a glass of wine at our "happy hour" together in the evenings and almost always drank wine with our dinner, but I noticed that since his retirement he was drinking more, which I attributed to his disappointment at not flying anymore. I thought once we started sailing it would get back to normal. It didn't. As our circumnavigation progressed so did his drinking. Perhaps it was due to the environment, perhaps to missing flying. Jokingly, I thought it could have been financial—local beer and often wine and rum were cheaper than Cokes and safer than water. But from my perspective, it felt like abandonment.

My husband, who had been my fun-loving companion for eighteen years, was no longer there for me. His behavior brought me a sense of loneliness that was difficult to shed. Having experienced a difficult childhood with an extremely abusive father and a mother who was unable to protect me, I knew abandonment only too well. To quote Yogi Berra, "It was déjà vu all over again." But I wasn't able to have a sense of humor about it. I wanted to complete the circumnavigation. I loved sailing. I felt peace during my night watches in the middle of a dark sea or snorkeling and diving among various fish and sea creatures. Perhaps I was one of the later ones to crawl out of the sea and start this evolutionary path to human form, for I am still of the sea.

Even though we worked as a team to bring Tommy safely through the pass at night, somehow Minerva Reef made me face up to my feelings. I think the isolation of the reef itself was a metaphor for my own emotions.

Panes of Sea: Minerva Reef

Panes of sea reflect
more than I want to know;
less than I want to see.

Island, gift of low tide,
grows stalks of shells,
meadows of coarse sand.

Solace, respite, small waves of words
lap at my toes,
free my heart.

Alone, I am
not lonely.
Together with you
that is loneliness.

Minerva Reef seemed like an anomaly of what was possible: a coral reef with not one coconut palm, not one beach, not one bit of dry land except when the tide was down and then just the rough top of the reef. Perhaps I loved it so much because it was how I felt at times, living below the surface, except for those glorious moments alone in the sun.

New Zealand: The End of Isolation Is Extinction

Under our feet, right now, the surface of Earth is moving, reshaping itself. A quarter of a millimeter where one plate shifts imperceptibly under another; a foot over here where a gully-washer loosens an overhanging bank and carries it to sea; acres out there as an underwater earthquake sends a tsunami crashing over a South Pacific island. Yet, we walk down our road as if it will always be there.

Before we could have memory, before any life as we know it, the land itself was cyclopean. Gondwana is the mysterious, other-worldly name for what was essentially the continent incorporating all of the southern hemisphere as we know it today plus India. Little by little, the islands that are New Zealand started their process of isolation, first still joined with Australia and Antarctica, then gradually moving off alone, some 85 million years ago. In the process of this continuing movement, a new plate was formed, and now New Zealand is balanced, geologically precarious, on the pivot point of the Australian Plate and the Pacific Plate. The Southern Alps are one of the newest results—being only ten-million-years-old—of the collision of these two plates, measured at about 40 millimeters per year. This land, this pint-sized country, considered by some to be a biogeographical continent, has glaciers with turquoise crevasses and white sand beaches with that same color—turquoise—for the water; fjords like Norway's; and a mountain, Aorangi, also called Cloud in the Sky or Mt. Cook, at 12,349 feet above sea level. It has straightforward, tall hardwood and conifer forests as well as lazy, rolling hills. There are neatly eroded rock walls, racing rivers, and underwater caverns and labyrinths to complicate the landscape.[2]

New Zealand: Statue of Sir Edmund Hillary and the Mt. Cook range, where he trained for Everest.

This biogeographic isolation suggested my own loss of companionship. Within it I searched for some meaning and understanding of how and why I had gotten to this emotional place, not to mention the question of just what was this place where I had found myself.

What I learned from New Zealand's isolation is the oddities it creates, one of which is flightlessness in so many of its birds. When that flightless characteristic is followed by the introduction of the most efficient and destructive predator of all time—humans—we end up with extensive extinction. Of course extinction has always been a factor of life, like death; yet there seems no question but that *Homo sapiens* have propelled it into a much faster process.

New Zealand, with its two main island land masses and a few smaller habitable islands plus untold rock masses poking up off the plate floor, had been isolated for a long time. But a place isn't created by plate tectonics alone. Plants and animals enliven it, and people add the ethnocentric interest. When the Polynesians arrived in the 1000s CE, the preponderant flora and fauna species were endemic, that is, they existed nowhere else on Earth. Some species had genetic roots in Gondwana; others arrived millions of years ago by sea, air, and island-hopping during times of lower sea levels. Whatever their means of arrival, they had a great deal of time to evolve independently after isolation.

And that's exactly what they did. Due to the transportation available and the changes in environment over millennia, there was a glaring absence of both large grazing animals and mammalian predators, like lions. Instead, birds and insects played those roles, including: eleven species of moa, a large flightless bird; colossal, carnivorous land snails; behemoth, flightless crickets; Earth's largest gecko; and the giant Haast's eagle (*Harpagornis moorei*), with a ten-foot wing span and talons "comparable to a tiger's."[3] This was the moa's only predator. But not everything was large. There were tiny wingless wrens and primitive frogs, too. And when thinking oddities, there is the tuatara (meaning *spiny back* in Māori), a lizard-like reptilian remnant of the Triassic period now extirpated from the North and South Islands of New Zealand, but surviving on offshore islands in sanctuaries. They look a little like the marine iguanas of the Galápagos.

The oddities don't end with specific species. New Zealand has more flightless birds than any other country including Takahē, Kakapo, Weka, Kiwi, two flightless ducks, and six of the seventeen penguin species. It's easy to agree with the theory that many flightless birds evolved from their flying ancestors due to the absence of predators. Another theory for flightlessness and becoming a swimmer is that food sources were in the water, and swimming makes more sense than flying, as the penguins figured out.[4]

Moas have a few world records: the largest moa species, *Dinornis giganteus*, was the tallest bird ever known on Earth, at six-feet tall at the top of its back, but over thirteen-feet tall with its neck outstretched, and weighed some six hundred pounds. This bird also experienced the fastest extermination in human history—all species of moas were wiped out within one hundred years after the Polynesians arrived.[5]

As predators, we humans have no competition. At least fifty-one avian species have become extinct since the Polynesian Māoris first settled in Aotearoa. Along with their alien plants, they brought their alien dogs, pigs, and, unintentionally, rats. The Europeans settled in during the mid-1800s and contributed to the extinctions, primarily due to habitat destruction and introduction of multiple predators. One aspect of colonialism often forgotten: the introduction of nonnative species.[6] The Brits, like all former colonial powers, have much to answer for, including the lesser-known evil of introduced species. In New Zealand these included stoats, possums, and probably rock doves (better known as pigeons and the scourge of most of the world's cities), and the blasted

sparrows. At least they sing; but all over the world, I saw sparrows, pigeons, a few species of crows, and a species or two of swallows. In many places, we were lucky to see anything else. If we're not careful, these adaptable nonnative survivors are going to be all that's left of avian species as they crowd out the local diversity.

New Zealand is the size of my home state of Colorado, but has almost as many threatened bird species as the entire United States: some seventy on the IUCN (International Union for the Conservation of Nature) Red List for New Zealand and seventy-four for the United States. But the end of isolation doesn't only mean extinction for birds and other fauna; it ends cultures too. The Māori, however, have worked hard to maintain their selfhood. Certainly there were ups and downs in this process, and they suffered the usual fates at the hands of an invasive colonial power. Yet, somehow the Māori often outmaneuvered the *pākehā* (white intruders) at their own games. Today, Māori language is taught in many schools and universities, and there are Māori-English bilingual/ immersion programs in some areas. So even with the end of isolation, Māoris beat the odds, and their culture did not become extinct. There are lessons for all of us there.

It seems that what made the difference were a few dedicated people in each generation who focused their energy on this cultural maintenance and preservation. Some were in tune with using *pākehā* ways to get what they wanted; others bulldozed through obstacles. But it seemed clearly the province of individuals, not large major movements or massive demonstrations—although using the term massive for any large number of New Zealanders seems unlikely, given the whole country is only four million people. Nevertheless, it clearly is the lesson of the pebble in the pond and the ripples it creates, so there is hope for us.

Listening to, seeing, and learning about these birds and trees with the enchanting, rhythmic sound of their Māori names helped me move past my isolation and embrace the world I was in.

Names of Wings and Wood

Kauri, kea, kaka
Kiwi, rimu, rata.

Māori mouths send these names
Of wings and wood
Whispering through the bush.

It is the sound of the kererū,
A feathery heartbeat of a sound,
Breathing through the bush.

Weka, hihi, titi,
Tawa, kakariki

Always tui moves
Branch to branch with two voices
Singing through the bush.

Caught by wind, now these sounds
Out of reach,
Spinning in the open sky.

There are still those for whom the end of isolation brings extinction nearer. Kiwis, New Zealand's icon, are quickly succumbing to the aliens, especially dogs and cats. One night we took a guided walk in a protected area. There were about ten of us and our volunteer guide, who was a dedicated wildlife advocate in his fifties, slightly balding under his cap. Even in the dark his eyes sparkled as he prepared us for our little foray. He warned it would be quite special if we actually saw a kiwi; we were not to get our hopes up. We had our flashlights, understood the drill, and took off. I stumbled a bit over tree roots and such, but strained to listen and look. We saw the glowworm larvae like a miniature Milky Way flowing over a vine-covered crevasse. Suddenly our guide stopped; we all came to a sudden halt, ears pricked, eyes scanning the darkness around us.

Kiwis are odd little creatures, hardly birds at all. Monogamous, they can live ten to thirty years. Their physiology almost defies the avian category. Kiwis have several characteristics that are unlike those of other birds including: nostrils at the end of their beak; a well-developed sense of smell with an olfactory part of the brain more similar to mammals than birds; strong little legs with claws—they can run fast, fight, and swim— that are 30 percent of their body weight; two functional ovaries; whiskers; plumage that is more hair-like than feathery; a body temperature closer to mammals than birds; and bone marrow rather than air in their bones. They're unusual enough to be the only members of the same family (Apterygidae) and order (Apterygiformes) taxonomically and include three species. They apparently evolved in the Australia-Antarctica-New Zealand break off from Gondwana.[7]

I never saw a kiwi in the wild, but that night I heard two, a male and female keeping in touch as they foraged in the night. We were listening carefully. Our ears—a poor excuse for hearing compared to other earthly species—became attuned to the male and female vocalizations as they called to each other. This connection, this vocal reinforcement of their bond struck me in a poignant way. My husband and I used to have such back and forth conversations, staying in touch, but of late, he delivered monologues and lectures and complained that I did the same. Like humans, the kiwis transmit a range of needs in their tones, and I imagined hearing: "Where are you?" "Did you find something good?" Look out; I smell a dog!" "Let's go home."

For now, New Zealand manages to hang onto its diversity. Among the most endearing are the little Blue Penguins. I've watched them in a few places in New Zealand and Australia as they returned from the sea and trooped up a small hillside to their burrows. They're little fellows, only about a foot tall. It was Johann Reinhold Forster, the naturalist on Captain Cook's second adventurous voyage, this time on the H.M.S. *Resolution*, who "discovered" these appealing little birds for the Western world in 1773.

Little Blue Penguins

We use bated breath
just after dark
to catch the tiny Blue Penguins
after they have fetched
a craw full of fish for their chicks;
after the group flotilla to shore;
after preening of those almost blue feathers;
after their fear.

We watch the mad little hatters
shoulders angling into the hill,
as they paddle their way
into their burrows.

We keep the silence;
we avoid the flash;
we follow the rules;
just to hold our breath
for the little Blue Penguins.

Then we shuffle up the slope
in scattered groups expressing our amazement
in whispered phrases.
One or two stand alone in shadows
to ponder what they witnessed
and let the lives of those now nestled in burrows
slip through their souls.

That intrepid and brilliant explorer, Captain James Cook, charted most of New Zealand quite accurately in 1769. The English name for Mt. Cook is no accident. But his story is of a classic self-made man, and he was singular in his accomplishments. His father was a farm day-laborer. Cook volunteered as an able seaman in the Royal Navy in 1755 at the age of twenty-seven, and in 1768 he was chosen to command the H.M.S. *Endeavor* on a scientific expedition. Promotions continued as his accomplishments racked up. His career was particularly unusual for those times, as officers were from upper class and noble families. Cook managed the following, among many other accomplishments:

Completed the first circumnavigation going east from Europe,

Captained the first ship to sail below the Antarctic Circle,

Determined that there was no land mass in the Southern Hemisphere comparable to the Northern Hemisphere,

Determined accurate longitude and use of a chronometer,

Completed mapping most of the South Pacific, and

Lost no crew to scurvy, which decimated personnel on most voyages until the late 1800s.

This last accomplishment was quite notable. For example, in April 1773, Cook had his crew set up a brewery along a clear stream in Dusky Bay by Queen Charlotte Sound on the South Island of New Zealand, a place where we walked and breathed in the musky scent of sea and land combined. We imagined where the site of the brewery might have been, where the long boats were pulled ashore, where his ship would have anchored.

He directed his crew in using spruce bark, tea leaves, molasses, and wort (an essence of malt) to create an anti-scurvy drink. He stocked extensive supplies of sauerkraut prior to leaving England, and when anchored had his men collect certain grasses and plants, which were cooked. When the crew refused to eat or drink any of these concoctions, he declared such food was only for the officers, which quickly changed it into being desirable by the lesser crew. Although the British Admiralty clearly recognized his skills, talents, and leadership ability, they unfortunately stuck to their old ways of ineffective scurvy protection and so it continued as a major cause of death to British seamen—those not under the command of Captain Cook. He also was a brilliant cartographer; in fact some of the charts we used in New Zealand and the South Pacific were from his original work. He was a supporter of naturalist and sociological findings too.

Both Wayne and I considered Cook a hero and enjoyed re-reading about his voyages as we sailed the same waters. Because of our joint interest in history, we visited museums from small and funky to large and sophisticated throughout our voyage—it was something we could still share.

6

Melanesia: Dinner and Destruction

I'll bet what motivated the British to colonize so much of the world is that they were just looking for a decent meal.
—Martha Harrison

The spirit cannot endure the body when overfed, but, if underfed, the body cannot endure the spirit.
—St. Francis de Sales

Sharing Food, Choking on Mores

Toughened brown hands grabbed the toerail running along the edge of our deck; the body they belonged to was no stranger to work either. His face masked shyness with a serious, formal look. "Will you," he coughed slightly, "Won't you come for lunch at my house? I am Johnny, the chief's son. He is not well and sent me to greet you."

"Of course," my husband, the man of the family, answered appropriately. "We would be honored."

We were the only boat anchored in a back little bay on a back little island in the Solomons. Johnny looked to us to be in his fifties, but probably was barely thirty. The country had just been through a devastating civil turmoil, basically a tribal war. One islander group had the political power and the money, although they were in the minority. According to Johnny, "Those people are smarter than we are; that's why they have all the money." The majority was at least smart enough to resent this concentration of power and wealth, and started a revolution. We learned that the revolutionaries dug up old guns and ammo left from World War II. As many were killed or injured by trying to use the old weapons as being shot by them.

Poverty existed before, but when we were there, it was thoroughly entrenched. Australia had stepped in, not to fight, but to broker an elected government; a lesson for other global interferers—like my home country— to learn.

"It is settled then; please come about noon." Johnny gave a short nod as he pushed his handmade dugout away and used his rough-made paddle to return to shore.

At the appointed time, we dinghied ashore, were met by Johnny, and followed him up the sandy path to his house. It was built above the ground for protection from water in the rainy season, as well as from crocs, which might get a little too hungry. It was built high also in hopes that the snakes, rats, and whatever else wouldn't be in such a hurry to climb the rickety stairs for a quick meal or cooler place to sleep, although there were no guarantees. The flies and ants certainly weren't put off at all.

The structure itself was put together with odd-sized pieces of wood: some were thin, round tree trunks; others were boards, often seemingly torn, not cut in any standard way. We saw many gaps, some holes that may have been meant to be windows, two door-width openings in front and back, and a little stoop on which to leave shoes. Sagging a bit, the floor was worn from use, and likewise sported its share of gaps—but none big enough for their baby to fall through.

I was seated on one of two benches at a handmade table, exhibiting handiwork that looked like it belonged in this haphazard, worn-out setting. Wayne was beckoned onto a creaky, white plastic chair at one end of the table. Dead palm fronds composed the roof, which was held down by some boards, not at all like the meticulously woven rows of palm fronds plaited together that we had seen in parts of Vanuatu and Fiji. Their home resembled this family who appeared randomly put together too: here skinny arms and legs; there a big tummy (a seemingly odd result of malnutrition, not overeating); a raggedy T-shirt, but no pants; a frighteningly untreated open sore on one of the children, but dark smooth chocolate-pudding skin without a mark on someone else; two tattered skirts equaling one cover up.

Our meal consisted of rice and manioc root; our chipped, pale green plastic plates were covered with mounds of white starch. I was sure they were wondering, "Would they like this meal? Was everything OK?"

I wondered, "How do they survive? What is the infant mortality rate? Is domestic abuse as big a problem here as it is in other parts of the remote South Pacific?"

The family, comprising the chief's son, his wife, and two small boys—one a baby about eight months old, and the other about four—cautiously watched us eat. Even the baby was looking at us wide-eyed. We smiled a lot and were careful to eat enough, but not too much because we knew this would be their meal also. As we pushed our plates back, I could almost hear a collective sigh of relief from the family: "Ah, they liked it; we have provided for them. Everything is OK, and there is some left for us."

Johnny asked worriedly, "Have you had enough? Can my wife get you anything more?" Meanwhile she smiled unsurely and nodded her head in compliance as she peeked around from behind her husband.

"Oh, no, thank you so much. This was quite a treat for us to be welcomed into your home. You are fortunate that you can grow manioc."

Johnny smiled, proud and now confident that he had done his duty as the chief's son. "Manioc is our staple crop; we can always count on manioc if all goes well."

"What else can you grow here?" I asked.

"We had some seeds from a pepper, but they didn't grow. We have pawpaw and banana, and my cousin has a breadfruit tree."

It didn't sound like much to me. Johnny himself was fairly hefty, but his wife was thin to the point of being gaunt, and the boys didn't look all that nourished either.

"Fishing is not good anymore neither," he volunteered, "but we get crabs sometimes."

We gave gifts to show our appreciation for their hospitality and our respect for Johnny's position as representative of the chief—some toys for the boys, a kilo of rice, some tinned meat, and a tube of antibiotic cream.

Our meal over, they showed us their home—the rest of it that is, which amounted to another room of sorts divided by a shabby curtain nailed up and a few boards on one side. The baby had a little nest of rags under a torn netting to protect him from mosquitoes, but when put down to nap, he cooed and drooled like any baby the world over. Clearly he was loved and as protected as possible from the main killer here—malaria.

Solomon Islands: The baby's nest.

We visited for a while and then followed Johnny, who presented us to his cousins and more family. Not for the first time, we felt as if we were medals or trophies from a sporting event. We smiled some more and told a little of our sailing adventures and presented a few more smaller gifts, balloons, pencils, and school exercise books for the children.

Before we left, I asked Johnny about swimming by the boat. "Are there crocs here?" I wondered.

"Oh yes, they live over there," he pointed a short way away to the jungly area that came down to the water, "but they only eat the pigs and dogs they can get at night." I quickly passed on swimming even in broad daylight.

Solomon Islands: A croc (that could be a tree branch if you didn't look closely) floating nearby.

A day or so later as we were getting ready to leave the anchorage, Johnny paddled out and presented Wayne with a hand-carved canoe. It was a simple affair, unlike the carvings so frequently seen in other areas of the Solomons, but clearly a labor of dedication and responsibility. As the chief's son, he needed to do this, and we greatly appreciated it. He did me a favor too. When we had left our boat in Fiji the previous cyclone season, we had become inundated with small geckoes. I knew they ate bugs, especially mosquitoes, but they had a habit of jumping out of the most unusual places and startling me, and they pooped all over—neither of which endeared them to me, but, of course, I didn't want to kill them. We had liberated all but one, which I coerced up on deck, where Johnny thoughtfully grabbed it and put it in his canoe for a ride ashore. I was glad to be rid of the little rascal.

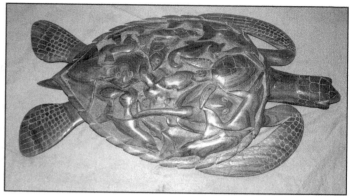

Solomon Islands: One of the exquisite carvings the author bought.

≈≈≈

Being able to invite local people to our floating home created a bond not easily forged in other ways. Our roles drifted among being amateur anthropologists, cultural voyeurs, and extended, albeit thoughtful, visitors, sharing meals in their homes and ours. Although we weren't expecting to penetrate the thick cultural core built up over centuries, this unusual relationship added an increased intensity and understanding to our insight. One impact of our responsibility of this more intimate cultural knowledge was that we then had to observe the cultural mores and at least pay lip service to the values. This, then, became a conflict for me because often they were 180 degrees from my traditional thought and behavior patterns. For example, certain *kastom* (pidgin for custom in a ritualistic sense) sites in Melanesia were for men only. It was *tambu, tabu, tapu* (taboo) for women to go there. No problem. This was obvious, I did not go. But inside me there was a small flame of resentment. This built as I learned of bride purchase still being in effect. In some

Solomon Islands: A skilled carver showing off his wares on *Bali Ha'i*.

places, such as northern Pentecost Island in Vanuatu, three pigs—especially if one had the desired curved tusk—would buy a wife. I also learned that domestic violence was the most prevalent crime. If one's wife was property, it led to this kind of behavior.

Interestingly in some places, hierarchy was matrilineal and property was handed down through the women. This was uncommon, however, and I never uncovered why and how this developed. Women rarely ate with us when we were guests in homes. In a few cases, we never even met the wife, "She is in the cookhouse."

There were a few situations where the wife seemed to be more of a partner as she whispered prompts in her husband's ear about what to do. Mary was like that, on a small island in northern Vanuatu, as she discretely coached her husband in the proper behavior in dealing with us as guests. She was one of the few healthy-looking women I met in Melanesia. Overall, however, in the rural areas and in the squatter villages around the cities, women were less than second-class citizens; they were possessions and not necessarily prized possessions. For me, as for many Western women, this was a difficult concept to swallow. If local custom stopped at some sites being sacred for men only, I could live with that. It was all the tendrils that spilled over from this concept of a woman as a body owned by a man that tripped me up.

So often the world over, I observed women treated as objects, unpaid workers, something to be used, and, too often, abused. It wasn't all that long ago that situation described the West also—and still does, but rarely. What a loss to civilization when half its population is constrained, restrained; their creativity, ideas, spirit, spark never allowed to ignite, to glow in the world. What a

different place it might be if that femaleness were free to temper male domination. Often, even in the West, women seem to have to be like men to succeed, losing their feminine spirit in the process.

≈≈≈

Another interesting visit ashore took place in a fairly remote area of Vanuatu; as so often *Bali Ha'i* was the only boat because we sought out these remote places. It wasn't a particularly attractive spot, but we had heard it had a place to snorkel with unusually giant clams that were, presumably, protected. They were still there, and they were colossal. We went ashore and met the local fellow who was the land-sea ranger, paid a small salary by the government. He wore a neat shirt and shorts without a tear or ragged edge, unusual in itself. As we walked across the island, he pointed out various trees and plants, then we came to an area where scaup ducks nested.

"Have you ever eaten a scaup duck egg?" he asked as he pulled one out of a nest and held it up.

"No," I murmured thinking it was big enough to make an omelet for two or three people.

"Here, you take this and try it," he instructed as he thrust it at us.

"OK," we conceded and pillowed it somehow in the daypack. Then we continued on to his home for a green coconut refresher and the creamy custard inside that is my favorite, which I scooped out using a husk chip, cut with the machete that opened the coconut. Here we met his family including several children, but how many were his and how many were his brother's wasn't quite clear. They were all playing with a large sea turtle kept in a small plastic pan barely big enough for it to fit. I suspected it was to become a meal at some point, although part of his job as ranger was to protect those turtles. Later we saw a sign about the scaup ducks; they were protected too. I cringed at the thought of the illegal egg in our pack. We did eat it because it was already too far gone to return to the nest, if we could even find it again. The egg when scrambled was quite gamy, and even if not protected, it was not a gastronomic experience I would care to repeat.

Incongruity Speaks

Incongruity speaks
in a trustful voice,
an authoritative voice;
but it doesn't speak the truth.

It tells of tagged turtles,
none eaten;
well, only a few.
(So many, remote officials reprimand.)

And the scaup duck eggs?
No, we've never tried them.
Now this giant egg is nestled
in a pocket of our pack.

A poster puts us wise.
Endangered, not to be taken.
The story this time is, "We only take one."

So it is that the *vanua-tai* manager
gives us the scaup duck egg,
and eats turtle.

The fish are not so plentiful now,
what can they do?

His family is hungry,
not only his children,
but his brother's too,
and then there is old aunty.

Our brightly colored perceptions,
butterflies of the mind, are transformed
into shrouded truths with lingering shadows,
hovering gray ghosts, wondering
when will there be
no more scaup ducks,
no more turtles?

Who will go hungry
and when?

Note: *vanua-tai* means land-sea.

Monkey on a Stick, Boiled Viper, and Lamb Flaps

Scaup duck eggs and barbecued dog weren't the only unusual food we've eaten. Many of our more exotic culinary experiences took place inland, as we usually explored the countries we visited on land as well as along their coasts. In Bangkok and other parts of Thailand, monkey meat on a stick, like a kebab, used to be common, and we've eaten it there. Wayne was quite fond of it and had first discovered it in his flying days. I found it rather greasy, and it didn't taste like chicken either. Now, it's rare; they've probably killed off too many monkeys, like so many other local foods. Another case of "The fish are not so plentiful now."

In Pago Pago, American Samoa, Wayne had found a local hole-in-the-wall cafeteria with diverse food and cheap prices—his favorite kind of place—and he dragged me there for lunch one day. Looking through the steamy glass-covered trays of food, I saw something that looked like croquettes. I asked what they were. "Turkey," was the reply. It took me back to my college days and turkey croquettes with gravy in the dining hall. I suspected its role then was to be filling and cheap, not necessarily tasty, but why not, I would try it again. Wayne thought it looked appetizing and told me to get two, he'd eat one. With our heaping plates of various dishes, we found a small, semiclean Formica table and sat down. I bit into the turkey and almost gagged—actually I did gag, and I spit it out into my serviette. It was turkey all right, but turkey tail (also called the Pope's nose), that fatty lump at the bottom of the turkey under which we stuff the stuffing at Thanksgiving, then cut off. It was something we didn't even throw into the soup pot.

In Tonga I bought lamb flaps from New Zealand. How bad could lamb from New Zealand be? Pretty bad, as it turned out, and the reason lamb flaps were in Tonga was because they wouldn't eat them in New Zealand. They're fat and bone from lamb bellies. Locally called *sipi*, they are part of the reason for many of the oversized Polynesians.

Sipi is just one type of low-grade meat exported to the Pacific, in a practice that Rod Jackson, professor of epidemiology at Auckland University, calls "dietary genocide." Courtesy of New Zealand and Australia, islanders have acquired a taste for turkey tails–highly fatty pieces of skin – and chicken frames, or carcasses. The result is an epidemic of diet-related illnesses. In Nauru, more than half of adults have diabetes. Pacific islanders have the world's highest obesity rates; 77 per cent of adults in Nauru, 74 per cent of women in Samoa.[1]

En route from Phnom Penh, Cambodia to Saigon via boat and bus, we stopped in the Mekong Delta in Vietnam. In between buses, we were at a boisterous, get-them-in-and-get-them-out restaurant when I decided I really needed the WC. On the way through a long, dark, dank hallway were cages of various kinds—holding-pens, of a sort, for various meals. One held several poisonous vipers. Some young fellows from Germany who had been on our bus ordered one, and gave Wayne a taste. I passed, but I wondered how the cook got them out of the cage and into the pan.

Octopus was something I've enjoyed the taste of, particularly in the Med from Turkey to Spain, but it's something that has to be cooked just right. It really needs pounding, like conch and whelks, to make it edible. Earlier at one little island in the San Blas, an autonomous Kuna Indian island group that's part of Panama, we would eat lunch at a small local place—one of Wayne's finds. It was one room with whirring refrigerator and generator, torn linoleum floor that may have once been lime green, four rickety Formica tables (somewhere there's a place that sells them as we sat at them the world over), the ubiquitous grimy plastic chairs, and a homemade charcoal stove outside. Although Wayne loves whole fish with its head and all the little bones, I am not fond of it. One day that was all there was plus octopus, so, of course, I ordered the octopus. It really was inedible; something akin to chewing rubber; but we were helping the local economy if not my hunger pangs.

Cruising Life: Fish head curry, an example of some of the interesting food on the menu, this in Singapore.

Cruising Life: In Thailand fried grasshoppers, grubs, and crawfish claws available from a street vendor. Photograph by Martha Eubanks.

In Fiji, the Polynesian gift-giving was done in reverse, perhaps because it was on the cusp and more Melanesian than Polynesian. There we had to take a gift of kava root to the chief. Kava is a mild hallucinogenic made into a disgusting-looking and -smelling drink, something like dirty dishwater. The ritual, which was repeated at almost all our many Fijian anchorages, demanded that once we anchored, put our dinghy in the water, and dressed appropriately, we went ashore and waited on the beach for someone to come and meet us.

The male representative of the chief's walked up and asked: "What are your names and where are you from?"

Wayne answered appropriately.

"What do you want here on our island?"

Wayne responded that we wished to anchor and (if no crocs) we wanted to snorkel, dive, and fish if allowed. Wayne then handed him our bunch of kava roots. "For your chief."

This fellow then took us to the chief's *fale*, (a thatch-roofed, open-sided building). There the chief and his elders were seated in a half circle. We sat on the floor with feet pointed away from the chief and, as for me, carefully covered with a *sulu* (like a sarong) and at least a short-sleeved decorous blouse. Wayne wore a collared polo shirt and long shorts, and combed hair. Our greeter explained to the chief in their language who we were and what we wanted, and then pushed our kava gift across the floor toward the chief. If he accepted it, we could stay; otherwise, we were "outta' there" immediately. Occasionally, the chief wouldn't accept someone, but only if they had committed some major wrongdoing. Someone made up the kava drink, and the kava bowl was passed around. It was necessary for Wayne to take a sip, but not for me. In fact, in some places, as a woman, I specifically may not sip from the kava bowl. Finally on one island where there was a party, rather than the traditional ritual, and most of the locals and the cruisers were already drinking kava, I was induced to have a sip—definitely dirty dishwater. I'm willing to try many unusual foods, but I'll pass on kava, poisonous vipers, turkey tails, and lamb flaps in the future.

Fiji: The author drinking kava.
Photograph by Dar Caple, S/V *Saw Lee Ah*.

Fiji: Preparing the kava.
Photograph by Dar Caple, S/V *Saw Lee Ah*.

Finding Food

Our issues of finding food were quite different from those of Johnny and so many of the families we met in too many countries. Concepts of sustainability fade into memory when populations grow. How many times we would hear the refrains: "We don't catch so many fish anymore." "The clams are gone now." "Pawpaw, breadfruit, and manioc, that's all we have." "We can't grow taro here anymore; we used to have so much." "There was nothing for the chickens to eat, so we killed them."

Our small gifts of a kilo of rice, tinned meat and tomatoes, tea, sometimes fresh pelagic fish if we'd caught one on our way wouldn't last long. They were a small drop in the limitless, ongoing issue of survival. It seemed as if there should be answers, but cultures never think they are dying; communities never think they can change. Sometimes the reason for no action, no move toward finding sustainability is religion, sometimes tradition, sometimes memory, and sometimes it is just beyond our capabilities. Constant hunger not only limits our bodies, it confines our minds and binds our souls in dread.

≈≈≈

There was another side to finding food, and that was my task of provisioning, sometimes for a few months at a time. Provisioning was really a challenge when I not only didn't speak the language (except for the basics), but the alphabet was different. It was fine when I was buying a can of tomatoes (providing there was a picture, of course), but what about bleach! Provisioning was quite a long, exhausting process requiring trips to various stores and markets. And then, there was always the challenge of putting all the supplies away, which on a boat became a significant task. Often the informal cruisers' network would be a source of where to find what at the best price.

My mother used to tell the story of how the Navajo wouldn't buy tins of Carnation milk or even take them if given. They knew milk didn't come from a flower. I had bought some tins and bottles like that, and it was always a bit of a surprise to see what I ended up with. Often it was more complicated than just not knowing what was inside, but even if I was given a name for it, what was it? How did I cook it?

I particularly enjoyed shopping at the public markets with multiple stands, each owned by individual families, and the bartering ritual that went on with any purchase. There's nothing like these markets in the United States; even our farmers' markets don't match up. At first, I found it difficult to negotiate over what might amount to five cents, but I soon learned that it was part of so many of the various cultures where I shopped. Bartering extended the conversation and established a relationship, although somewhat temporary depending on how long we were staying there, but sometimes that might be months. This back-and-forth conversation gave the seller a chance to extol the virtues of her products. Even if I couldn't always understand all the nuances of words that were foreign to me, we understood each other.

I really had trouble with tinned tomatoes in Turkey. I bought tins that looked exactly the same in terms of words and pictures, but one turned out to be tomato sauce and the other whole tomatoes. I never did figure out what was different, but I did learn how to read "without sugar" in Turkish. In Thailand, I ended up with three large bottles of oyster sauce, trying to buy something else.

Cruising Life: A fish market in Thailand.
Photograph by Martha Eubanks.

Cruising Life: A legumes and
grains market in Yemen.

Cruising Life: An olive market in Turkey, one of the author's favorites.

Shopping was an adventure, not a chore. I heard later from other cruisers that a woman was killed by a cobra at a large market where I used to shop in Phuket, Thailand—sometimes the adventure could get out of hand. But every once in a while, we would luck out. In the Louisiades, a remote archipelago of Papua New Guinea, a local fisherman paddled up in a leaky canoe and offered us six lobsters, and all he wanted was a deck of cards. We gave him the cards, along with a kilo of rice, some tinned meat, a baseball cap, and a T-shirt. He left smiling, and we continued smiling through our feasts for the next two days: steamed lobster for dinner, lobster and scrambled eggs for breakfast, lobster salad for lunch, and more steamed lobster for dinner. Just writing about it, makes me hungry for that again.

At one open market in Tanna, Vanuatu, almost everyone had mostly limes and taro and one or two other items, but by one tree was the most beautiful rooster I've ever seen. He had absolutely shimmery purple feathers with brilliant green and red ones on its side, but was trussed up in such a way that he clearly had lost his pride. His head was down, seemingly ashamed of what had become of him. Of interest also at this market was a fruit bat or flying fox. Furry, funny looking little critters, they often flew over our boat commuting to and from their roost to the jungle fruit trees. I liked them, and couldn't bring myself to eat one even if I had known how to clean and cook it.

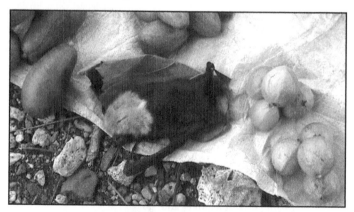

Cruising Life: The fruit bat for sale at the Tanna market.

Spiritual Food

"Do you know Tom Navy?" Chief Henry asked. We didn't, but we answered that we thought we might. This chief was sitting in the cockpit of our boat anchored in the eastern bay of Tanna, our first landfall in Vanuatu. Protected from the sun by the Bimini top, he squinted at us nevertheless, as if working harder to see us clearly. He awkwardly sipped the tea I had served him, to which he had added much sugar.

Vanuatu: The chief comes for a visit.

As he munched hungrily, but not greedily, on the biscuits I had put out, he told us, "A large American ship is coming—this is the second coming of American ships." He explained how three chiefs were drinking kava down by the south beach many years ago, and they had a vision. A man in a white U.S. Navy uniform came up from the water and told them to prepare for this arrival of the ships—thus started our introduction to Vanuatu's cargo cult religion, with its roots in World War II.

"I will sing you a song," he told us. "It explains our beliefs, our religion." He cleared his throat softly. "But, you see, of course, it is in my language. I will sing, and I will explain." We listened, one word stood out, a year actually, 1941.

"I wasn't born then." So he was younger than we were, but didn't look it. "But I have heard the stories, and I am a chief here so I am caring for them. This is when many of our men who could work went up to Espiritu Santo to work for $1 a day to unload the big American ships. These ships had everything— things we didn't know about then—Coca-Cola, machines to keep things cold, jeeps, guns, so many guns and ammunition. It was amazing to us. But we learned not to worry that we didn't have these things because some day we would. We go to church. You have seen our churches with the red cross in front? I will take you to a service if you want. But they last all night, on Fridays with much singing and dancing. For some people who are not in our religion, they get tired or they think it is a party. No, it isn't. We are waiting. Tom Navy is arranging this, for a ship to come and bring us everything we need that we don't have. I have to build a pier for the ship. That is my chiefly duty." He pointed to a shallow place by the shore and turned to my husband, "You are a captain of a big ship. Will that work do you think?"

Wayne chuckled, "No, this is a boat; much smaller than a ship. But I think that is too shallow for a big ship. I couldn't even bring our boat over there."

"Well, we have to do this thing. I am not sure

how." His eyes saddened; a failure of this duty weighed on him. But after a moment he perked up, "You know our volcano? I will arrange a guide for you. Not expensive, whatever you think." Perhaps he saw the money as a help in getting his pier built. We made the arrangements, and Wayne took him back to shore with gifts of a kilo of rice, tinned meat, and a box of biscuits. He was smiling again.

≈≈≈

Port Vila was a lovely place with French baguettes and classic melt-in-your-mouth French croissants, DVDs we could rent, and a lovely restaurant with the quintessential tropical patio where we often sat with Norwegian cruising friends for a sundowner. Nevertheless, parts of Vanuatu were the most primitive country I've been in. The cargo cult wasn't the only religion in Vanuatu. There was a strong belief in and practice of black magic. Sitting on the edge of the active volcano in Tanna—an intimidating experience, as huge burning chunks of molten rock shot up in the sky and landed across the rim from us—it was not difficult to imagine a belief in primeval forces at work. They were right in front of us. When a chief on another more remote Vanuatu island told us that his two sons were killed by black magic within months of each other, and we observed the now well-known land-diving ritual based on ancient beliefs of protection, it was all fathomable.

Land-diving inspired bungee jumping when a Kiwi visited Pentecost Island in Vanuatu some years ago. Legend told that it all started in the misty past when a young woman ran away from her abusive husband, who followed her. She climbed a tall tree and tied vines to her ankles, and as he approached, she jumped. Not seeing the vines, he jumped also with obvious results. At first it was a women's ceremony, but somewhere in the annals of time, the men took over to the point where the rickety tower they construct is guarded day and night to make sure no women come near, which would impose black magic on it. It has become a coming-of-age ritual for all the boys at about age ten.

Vanuatu: One village's protection against black magic.
Photograph by Gayla Morkel Phelps, S/V *Ariel*.

Vanuatu: The carver with the author's purchased protection against black magic.

seriously hurt, although one fellow was a bit wobbly when he was helped up, but death rarely happens. One of the interesting aspects about the elders' land-diving is that when a man is up there, he can say whatever he wants about anyone in the village, even the chief, and his words won't be held against him. This is something we ought to consider if we could do the revenge shouting without the actual diving. I didn't know their language well enough to understand the shouted critique, but I would have liked a translator for that. No one was willing, however.

The young boys climb the tower one at a time and stand on a small platform over empty space, while one of the elders ties vines around the boys' ankles. The dirt is softened below, but the hope is they won't actually hit it, at least not too hard. The women dance bare breasted in grass skirts, and the men wear only penis shields made of leaves. The youngest children, wearing nothing, try to imitate the dancers and the chanting. To me, they were the most captivating.

After all the boys are finished, which takes several days, the older men can prove their courage by diving. By this time, the vines are drying out, and it is getting more dangerous. When we witnessed this event, no one was

Vanuatu: Land-diving tower.

Vanuatu: The actual dive.

The Starvation of War

Ironically one of the survival techniques of the Allied troops during World War II in the South Pacific is now contributing to the hunger of those who were saved. GIs planted kudzu vines to provide camouflage over Quonset huts, hangers, ammo dumps, foxholes. Now these same vines have spread like a plague in some areas covering fertile ground, preventing planting, choking out native fruits.

It was in Honiara, the capital of the Solomons,

that we came face-to-face with another plague of that region—malaria. Wayne developed falciparum malaria, the most dangerous type that affects the brain quickly. He was so sick, he could hardly stand. Fortunately I was able to get him ashore and to a doctor the next morning. I, too, tested positive, but had only started to become ill. We were advised to take a Chinese herbal medicine made from *Artemisia annua,* Sweet wormwood. We had been taking prophylactics, and been careful, but the mosquitoes that carry it are so prevalent, it's difficult to avoid. Fortunately the medicine worked well and fairly quickly. We immediately bought extra to add to our medical supplies.

Wayne and I happened to be in Honiara on August 7, the anniversary of the U.S. Marines landing on Guadalcanal—the first major U.S. campaign in the South Pacific and a climactic turning point of the war. On a hill overlooking the ocean and the jungle, both of which were scenes of horrendous death and destruction from August 7, 1942 until February 9, 1943, stands the red rock American Guadalcanal Memorial. The Solomons and the Battle of the Coral Sea are iconic words for memories of World War II.

The night before the ceremony marking the Marines' landing anniversary, Wayne and I were invited to a reception given by the U.S. consul where we met two veterans who had actually been part of the battle. Every year they make the journey back with a small group, often of children and grandchildren of men who died there.

I listened carefully to a Navy vet, who haltingly told the story of how the landing craft he was on, taking Marines ashore, had been hit by the Japanese, but they managed to get the front part of the craft to the beach.

Solomon Islands: August 7 anniversary ceremony.

of planes, jeeps, and other military equipment—and the kudzu.

Solomon Islands: World War II Quonset hut in the jungle.

All his Navy buddies were killed, but the Marines got ashore and were able to drag him from the water. Every year, he comes and puts a wreath on the still-visible wreck of the landing craft.

Later Wayne and I went in our dinghy to where the wreck of this landing craft lay in a swampy, crocodile-infested area. It was an emotional experience having just heard the story. I added a small bouquet of lantana and watched its orange and pink blossoms float over to the rusted hull, the number still visible. I thought again, as I would so often throughout this area, of all the young men who had died here: seven thousand U.S. troops and thirty thousand Japanese, as well as an unknown number of local people.

We walked up on Red Hill and saw the foxholes that remain. Quonset huts still stand in both the towns and odd spots in the jungle. We saw the rusted wrecks

Solomon Islands: World War II wreckage.

Burning Land

Land first formed by fire and lava flow
Melanesians found this place
banana paw-paw kava need space to grow
fire used to clear this land.

Colonial powers force coconuts
in ruler-rigid rows put there by dark-skinned
sweat for copra silver it brings
fire again creates these palm-tree parks
market fell plantations gone
to feed their hunger Melanesians burn anew
ages pass generations too then war
brings bombs and flaming guns but worse
the planted vines enemy can't see through
covers guns manioc too.

These vines still they cover bush and thorn
not just rusty guns and human bones
yet today no embers glow
just machetes dull dark worn
like the men who learned what fire leaves.

Mournful murmurs echo through this land
formed by lava flow
and fire's flames.

I learned more World War II history when we
were in Darwin, Australia the following year. Few people
knew that Darwin had been bombed over fifty times by
the Japanese; nor did they know that a few members of
the Australian government had suggested establishing the

Brisbane line limiting how far they would let the Japanese
go into Australia, which many thought was inevitable—as
if that line would have stopped the Japanese. General
Douglas MacArthur, commander of the Allied forces in
the Pacific, quickly killed that idea although it appeared
not to ever have been a formal policy of the Australian
government.

The United States has never again shown itself so
finely as we did in World War II. Older Aussies know, as
do the French (except they won't admit it), that we saved
them. It is something to be proud of. War brings out the
best and the worst in humans.

The atrocities, the rape, the pillage, the unwonted
violence—for some, war is carte blanche for inhumanity.
One Aussie told us, while sipping a gin and tonic on
the purple bougainvillea-draped porch of a small resort
bungalow, about his father who had been captured by
the Japanese and buried up to his head, then was made
to watch the Japanese soldiers play soccer with his best
friend's head. How either the players or the forced
spectator survived and returned to live normal lives is
beyond imagining. When will it end?

7

Australia: Down Under to the Extreme

Out here, we hear the ants breathing. Land is somethin' the black fellas need. We came from the land, we go back to the land; it's part of us. Whites just use up the land.

—Aboriginal elder in radio interview

Poison, Tides, and Space

Everything I ever read about Australia is true. I can say this with certainty because it is a land of such extremes that indeed everything is true about it. Much of the wildlife in this country-continent is treacherous or poisonous. For example, of their approximately twenty-six varieties of snakes, twenty-three are poisonous—including the ten most deadly snakes in the world, a few so deadly one cannot possibly survive—and the other three are pythons. But it's not just snakes. Australia's sea is full of sharks, with a relatively large concentration of the Great white, (although emptying fast of that "threat," thanks to predation by humans). Great white sharks are a much over-rated killer of people, frankly, but they do make headlines. Making their home here are salties, aggressive Saltwater crocodiles, which are much more likely to make a meal of us than the sharks, and one of the most lethal animals in the world, the Box jellyfish. This creature reportedly kills more people worldwide than the sharks, snakes, and spiders put together. Although it averages only one person per year in Australia, it reportedly kills twenty to forty in the Philippines. One second is all it takes for the stinger to find its target, and about three minutes for a person to die. When we were in Australia at least two people were killed by crocs and a few more severely injured. I didn't read of any Box jelly deaths, so the crocs may be upping the stats, but it's the snakes that are responsible for the most deaths in Australia.

Australia provides habitat to the deadliest spider, tick, jellyfish, fish, shark, and snake in the world. The Funnel-web spider can actually inject its venom through shoes, and the Blue-ringed octopus is quite tiny and curiously attractive—something I might have been tempted to pick up and examine. It can kill in minutes. The Irukandji, another lethal Australian jellyfish, is the smallest animal known to kill humans.[1]

As well, there are mosquitoes—*mozzies* in the local jargon—the size of attack helicopters. In the outback, the next gas station may really be over 450 miles away; where during the rainy season a 4-wheel drive vehicle needs a snorkel to get across an otherwise dry river bed. Remember that storm I wrote about in the first chapter? That happened in Australia.

So how do Aussies and tourists survive? Australia is one of the few countries left on Earth where there is space for both its human population and its wildlife, poisonous or not. Not discounting the Sydney opera house, the fascination of Tasmania's Port Arthur prison museum, or other human-type sights, Australia is a country of unfathomable space. The wild beauty of the country, whether its immense barrier reef or its Outback, is transforming.

Australia: A valid warning.

≈≈≈

Australia: A saltie seen during a boat trip in the Yellow Water Billabong.

In Darwin, where we sailed from Bundaberg in 2006, there are tides of over thirty feet. When we first arrived in Darwin, we anchored and took our dinghy ashore for lunch. We put the dinghy anchor out within a short and shallow walking distance of shore. Wayne was on his second beer when clearly the dinghy was getting in deep water as the tide was coming in, but he didn't think it was necessary to pull it closer to shore, in spite of (probably because of) my insistence that he should do so. Some time and a number of beers later, we left, and he had to swim out to bring the dinghy ashore. Later we remembered that a young woman had been killed by a croc near that same beach. After that when anchored out and coming ashore by dinghy, we spent several sweaty minutes pulling it far up on the beach.

Several days later we took *Bali Ha'i* to a marina to facilitate provisioning for our next passage and time in Indonesia. With the excessively high tides, the marinas have locks through which yachts must transit to get to the marina basin. Not even floating docks can handle tides like theirs.

Continuous motion of planets and moons in space translates into continuous motion between land and sea: tides. Tides are actually a very long wave—half the circumference of the Earth. Although entrenched in the science of oceanography, to me, it's quite a magical thought to imagine a high tide as the crest of a massive wave. Oceanographers, fishers, boaters, and those who wander beaches and rocky intertidal shores know much about tides. Tide tables for various specific places can be predicted long into the future. Yet there is a certain leap of faith we take to accept this knowledge. That leap carried us into anchorages and harbors around the world.

Since tides are waves, it fits that high tide occurs when the crest of the wave reaches the shore, and low tide when the trough reaches shore. But it is the relationships of moon and earth and sun and earth that create these waves in the first place, thanks to gravitational pull and the movement of the Earth and our moon through space. Being closer to us (thank heavens), our moon has a stronger influence than our sun.[2]

What was fascinating for me about tides, aside from the fact that they are one long wave, was what can live in that space and time between high and low tide. Imagine: sometimes sea, sometimes land; saltwater or oxygen; wind waves that pulse gently like a small steady heartbeat or those times when they are the equivalent of a Muhammad Ali knock-out punch. How much variation can an organism take? Apparently quite an exorbitant amount when we consider the hundreds, possibly thousands, of intertidal species.

We spent many hours walking intertidal areas, from clear sand to pebbly to shell-covered to slippery rocks. Every type had its own special feel, its own life with stories to tell. One of the events that used to amuse us on many of these intertidal beaches was what we called the hermit crab conventions. We saw these in a variety of places and environments. We would see here and there solitary hermit crabs, then suddenly they would all assemble. It would be a big flea market of real estate for the hermit crabs, each looking for a better, possibly bigger, shell to call home.

Australia: Arriving for a hermit crab convention. Photograph by Gayla Morkel Phelps, S/V *Ariel*.

≈≈≈

Extreme poisons and extreme tides are just part of Australia's story. There is also extreme space. From Darwin, we flew to Alice Springs, considered the focal center of the Outback. For those who live in this space out of reach of the few towns, the basic needs of medicine and education are handled by air.

The Australian Inland Mission Aerial Medical Service, which later was renamed the Royal Flying Doctors, began in 1928 based in Queensland, serving the remote Kimberly region in the northwest using chartered airplanes and pilots. Today the not-for-profit organization owns sixty aircraft, has twenty-one bases throughout Australia, covers a range of over 7.2 million square miles, serves over 270,000 patients a year, and, according to their reports, their pilots fly almost 16 million miles a year. It's such a remarkable story that a long-running TV series was based on the risks and adventures of their intrepid staff. They take to heart the quote from the Reverend John Flynn, a Presbyterian minister, who started the service back in 1928, "Do not pray for tasks equal to your powers; pray for powers equal to your tasks."[3] Their history is a story of compassion, action, and heroism.

Education in the outback is accessible via a variety of communication technologies from television to satellite and originally radio from the remarkable School of the Air, headquartered in Alice Springs, which I visited. Started in 1951 using basic radio technology from the Flying Doctor base, it now uses complex, interactive satellite technology. The school reaches approximately one hundred and twenty students per year hundreds of miles away who would have no other access to an adequate education. It covers an area over 380,000 square miles.

When I visited, the furthest student was over six hundred miles from Alice Springs. Their teachers and staff are dedicated, compassionate professionals—also heroes in Australia's world today.

Aboriginal Conundrum: Songlines vs. Scorn

This antipodal land has many layers of meaning. Sometimes it seemed so basic and down-to-earth that symbolism could have no place here; but its space, once past the eastern coast, is so vast and unforgiving that the only way to survive it would be through a metaphysical connection. The physical connection becomes exhausting with its antithetical characteristics: extreme heat and cold, swirling dust devils and waist-deep mud, parched dryness and torrential rains, the long-burning dry crackle of wildfires and the quick flash of lightning and booming crash of thunder, and, of course, all those snakes in all that space.

I touted some of the accomplishments of Captain James Cook earlier. In 1770 he was the first European to explore and chart the east coast of Australia. He wrote of the Aboriginals, "I think them a timorous and inoffensive race.... [All] they seem'd to want was for us to be gone."

No wonder. "Wherever the European has trod, death seems to pursue the aboriginal," wrote Charles Darwin in *The Voyage of the Beagle*. I have to say that of all the countries I have visited on this circumnavigation and other trips, I have never seen a conquered people as debased, disrespected, and poorly treated by their conquerors as the Aboriginals by the white Australians.

Granted I wasn't around when the Spanish decimated the Central American native population; and when in Sudan, I wasn't a witness to the crimes against humanity in Darfur. Historically and in modern times, there are worse examples, but I wasn't watching them. Quite recently, there seems to be somewhat more interest from both the Aboriginal and the white perspective in exploring the Aboriginal cultural heritage, particularly of music and art.

The movie, *The Rabbit-Proof Fence*, is the tragic true story of one of the means used for subjugating these original inhabitants of this continent. Australian authorities took—kidnapped by any other standard—the mulatto children, selected by lighter skin color, and raised them in compounds teaching them to be servants. These children are the Stolen Generations of the Aboriginal people. It wasn't until 1969 that the laws allowing these children to be taken from their families were repealed.[4]

Today, there is a different story. Many Aboriginals use desperate means to escape their existence. Alcohol, gasoline, glue, paint, whatever is available, all of which separate them from their traditions, their self-respect. Although I understood this, I felt fear and disgust when several Aboriginal black-as-a-crow, dread-locked-greasy-haired young men, with faces planed differently from mine, dressed in torn rags, came careening past me in Alice Springs swearing loudly in the Queen's English. Only when my uneasiness abated did I feel sadness and some compassion for the hopelessness of their lives.

On a camping trip from Darwin to the Yellow Water Billabong, we had an Aboriginal guide on a river tour. She amazed us with her ability to spot wildlife including a small snake lying on a branch of a tree some distance away. Her winsome face was classic Aboriginal, but with a smile and none of the vulgarities of the lurching, drunken young men of Alice Springs. She epitomized for me through her ability to see, her words, her actions, and her demeanor, the impressive qualities of these people.

I saw these two examples as expressing a range of types of a people, which seemed callow of me at best. These stereotypes are truths, but only part of it, of course. The issues of maintenance of traditional Aboriginal culture and the inbred prejudice against the Aboriginals by the whites are complex problems that Australia must face. As of yet, the country seems to not have found solutions. My own country has little to offer in that regard either.

The Southern Cross Watches

So much has she seen
under her watchful stance
of those who cross her path

Invasion only one of those
that makes her want to turn away
dark, dense, green kudzu vines covering
and suffocating life
out of struggling hibiscus
she watches as invaders win again

white Australians only one of many
to commit these particular crimes
of slavery, executions, disease
in the territory she watches over
and listens to

"We had no choice. We stole
a loaf of bread for a child, a hungry child,
and were deported here, to this
truly God-forsaken land."

　　"You stole our children, you killed us
　　with your diseases, your guns, your hatred
　　of our ways."

"We needed to survive. Some of you
were in the way. Others we tried to help. We gave
your children clothes and homes."

　　"Don't you understand! Their home is with us,
　　in this space of ours. Not in your boxes.
　　The stolen ones—you broke our souls."

"It wasn't...we didn't mean...
we lost our homes, our families. We
are lost and broken too."

　　"Then where is your compassion?"

"We apologized, what more do you want?"

　　"We do not believe
　　you can hear what we want."

This night as all others
the Southern Cross
anchors the Milky Way
and all who cross her path.

Possibly as much as seventy-five thousand years ago, the Aboriginal people separated from other *Homo sapiens* and migrated to Australia from New Guinea when those land masses were still connected. To get to New Guinea, they probably island-hopped from Indonesia. Whether one or multiple migrations isn't known, but once there, groups separated and even went as far south as Tasmania about thirty thousand years ago. By the time of the European invasion, there were multiple indigenous peoples with different languages and cultures. Today they are lumped together as Aboriginals, although the Torres Strait Islanders are considered separately.

According to an online article in *Science*, Australia's Aboriginal people are "likely representing one of the oldest continuous populations outside Africa."[5] Like the isolation of New Zealand's birds creating their own physical characteristics, and of mine at Minerva Reef affecting my emotional character, the Aboriginals' long-term isolation in this place of extremes created a worldview in which they saw a place for everything, and made that place part of a person's heart and soul. To put it intellectually, as Australian historian and anthropologist Inga Clendinnen does:

> Traditional Aboriginal culture effortlessly fuses areas of understanding which Europeans 'naturally' keep separate: ecology, cosmology, theology, social morality, art, comedy, tragedy—the observed and the richly imagined fused into a seamless whole.[6]

Max Dulumunmun Harrison wrote in his book, *My People's Dreaming*:

You see these rocks and this tree here; the rock says to the tree, 'Hey, you can come down here, and I will support you.' This is how we work with the land, supporting and helping each other. Trees live in tribes, just like people. When a tree is born and then it is moved to another area, for whatever reason, that's like taking a person out of their country and putting them in a different country. They become like refugees.[7]

And then there is listening to the ants breathing, a phrase I heard used from an interview with an unidentified Aboriginal man quoted in the epigraph for this chapter, and which led me to write this poem.

I Hear the Ants Breathing

I pause in the openness of the earth
to hear the ants breathing.
I watch my brother, koala,
dozin' in the eucalyptus,
what that fella does best.
I move slowly, drawn by threads
of power, unbreakable
by wire fences, railroad tracks, power lines,
coal diggers. Unbreakable, I sing
these Songlines, this path I walk
is sacred, I have known it for centuries.

I pause to hear the ants breathing.
This place is my strength.

The Aboriginal people are different. I do not mean those lost in hopelessness, thanks to the conquerors and their own choices. I mean the song people, artists, musicians, wanderers, guides, sheepherders, and all those who nourish the flame of their innate knowledge in their souls. They know something of this Earth that all other cultures have lost in their evolution toward civilization.

Everyone has heard of the Aboriginals' walkabout, but few outsiders truly understand it. Of course we don't understand it; it's like explaining subatomic physics in English to a three-year-old child who only knows Thai. This web-like connection—their walkabout, their songlines, their art—all support not only their worldview, but who they are as a people and as a person.

Australia: Early Aboriginal drawing at Uluru.

Australia: Uluru at sunset, a spiritual place for the Aboriginal people.

of its continuing physicality. But it is dead, it's not what it was before. Isn't that what air, water, and soil pollution, as well as habitat destruction are—using up the land, the Earth, our planet? We use it and discard it, as if this is our right; and we do not accept responsibility, accountability, or stewardship for it.

We have disassociated ourselves from the very substances that nourish us—our air, water, oceans, wildlife, wild places—in our greedy search for material goods, for a life of comfort. We barely feel connected to our own families, let alone our neighbors, or the wildlife that may exist near us. Our disconnection extends to what we eat, what we use, what we wear with no sense of what it really costs. Yet, what a price we have paid for our neglect, our refusal to be responsible, accountable.

What will it take to understand essential ecology, the interconnection of all life on Earth? I had understood this concept academically, intellectually, but through this voyage it grew to become the center thread of my spirituality.

When I see an uninhabited, classic South Pacific island with all the usual accoutrements—swaying palms, white sand beach, nesting terns, shimmery turquoise water—and the whole place is covered with refuse, mainly plastic bottles; or when I sail through acres of trash, again mostly plastic; or when I see within a day's sail excessive

Dulumunmun also noted that the songlines came first, before the art, and are a part of Aboriginal "mental and spiritual structure. They are lines of energy that run between places, animals and people."[8] Most importantly, this connection or definition is all-encompassing with the Earth and all its living beings, including rocks.

In another radio interview that I heard, a woman with the charming name of April Bright said:

> In our heart, from long time, all our Dreaming stories, no matter white man got fence lines everywhere, they cut this country up. Aboriginal way, our way, that country goes right past Dreaming tracks, and you can't cut it off with fence lines.

We do cut the land up; we use it up; we forget what it is, what it was. We think it is still there because consumerism opposed to the basic survival needs of so many; or when I can't eat the oysters or swim because of pollution; or...or...or...I become a missionary, a zealot, a proselytizer. It is all worth saving. I am as furious as I am mournful. We are all threads woven into this tapestry of life, but our species isn't the only thread. Every thread plays a role, has a purpose, and they all fit together to create the tapestry, which is inordinately beautiful and irreplaceable.

Things

What do we do with all these
things?
How can there be entire TV channels selling only
things?
The Internet selling
things?
Side-by-side stores selling the same
things?

In Cambodia, what is needed for life
is found in the trash or the gutter
by scab-faced children wearing holey T-shirts
from some Hard Rock cafe.
No one sells
things.

In Vanuatu, what is needed for life
is picked from the reef at low tide
by brown barefoot women in long threadbare skirts
wrapped up to their knees.
No one sells
things.

In the Kimberly, Aboriginal artists
walkabout for the red ochre
intent on the ground and where to dig for this,
the blood of their ancestors, to paint
their dreamtime souls.
They don't sell
things.

But we buy things and more
things
creating such a mountain of
things
we only see
things,
while the rest of the world treads by, eyes downcast,
searching for life.

I'm not suggesting we adopt an Aboriginal culture; not possible. But it is time that all the institutions and adornments of our culture be examined more closely: religions, governments, the quality of national leadership, education, commerce, economies, our tendency to create revisionist history, the insanity of war, the structure of the family—everything. What do these institutions say about us? Where have they led us? Possibly it is time for some focused and disciplined Socratic questioning with enlightened and wise Platonic responses. We could learn from the Aboriginals as they may wish to learn from us, if there is any way to align their culture with the modern world. If Alice Springs is any example, perhaps there isn't, and self-destruction is what we both will continue to do best.

There was one particular experience in Australia that focused on preservation and provided me with another image that will stay with me forever. A few dedicated people and then the government came to the rescue of Loggerhead turtles that lay their eggs on the same beaches year after year for, probably, centuries. Some of these areas, including Mon Repos Conservation Park, are now protected and guarded carefully. We were fortunate to be able to accompany a ranger with a small group to watch a female Loggerhead come up from the sea, dig a hole, settle into it, and lay her hundreds of Ping-Pong-ball-looking eggs. While she is laying her eggs, she is in a daze and can be measured, tested for DNA and health, tagged, pictures taken, and petted. What I remember most, however, is the sight of her heaving her giant body down the beach in a narrow path of moonlight back to the ocean. For me, it was as special as looking into the eye of a baby whale.

Australia: Loggerhead turtle laying eggs at Mon Repos.

8

Southeast Asia: Death and Hope

"Hope" is the thing with feathers –
That perches in the soul –
And sings the tune without the words –
And never stops – at all –

—Emily Dickenson

Indonesia: Corruption Means Dead Orangutans

She was a beautiful auburn wild female with a new infant. She nibbled a tough shelled pandanus fruit and shifted the baby around as she melded into the luxuriant riverside greenery. She eyed us, but didn't flee. Possibly she sensed that there she would be protected. We looked, we photographed, we smiled, but kept some distance. She took us in with one eye, the other on her meal and her baby. I wanted to help her somehow, even more than I wanted to help the young beach hawkers in Lombok, the Indonesian women with their babies tugging at our sleeves in Ubud, the wide-eyed children in Samoa.

This orangutan didn't have a name; she hadn't been rescued to be rehabilitated, guided back to orangutan life, and named like Kusasi, Tom, Princess, or Percy. But she has 95 percent of our DNA, as all orangutans do, thus they are among our closest relatives. Chimps and bonobos, two other species of great apes, have a little over 98 percent of the same DNA as *Homo sapiens*. In fact, they are closer to us than they are to monkeys. These species separated from our direct ancestors only twelve to fifteen million years ago, a short time in Earth's history.

Wayne and I were the only passengers and royally treated guests on the little putt-putt *klotok*, a local riverboat, that took us from our anchorage off Kumai up the Sekonyer River in southern Borneo, part of Indonesia. "I'm Jenny," our captain told us, "like Jennifer Lopez," and giggled, always a smile on his face. We sat on the roof on small benches under a canopy. I suspected the canopy was not only to protect us from any sun that might slip through the tangled jungle overhanging the river, but to keep the snakes from dropping down on us as we passed underneath. There the first mate served us our flavorful and nicely presented meals, which he cooked on the aft deck over a simple charcoal grill. Also on the aft deck was a simple shower and closet-like room with a toilet, and on the small open deck Jenny and his crew of one slept. In front was the engine room and our sleeping cabin: two simple, but tidy, small (but big enough for us) beds against each wall with their own mosquito netting, much needed, and an open window to listen to the jungle noises and the lap of the water when we tied up against the shore at night.[1]

Indonesia: The *klotok* that took us to Camp Leakey.

This narrow, muddy, flowing, jungly rivulet, the Sekonyer River, is the path to one of the special places on Earth—Camp Leakey. Located in Tanjung Puting Reserve, it is the result of the dedication, persistence, labor of love, and just plain grit of Biruté Galdikas, PhD—one of the three "Leakey girls," along with Jane Goodall, PhD, and Dian Fossey, PhD. Starting with next to nothing in 1971 in this inhospitable jungle, Galdikas and her first husband built a compound for continuing scientific research, and started what has become the

longest continuing study of a primate. Galdikas has brought to world attention the sword of extinction that hangs over these glorious relatives of ours.

The reserve was a combination of peat and freshwater swamp and solid ground below the immense canopy of the jungle, which often rose to one hundred feet. The water was brown to black. The land was shades of green with flashes of color from the myriad birds, such as the brilliant turquoise-blue and yellow Stork-billed Kingfishers with their extraordinarily large bright red beaks. Then there was the Rhinoceros Hornbill, the ultimate in evolutionary bizarreness, with its large bright yellow beak, and, as if that weren't enough, on top of that an appendage perched like an afterthought as one sets off for the Queen's garden party, the gaudiest of bright red and yellow hats curving upwards making the bird look perpetually uppity and rather comical at the same time. In this world of browns and greens, it did stand out. But I wondered why they didn't just tip over with all that hornbill weight up there. There were many other species too, including the Edible-nest Swiftlet, whose nests made of their spittle, mud daubs, and small twigs are captured for bird's nest soup. Knowing the nest's composition would make me think twice about ordering that gourmet extravaganza, as if stealing their nests wasn't bad enough.

Along the river, we watched crocodiles sunning on nearby logs, snakes slithering along branches, and the ever-amusing Proboscis monkeys with their most bizarre noses, looking like a big—very big—wad of clay stuck on the end of what might have been a normal monkey nose.

Indonesia: The author with Princess and Percy.

bodies considered an aphrodisiac. Haven't these Asian men ever heard of Viagra?

I was fascinated by the story of Sam, an orangutan who had been traumatized by a large male when he was a toddler. Generally orangutan mothers care for their young for three or four years, but at age twelve when we were there, Sam was still cared for by his mother, who clearly knew he needed special help. Percy captured my attention too. He was about two and the son of Princess. I watched him play with an empty plastic container using it in many of the same ways a human child would: a hat, a boat, something to toss back and forth. He was much more adept than my children ever were, using his feet and toes as well as hands and fingers. This led me to think of the way human hands and fingers are used in so many of the story-telling dances of Southeast Asia and Polynesia.

But birds, crocodiles, and monkeys weren't what brought us there. It was the orangutans. *Orang utan*, person—or in some translations, man—of the forest. This is one of their last holdouts. In spite of the work of Galdikas and her associates and volunteers, the orangutans are declining. Many of the orangutans there have been rescued, often from the exotic wild pet trade. How could anyone possibly think that they could manage a full-grown orangutan as a pet? A grown male could weigh up to three hundred pounds and have an arm span of eight feet, and they are wild, a fact they don't forget. Others were orphaned when their mothers were killed either for venturing out of the park into a farmer's province or for some ridiculous, obscure part of their

Indonesia: Princess relaxing while Percy plays.

The Length of Fingers

The Nuka Hiva women dance for us
lengthened fingers are fluttering butterflies
telling their stories.

Special memories linger from Toau,
home of two families,
where young Violet dances for me,
her graceful hands older than her giggling face,
while her aunt stretches her work-hardened tan fingers
to spread crimson hibiscus flowers
on the cake she baked for my birthday.

In Ubud, the stylized Hindu dances tell of legends
of Rama, Shiva, and the powerful,
rambunctious monkey god,
Hanuman. Here the fingers are floating golden swans
tacking purposefully down a glistening canal
pausing here and there to make an imperial point.

Then we come to Princess with long,
well-jointed, dirt-red fingers
stretching them out to pick up bruised bananas,
reminding her small son Percy where she is
as he makes a plastic container a boat, a hat,
an object to juggle,
a toy using his feet and fingers equally well.

Our closest relatives with talents we could use,
yet, we kill them
for space to plant palm oil,
for the orphaned pets until they get too big—

then they go the way of their mothers,
for added strength to sagging penises,
often for no reason,
we kill them.

Indonesia: Dancer in Bali.

124

There were several small buildings at the camp itself, mostly for research and the care of those orangutans that needed help. The human inhabitants had only their basic needs met; if they were not dedicated researchers and caregivers to the orangutans, they were not there.

Feeding platforms were located throughout the park area near the camp. Every day they were stocked with bananas and small tubs of fortified milk for the babies. The point was to try to keep the orangutans inside the park boundaries, for if they ventured out, they would inevitably be killed. Even within the park there were dangers: poachers and illegal loggers topping the list.

Malaysia and China are the primary beneficiaries of the rape of Indonesia, their money going into the pockets of a few in government and even at least one park manager, and their products going to the Western world, particularly the United States. The orangutans are an eco-tourist attraction, which, when local providers are used, puts a lot of money into the local economy, but those that kill them or sanction their killing ignore this. There is a touching and informative documentary, *Kusasi: From Orphan to King* by PBS, about the former alpha male at Camp Leakey. In the documentary, Galdikas points out a photo of the then-park-director on top of a pile of illegally cut timber receiving his payment—more orangutan habitat destruction.

It was clear that all this damage was for money, not merely survival. We must ask, "What are we doing? Is it really worth it? What will we have left?" The answer to the last question is: Nothing.

Indonesia: Tom, the current alpha male.

Thailand: Food, Sex, and Death

Thai cuisine, known now throughout the world—there's even a Thai restaurant in the little Colorado mountain town near where I live—is certainly one of the industries, at least of Chiang Mai, where cooking schools abound. My friend, Martha, who visited us on the boat, then toured north Thailand with me, took one of these classes with me, and we thoroughly enjoyed ourselves. The class started with a visit to the local market, where our teacher-chef introduced us to his favorite suppliers and to some of the unusual foods here, which we might not know. He passed on the grubs and crickets, which get sizzled in woks street-side, thinking, rightly so, that most of our Western taste buds weren't up to that. The best part of this class was that we got to savor the full meal after. Among other dishes, we prepared a red curry chicken, which can almost be duplicated in the United States.

As much as Wayne and I loved Thai cuisine, we had to be sure to ask for "not hot," even though we liked spicy food. In Thailand, hot is beyond what most Western mouths can survive.

When trying to replicate some of my Thai recipes in the United States, there were two ingredients that were difficult to find: galangal and kaffir lime. Galangal grows like ginger, is sometimes called blue ginger, looks sort of like ginger, but it doesn't taste like ginger. It's rather peppery. There is a galangal sold in the West that comes from Indonesia, but it is quite different, and has been described as somewhat piney in taste. Words fail me with kaffir lime. It's not like any common citrus in the West; an approximation would be a cross between what we know as lime and a blood orange. I loved it and stocked up in Thailand on dried kaffir lime leaves, but they aren't nearly as savory as the fresh. I would guess any city that has an Asian market would carry these ingredients fresh.

In spite of some seriously negative experiences in Thailand recounted later in this chapter, which had nothing to do with the country itself, Thailand had much to offer besides its spicy, flavorful cuisine, boat work, and friends. It was a comfortable place to be with friendly, easy-going people, interesting sites to visit, and the calming sight of the saffron-robed Buddhist monks on their morning walks for alms.

≈≈≈

Another industry besides cooking schools in most of the tourist areas of Thailand was sex. We saw white males proudly walking down the streets of Chaing Mai, Bangkok, Patong, and other Thai tourist areas, their bellies hanging out, their faces needing a shave, clutching slim, young, lovely Thai girls. To me, it was nauseating, but it certainly helped the economy, for these men often find they were not only paying for their concubine, they were supporting her family as well. This "industry" existed in Cambodia also. Of course, there are many successful interracial marriages, but those are definitely not the relationships I'm describing here.

≈≈≈

For us, our stay in Thailand meant work—work on the boat, not that one isn't always working on a boat, but this was more intense than usual. Here *Bali Ha'i* was to be hauled out, the hull repainted, and many repairs completed. During the hot, sweaty days of getting her ready for her new beauty treatment and necessary repairs, images of the turquoise, shimmering pool by the hotel next to the boatyard floated before my eyes; but when could I float in it?

Before we hauled out, Wayne's son Ron and his family came for Christmas, and we celebrated our grandson's tenth birthday on the boat. It was always a treat for us to have family and friends visit, but we would only do so when there wasn't much sailing involved. At one anchorage with them, Wayne and I were lowering the dinghy into the water as we've done hundreds of times: I handled the line on the winch, and he manhandled the dinghy into the right position. Wayne yelled angrily, "Come on, hurry up, let it down faster!" Foolishly, I thought, *OK, you want it faster, here it comes.* I let go of the line and stood back, but not far enough. The stopper knot at the end of the line whipped around and smashed my hand, but the dinghy was definitely lowered faster.

Bali Ha'i was to be hauled out at 8 a.m. on January 2, soon after Ron and his family left. Before the hauling out, there was work to be done! With my left hand in an air splint, I spent New Year's Day going through the boat carefully packing and sealing everything that would stay on board, be put into a storage shed, or be moved to our studio apartment. Wayne served as the mule lugging items here and there. Finally, a week or so later, I was able to go to the hospital to learn my hand wasn't broken, just badly damaged.

Once the boat was on the hard (after the boat is hauled out and propped up with lots of supports on dry land) in the boatyard, the mast and all the sails, lifelines, stanchions, and hardware were stripped off. Down below all the shelves were bare and the lockers filled with plastic-encased nonvaluables, while anything of interest to anyone else was locked in the storage shed, where, on advice from other cruisers, we left no food, but lots of rat poison. What remained was piled up in our tiny apartment. I only hoped there would still be room for us.

As the hull painting contractors got to work, Wayne was there as they removed everything from the decks, saving the radar wires from being cut just in time, disassembling the anchor windless, and all of that. The contractors were a husband-wife team with various cousins doing much of the work. Only the wife understood English, so there was always a bit of translation going on. I picked up a little Thai, but my accent was terrible, and I never could quite hear the difference when my Thai friends corrected me laughingly.

I was busy meeting with contractors to make new upholstery for the pilot house and new ceilings down below after they had sagged from six years of heat and humidity, the foam backing disintegrating. In between I hand-laundered clothes in the shower, cooked on a one-burner hot plate, and washed dishes in the bathroom sink. But I had WiFi, which worked most of the time, and air conditioning when the mosquitoes and humidity got too much.

Along with other cruisers in Phuket that season, who were in the same boat, or, to be more exact, out of their boats, we would sojourn in the heat of the day to Rosie's. This was one of several shacks behind the boatyard with the usual cracked plastic tables and chairs, where we would order one of several mouth-watering choices of Thai food for about US$1.85, maybe a little more if we had shrimp instead of fish or chicken. Rosie had one helper and cooked everything to order in a large wok over a single charcoal burner. We helped ourselves to water, lemonade, or beer, silverware, and serviettes (in the United States we call them napkins, but everywhere else in the world that means a feminine product, not something to use at a meal).

At Rosie's there was always someone to discuss where to find a replacement stanchion, a certain size line, a specific metric-sized screw, or get some welding done. Anyone not into boat maintenance would find the conversations unfathomable and boring if they understood at all. It was a time when days stretched into weeks and weeks into months. The cruising community was expanded there, although most of us were working hard on our boats. We shared not only information and meals, but assistance, and, of course, social time. Within the incomparable, cooperative cruising community we made several friends for life.

Cruising Life: A holiday season dinner at Yacht Haven Marina in northern Phuket, Thailand with close friends from S/V *Ariel*, S/V *Briana*, and S/V *Strider*.

≈≈≈

This must have been the place for accidents for me. Obviously I had not invoked the right spirits to watch over me or was working too hard in the heat and humidity. Another accident occurred the following Christmas at the marina on the northern end of Phuket where we went after the boat haul-out work was completed. I thought as it was happening that I was going to drown, which seemed odd at the time as I do not fear the water at all and it has seemed a place of renewal and safety for me. During the circumnavigation, I often escaped to swim, snorkel, or paddle my sea kayak away from everything and everyone. This Thai accident became my second close-to-death experience—the first being the storm in Australia, ironically another potential watery death.

The sunny and exceedingly hot morning of December 24 was a busy one with chores to be completed. First, I crawled into the cockpit locker then into the lazarette (a deep storage area under the stern of the boat) to clean them out. I had to slither into the cockpit locker (Wayne couldn't fit, so it always had to be my job), contorting myself to grab something, re-contorting myself to hand it out to Wayne, cleaning the inside of the locker as best I could, repeating the process to re-store the gear. The lazarette was particularly demanding with heavy scuba tanks, coils of line, a large nylon net bag of extra fins and masks that moved like a giant octopus squirming to get away, a drogue anchor, as well as many other items, making it awkward and difficult work in the hot, confined space. I expected scrapes and bruises and got plenty.

Those tasks done, Wayne and I showered and changed. We were planning to ride our bicycles to visit some cruising friends on their boat and then drive to the anchorage at the southern end of Phuket to visit our close friends on S/V *Ariel* for Christmas. We had bought second-hand—probably more like fifth-hand—ratty old bicycles from other cruisers at the boatyard where we had our boat painted.

I got on my rickety bike on the rickety dock (not because it was old, but because it was floating on pontoons and there was a little swell in the marina). Being a bit rickety myself from the heat and the morning's work, I stumbled and fell. The bike fell on top of me and pushed me over the edge into the water; my leg was caught in the bicycle, and it sank with me attached under it. It seemed to be happening in slow motion. I remember seeing the light of the sun on the water above me as I was sinking down. As I struggled to free my leg, which took a little more than a minute, but felt like several, I expected that I was going to die. When I first came up I was under the dock and hit my head, not badly enough to knock me out, but enough to push me under again. I fought my way to the open surface as I had run out of air. Wayne and two young Thai men came running over and pulled me out. Nothing was broken, but my leg was badly bruised and swollen.

A cruising friend of ours who was a retired surgeon monitored it for me over the next few weeks. The swelling finally went down, and I, more or less, recovered from the fright, although I continued to have nightmares about this potential watery death for several months. Now it's just another cruising story.

Just as on land, sometimes at sea accidents end tragically. But somehow, accidents seem more difficult and require more of us on a boat; perhaps because we're often isolated without a support system. I've heard many people react to our circumnavigation as being romantic, fun, relaxing. At times it was. Yet like life, it had its dark side too. Two tragic events struck close to our own lives: the death of the seven-year-old granddaughter of Kiwi friends of ours whom we had shared an anchorage with the day before and the murder by pirates of a Brit friend of ours at an anchorage we had been at two years before in much the same circumstances.

The first incident was in Vanuatu. We had been all together at an anchorage, then as our yachts sailed in opposite directions, their wakes separated with waves good-bye and "See you soon, somewhere." To our shocked surprise, it was to be the next day.

Imagine little Sophie bobbing up and down in her orange water wings, her sister and brother playing on an upturned canoe ashore, parents relaxing on bright blue beach towels watching, grandparents, Liam and Ella, on their boat cleaning up after ham and eggs.

Where such a big shark came from, no one could say. Sophie was in shallow water, but it ripped her apart mistaking her for something else in an attack not typical for most shark species.

We heard quickly, the news surging along with the speed of a fast canoe. The parents with the body of their daughter were somehow getting to Port Vila to start arrangements for returning to New Zealand, and our friends were sailing to Espiritu Santo with the other two grandchildren where they could leave their yacht. Then, they too, would fly to Port Vila. At first light next morning, we saw them and went over to help. Liam's hands were shaking as he tried to tie the dinghy down, Wayne took over, "I'll do it." I hugged Ella and started on the many chores to close down the boat to be left for who knew how long. Nine-year old Emma told me, "A shark bit Sophie right here." She drew her hand across her stomach. "I know, love," I turned, bent down, and whispered into her curly brown hair, "but you are safe." Her little brother was playing with a yellow plastic car, moving it in steady circles, "Where's Mama and Papa?" he asked over and over. I could not speak the gruesome truth.

In the corner of the cabin was a large, shiny black plastic bag holding the bloody clothing, towels, and clean-up rags used after fatally injured Sophie had been lifted to the deck. Ella threw another rag into the bag, without looking. Soon the runabout came for the grieving family. We handed them their luggage and promised to finish up and lock the boat behind us. Ella called back, "The bag…" "I know," I yelled, "I'll get rid of it." She tried to smile her thanks.

As soon as they were out of sight, I grabbed a rag and soap, and started scrubbing every little spot I could find on the deck, as if erasing these last blood stains could erase the pain of death. Finally done, I added my bloody rag to that insidious bag and handed it to my husband, "Get rid of this ashore!"

The second tragedy occurred in an anchorage on the way to Phuket from Langkawi, Malaysia that we knew well, having been the only cruising boat there ourselves two years earlier. Two Thai fishing boats had been anchored not far away, just off the uninhabited rocky shore, tightly knit trees blocking access to the land.

It was this same scenario that ended in tragedy for our friends. Around midnight, three Burmese crew from the fishing boats—now pirates—came, grabbed a hammer from a project Richard had been working on before turning in, attacked him in his bed; Holly sleeping elsewhere due to the heat, cowered under the sheets, afraid to move. When Richard regained consciousness, he struggled up, yelling in his clipped Brit voice, "Get off my boat, you thieving pirates!" Holly heard Richard's scream, then the young men with hammer, knife, and rope were at her and bound her. Later they dragged her out briefly and ordered her to start the yacht's engine. Slipping through her husband's blood, she knew what his last scream had meant. Much later, dawn almost, she got herself undone and heard them starting off in the dinghy. She rushed on deck, the blood still wet, clinging to her bare soles, got the anchor up, the engine started yet again, searched through the night, finally finding a fishing fleet to help. Soon she was in the hospital, and almost as soon the pirates were

caught. Friends were called and rushed to her side; the children boarded a plane for Thailand from the green calm and damp of England.

I remember Richard with his bright, white mustache trying to hide his mischievous grin; eyes, gems of blue light flashing around wondering where to alight; arms spread out, embracing his world. Holly, hands on hips, a smile too, but saying, "What now, you rascal?"

That's what I remember. But what I see, what I see is more blood, more blood on the deck to be scrubbed away. After I can no longer read the words on this page, I will still see, still see, the last drop of blood on the bright, white deck.

Cambodia: Remembering History

Cambodia struggles to not be among those "who cannot remember the past [thus] are condemned to repeat it."[2] It is a country trying to heal itself, a country seeking emotional support, talking about its past, reliving the horror over and over, wanting not revenge so much as external acknowledgement and a collective memory that will not die. "We suffered this; remember us." As a report from Yale University's Genocide Studies Program stated:

The Cambodian genocide of 1975–1979, in which approximately 1.7 million people lost their lives (21% of the country's population), was one of the worst human tragedies of the last century. As in the Ottoman Empire during the Armenian genocide, in Nazi Germany, and more recently in East Timor, Guatemala, Yugoslavia, and Rwanda, the Khmer Rouge regime headed by Pol Pot combined extremist ideology with ethnic animosity and a diabolical disregard for human life to produce repression, misery, and murder on a massive scale.[3]

But now in Cambodia, people smile, children wave and say "Hello, howareyou, what'syourname, whereyoufrom, howoldyouare???" I hear laughter in the streets at the same time I see all the detritus of war, continual landmine explosions, and extreme poverty.

I discovered in my reading that Cambodian history, like so many former Western—in this case French—colonies, is difficult and confused. Prince Sihanouk gradually wore down the French through negotiation, not war, and achieved independence for the country in 1953, but was overthrown in 1970 by internal forces, supported by outside powers. As was done so often during the Cold War, we helped to destabilize countries and create monsters who eventually became bloodthirsty dictators and our enemies, or we killed them because they were socialistic or communistic in their governmental approach. There is evidence that it was the United States that first introduced the use of landmines in Cambodia via our support of rebels there.

The monster that was created in Cambodia was Pol Pot, who became the leader of the Khmer Rouge and was in power from 1975 to 1979. Khmer is the name for the indigenous people of Cambodia. One of Pol Pot's policies was much like Mao Tse-Tung's Cultural Revolution, but even worse, and was an attempt to revert Cambodia into a feudal peasant society. Pol Pot not only sent many professionals and artists out to become farmers, but executed many of them along with their entire families. Although there are others, the most dramatic example of an execution site was discovered at what is now called the Choeung Ek Killing Fields. The stories are horrendous and attest to man's continuing inhumanity to man.

In Pol Pot's society, all science, medicine, art, dance, and writing were to be decimated, and nearly were. One older woman who knew the traditional Khmer dances, through hiding remained alive. Later, after Pol Pot was removed from power, she returned and started teaching others. Traditional music, too, almost died out. Arn Chorn-Pond, a young, accomplished flute player, was nine when his musician family was killed by the Khmer Rouge. He survived only because they wanted him to play their propaganda music for them. After the Khmer Rouge was thrown from power, Chorn-Pond was adopted and lived in the United States. The documentary, *The Flute Player*, tells the story of his return to Cambodia and his work to restore the traditional music of Cambodia's culture. I heard this music at Angkor Wat, played by small musical groups made up of landmine survivors. It is one of my more poignant memories: these people with missing limbs, scarred, some blind, playing the remembered music of a country torn from its roots, trying to live again.[4]

In Siem Reap, where we had gone primarily to see Angkor Wat, I found many handicraft shops employing widows and orphans, disabled landmine survivors, street children, and others needing a safety net in a country with none. Such shops were among the various projects of the multitude of NGOs (nongovernmental organizations) in Cambodia. I followed the directions I had been given down a curving dusty street to such a shop. There I bought my Christmas presents for that year, much to the delight of the smiling young widow and mother, whose child wearing only a small torn T-shirt played quietly in the dirt nearby.

Cambodia: Evidence of the historic importance of dance and music in a detail at Angkor Wat.

Cambodia: An interesting perspective of the Angkor Wat ruins.

Cambodia: Landmine survivors' band.

There was even an organization called Seeing Hands, where I could get a massage by a blind masseuse or masseur. I can attest that it was excellent, one of the best I've ever had, once I got past the somewhat seediness of the physical facility. One of the most successful ventures when we were there in 2007 was Friends: The Restaurant in Phnom Penh. Not only could customers get deliciously prepared and professionally presented meals there; but all of it was done by former street kids who had been taught all aspects of the restaurant business. I observed a pride of work in the serving of the meal and cleaning up after that was rare to find in the West.

In Cambodia, I learned and felt yet another face of love. In an orphanage in Phnom Penh, I went to give, but really I received. How often that has happened. Although we shared what we had, I "taught" children, and we distributed food, school supplies, and medicine, I have always received so much more than I have given. It felt like a spiral—a waterspout in reverse, the deep blue of the water curling up into the paler blue sky. At the tiny orphanage—no more than one large room with a sleeping loft for the girls—I helped with an English class, played games, and hugged many children. The older boys raised money by performing in the park. On the way to the orphanage, which was located in a back alley, I asked the driver to stop at a store so I could get the children some treats. "No, aunty," he replied. "Buy rice and vegetables. They need those more." And so I did, although along with a few toys. Now, back in the United States, I still remember those experiences of giving and receiving. I send occasional packages to the orphanage, but rarely hear if they are even received. Communication is not easy there.

My arthritic-knobbed fingers reach for these moments as if they could be held, but they are only memories. I still see the faces of many of those children and wonder, now that they are older, what has happened to them, how are they faring in the world? I do not forget them. Cambodia is a country that does not want us to forget.

Cambodia: The older boys from the orphanage performing in the park.

I'm Hungry

I'm hungry for my family,
but since they're dead, maybe
I could have another family.
I'm hungry for someone who loves me to hold me.

Can we walk down the alley while I am
holding your hand?

I'm hungry for a place where
I can just be.
I want to belong to someone.

Can you buy me? My uncle sold me
when my parents died, but the man was mean
I ran away.
I won't run away from you.

I'm hungry to learn. I want to speak
English so I can work,
then I won't be so hungry. I'm hungry to learn
about children in America and India and Germany.
I'm hungry to learn
so I can dream about them.

Show me where you live on the map you brought us.
You live in America. That is so far away. Don't leave.

Oh, I'm hungry for so much,
but now
I'm just
hungry.

9

Sri Lanka and Yemen: Tea vs. Qat

*What would the world do without tea?—how did it
exist? I am glad I was not born before tea.*
—Sydney Smith, *Lady Holland's Memoir*

Sri Lanka: A Cup of Tea, a Drop of Water

I learned an entertaining story both from legends I was told and reading in various books about Sri Lanka's history. It could be a parable, of sorts, but it also gave a sense of the country and described a fascinating site we visited—Sigiriya.

There once was a wise and thoughtful king, Dhatusena, who ruled from 460–477 CE. He knew in this small island kingdom, water and agriculture were critical and irrigation was the key. He had a huge seven square mile reservoir built, the Kalawewa, with an equally large dam and long, wide canal to bring water to the then capital of Anuradhapura. It was but one of the many massive, cleverly engineered irrigation projects that he had built. Many are still visible and some are still in use in modern-day Sri Lanka.[1]

In the tradition of the time, Dhatusena had several wives. One of noble birth bore him a son, Moggallana (there are several variations of his name), who was the heir-apparent. But Dhatusena also had another son,

Kasyapa, whose mother was a commoner. Jealousy, lust for power, possibly insanity, we don't know what lurked in Kasyapa's mind, but he had but one single focus—to be king. He seized the throne by imprisoning his father. As soon as Moggallana was aware of this, he fled to India.

Kasyapa knew—he just knew—that his father had secret riches hidden away, and there was no point in being king if he didn't have all that went with it. Forced to reveal his wealth, Dhatusena, now old before his time and disillusioned with the horrendous behavior of this son, took Kasyapa to see his riches. They traveled with military guard. At the dam of the Kalawewa, Dhatusena threw open his arms taking in the great engineering marvel of its time. "Here," he yelled into the wind, "Here are my riches!"

Kasyapa was beside himself with anger. "You will die for this," he yelled back. His words were only too clear above the sounds of wind and water. Kasyapa walled his father, the wise and thoughtful king Dhatusena, inside his tomb—alive. But the story does not end there, for there was karma, as well as political intrigue, in early Sri Lanka.

Despised and disrespected for his act of patricide, and fearing the worst, Kasyapa built himself an intimidating and impressive stronghold on an impregnable massive rock formation over six hundred feet high, reached only by a winding path traversing up the west side of the rock. It was called "Simha-giri," Lion Rock—today spelled as Sigiriya. There was good reason for the name. The final stairway from the Lion Terrace, which is about two-thirds of the way up the rock, leads between two giant lion's paws still visible carved into the solid rock with claws sharpened to rapacious points.

Sri Lanka: The lion's paws at Sigiriya.

Sri Lanka: Sigiriya from a distance.

Along the path rising to Kasyapa's prison of his own making is a wall of paintings that is estimated to have been about 460 feet long and, at one point, about 130 feet high. All that remains today are two main areas with the top half of several female figures, *apsaras*—to us, a hybrid of angels and fairies, and, by their looks, something classically provocative as well. They are topless and extensively bejeweled. There are graffiti remembrances to the ladies dating to the sixth century. For example: "Their bodies' radiance/like the moon/wanders in the cool wind."

Sri Lanka: Two apsaras.

Sri Lanka: The Sigiriya walkway along the cliffside where the apsaras are located.

Meanwhile in India, Moggallana raised an army of mercenaries and followers and returned to fight the murderer of his father. Kasyapa assembled his forces. The elephants were prepared for war, frighteningly decorated, tusks intimidatingly polished. When all was ready, Kasyapa descended from his fortress aerie, mounted his war elephant, and led his assembled troops into battle. The two half-brothers and their armies faced each other some distance apart. Spears glistened in the sun, held upright, but ready to lower and plunge into the enemy. The battle cry was raised. Suddenly Kasyapa's elephant turned; he sensed a swampy area in front of him perhaps, or, it is known that elephants are smart and also have feelings. Whatever the reason, this elephant played a role in history, for when Kasyapa's troops saw that Kasyapa astride his war elephant had swerved in front of the enemy, they believed he was retreating. As is so often in war, all hell broke loose. Kasyapa's troops fled in all directions. Kasyapa—knowing the end had come—brandished his sword and cut his own throat in a final, dramatic, defiant gesture. He returned the sword to its sheath before he fell, dead.

All too soon the violence of the present will be the legends of history. And the cycle continues.

≈≈≈

The country's conflict theme was evident at the time we visited Sri Lanka. Because of this, entering the harbor at Galle was an adventure in itself, although not a reenactment of the Moggallana vs. Kasyapa battle. We arrived at the outer area of Galle harbor about 1:30 a.m. after a passage of six days. En route we had a range of conditions including 30- to 35-knot winds and ten-foot seas for about fourteen hours. During that time I saw our speed hit 11.3 knots (fast for a sailboat). On the other hand, for several miles along the south coast we motored only, due to light winds and the need to thread our way among the night fishermen in their small boats.

It was a typical passage with various failures and surprises. Autopilot 1 failed on Day Two (but fortunately there was an autopilot 2); a propane leak and no use of our stove on Day Three (then everything hot had to be done in the microwave, which became problematic during the big-sea period). On Day Two we had two separate pods of dolphins visit us for about a half-hour each. But the most interesting episode occurred after checking for traffic one evening (making sure no ships were going to run us over, which the watch person does at least every ten minutes), Wayne and I were both below, when I asked, "What is that noise?" Wayne started to give an explanation of some mechanical system, when a flying fish flopped around the corner of the galley. Unfortunately for the fish, he had managed to fly through an open hatch. Wayne quickly dispatched him back to the sea.

This small passage was so typical of our life at sea—diversity, challenge, humor, beauty, hard work, and so much more—all the stuff of life crammed into such a small space and time. I was used to it by then, but much later back on land I would find the differences between sea and land life disorienting. It was difficult for me to adjust to my return to land.

We anchored until morning in the outer harbor because the Galle harbor had a chain across the entrance, mines, and depth charges. The Navy used these means to discourage Tamil Tiger divers—the Tigers are the forces fighting for Tamil autonomy—from blowing up a ship, a dock, or some battlement, which had happened in the past. As we were anchoring, a small, dark, unlit ship approached with a machine gun mounted on the front pointed at us. It was the Navy just wanting to know who we were, where we were from, and what our intentions were. Once satisfied, they moved away, but we felt even safer than usual, as we were sure they were keeping an eye on us all night.

The Tamils are an ethnolinguistic group of people originally from southeastern India, who first settled in northern Sri Lanka about 300 BCE. They are primarily Hindu and have a unique Dravidian language. One could say that the evolution of the Tamil Tigers began when the first Tamil traders from southern India began settling in northern Sri Lanka. They found existing settlers, the Sinhalese, also from India, who had arrived about 500 BCE, and who had replaced the Veddah, the indigenous stone-age people. The Veddah have been variously ignored or destroyed, but have managed to maintain a small, primitive lifestyle in remote areas, when not trampled on by tourists or the government.

Like the Christian Bible, the *Mahavamsa*, a Buddhist story of the death of Buddha and the settlement of Sri Lanka by his followers, was written long after the actual events, in the sixth century CE. This document has had the contemporary impact of imparting a cultural belief by many Sinhalese that they are chosen to protect the Buddhist faith and that this is to be done on the island of Sri Lanka.

More Tamils settled in Sri Lanka both through invasions and as mercenaries to such leaders as Moggallana, who rewarded them with land and riches. As reported in the *Mahavamsa*, a historically rich battle in 161 BCE is represented as the story of the Sinhalese king, Dutugemunu, triumphing over Elara, a Tamil ruler. Evidence indicates that this had nothing to do with the ethno-religious character of these two leaders, but rather a political battle over centralization of the government. The refashioning of history to suit current interests is as old as the history itself. There have been more skirmishes back and forth between the Tamil Hindus and the Sinhalese Buddhists, enough to establish a historical context for animosity between the two groups in addition to their religious differences.

In the morning we called our agent, a requirement for yachts wanting to enter the country, and were told to wait at the breakwater for the Navy, but NOT to enter without the Navy. In typical fashion, Wayne, always wanting to push the edge, the envelope, and I, always wanting to follow the rules and listen to the local drum beat, had a disagreement about where to wait. Fortunately I persisted this time because when the Navy joined us, it was clear we shouldn't have gone any farther in the direction we were headed because it was mined.

As instructed, we closely followed the Navy ship in a zig-zag pattern into the harbor and then took a sharp right turn between metal nets. There was no room for us at the concrete pier so we dropped anchor and backed down to a rusty metal pontoon along with a few other cruisers already there. We tied off and put out stern fenders. That didn't work for long as there was a strong surge that jerked the boat back and forth. As a result we got the first major dent to our beautiful new paint job that had been done in Thailand.

Between visits from our agent with officials from Customs, Immigration, the Harbour Master, and Health, we did what we could to stabilize our position off the pontoon dock. We created a cat's cradle of lines to keep Bali Ha'i's stern from banging into the old rusty pontoon. Wayne set a second anchor, and it seemed to hold. Later when he picked up the first anchor to reset it, he found a large piece of wood jammed in the flukes. For me, it was an act of courage and derring-do to get on and off the boat via jumping in the dinghy between surges, then scrambling up the pontoon at just the right moment. Once I missed, and Wayne hauled my bruised body soaked in polluted water up and onto the rusty pontoon. It was night, and I hurt. Wayne proceeded me up the ladder off the pontoon, gave me a hand, and we went on our way, me in my sopping clothes.

At night, the Navy set off random depth charges, which sounded like rifle shots right outside our boat. They did get our attention. It was one of the worst dockages we ever had, but the time in Sri Lanka was worth it.

Our first night we were invited to attend a local *perahera* (a pageantry procession). Our new friend and guide picked us up about 10 p.m. and off we went into the dark. It was to start at midnight. We found a grassy place to sit above the road on which the procession would travel and within sight of the brightly and colorfully lit Buddhist temple some distance away, where the procession would be headed. About 1 a.m., we were ready for sleep after our passage and little rest at our outer harbor anchorage the night before. Should we stay? Fortunately we did, for about an hour later we witnessed a series of fascinating dancers and performers, each group representing a different small hamlet and village with ornate, colorful costumes.

One group was in sequined blues and turquoise

with feather-like wings representing peacocks and danced even more delicately than the ornate birds they were dressed as. Another group was composed of young men on impossibly high stilts in bright red and yellow costumes, dancing and performing unfeasible-looking gymnastics. On and on it went, these impoverished, tiny villages putting so much effort and resources into this one night, each group spectacular in its own way. As tired as we were, we were captivated by the color, the music, the achievements, and the artistic pageantry of each village group as they passed. We were transported into this world—this otherworldly world.

Sri Lanka: A peacock dancer at the *perahera.*

A few days later, we went on a six-day tour of the island by car with a driver, and part of it by train. Although used to driving in many different countries, to us driving in Sri Lanka was a free-for-all. There were no traffic rules and narrow, potholed roads filled with careening buses, speeding motorbikes, weaving bicycles, small garden-type tractors pulling large carts, cattle carts, water buffalo carts, pedestrians who never looked, a few tourist vans; and always an elephant or two.

On our way north, the stronghold of the Tamils and their Tigers, we passed several UN and International Red Cross vehicles going the other way—the direction we had come from—with their large identification flags waving and signs on their windows: *This vehicle contains no firearms of any kind.* I thought it a bit troubling and asked our guide, who was also our driver, "Should we really be heading this way?" "No problem, aunty, no problem." (Ladies of a certain age are always "aunty.") One of several cease-fires had just ended and a few days before, a UN vehicle had been fired on. Fortunately no one was hurt, and no one ever took credit for it, indicating that it had been a mistake. Nevertheless, those involved in international attempts at peacekeeping and care were high-tailing it out of there, but we continued on.

Our driver maneuvered us through the various roadblocks of police and military with whatever papers he had managed to produce. We continued bouncing north, past sandbagged checkpoints with soldiers pointing their semiautomatic rifles at our vehicle and guard towers among the tree canopies, until finally even they disappeared as the road became more potholed and narrow with little traffic other than the occasional farm cart. In the fields we could see small bungalows, farm families in their traditional long, skirt-like attire working their fields and paddies, often pulling plows by hand, occasionally with a water buffalo.

As a history major in college, I quickly learned that every colonial power had much to answer for, and from my daughter-in-law from India I learned many more details of the Brits in South Asia. The Portuguese and Dutch were most interested in money; the Spanish in gold, conversion to Catholicism, and slavery; the United States in power and dominance; and the Brits, with the largest empire of all, all of the above. In the process, the most tragic upsetting of the cultural and geopolitical applecart possible was executed.

Sri Lanka experienced first the Portuguese in 1505 until 1685 when the Dutch India Company took control, then the British for the longest period—from 1795–96 until independence in 1948. British colonialism and its plantation economy brought a new batch of Tamils to work on the coffee, then tea, plantations. These Tamils were of a lower economic class than the established Tamil population, making for more divisions. Brit colonialism had diverse fallout, but in terms of the Tamil Tiger evolution, it set up a dichotomy of "slaves" versus "cooperators/elite" within the Tamil communities.

The creation of one of Sri Lanka's greatest social problems of today resulted from migration patterns, gender work, and the destruction of family structure, and is the continuation of labor patterns established by the Brits. This pattern made the women the tea pluckers. The poorer Tamils who emigrated from South India for jobs in Sri Lanka found once they got there that the jobs were for the women, but few of the men could find work. Loss of pride and hope created an environment of both substance and domestic abuse.

Driving through the hillside villages, we saw many small groups of young, dark men sitting by the roadside, drinking from various bottles and cans, some reeling away down the road toward the shanties they lived in. Small children played in the dirt outside their stick, mud, tin, and cardboard homes. Sometimes there was an aunty watching them, but usually not.

Young boys sold bunches of flowers and ran up and down the steep, curving roads keeping pace with the few vehicles to sell their wares. I have a photo I came across recently of one such boy who shortcut several of our vehicle's hairpin turns by running straight down the steep hillside and offering me a beautiful bouquet of flowers at least at two places, and maybe three. He was about fourteen with black hair parted in the middle and slicked down neatly to each side, dark brown hopeful-looking eyes, medium brown skin glistening slightly from the sweat of running so fast down the precarious hillside, and the faint hint of facial hair, perhaps to be a mustache someday. I no longer remember how much he wanted for them, but what I do remember is that I didn't buy them. We were traveling, I had no place for them; I wouldn't even have been able to keep them alive for long.

I understood the culture enough to know it would not have been acceptable to give him some money and tell him to keep the flowers. There was pride among those with something to sell or a service to provide. That boy was not a beggar. I wonder now how I could have been so thoughtless, so stupid. It is one of those small actions not taken, and I would give anything to go back and buy those flowers. We live with what we have done or not done.

Sri Lanka: The young flower seller.

After independence, with the usual maneuvering for power, Sirimavo Bandaranaike, the powerful widow of an assassinated leader, ruled from 1960–1965, 1970–1977, and 1994–2000. It was during her second term that Ceylon was renamed Sri Lanka. Her various rules increased the Tigers resistance due to her insistence on a single Sinhalese language ignoring the Tamil culture and language, strengthening of the Sinhalese-Buddhist position, cracking down on Tamils, and nationalizing some minority-held industries. The Tamils were and continue to be treated as a second-class minority. Their fight continues to be one for civil rights. Of course, there were extremists on both sides, and, like the IRA in Ireland, there was definitely a terrorist side to the Tamils. There was also the under-reported story of the cruel and harsh treatment of innocent Tamils by the government's security forces. The Sri Lankan military

and "anti-terrorist" activities were funded in part by the United States, who viewed the Tamil Tigers as "one of the world's deadliest terrorist groups."[2] But they were no worse terrorists than the Sri Lankan military. How much there is to answer for, but no one does.

When we were there in 2008, the warfare was winding down. As I wrote this, a tenuous peace existed, and, in fact, in October 2013, the Tamils won a significant majority in an election in the Northern Province. The majority of Sri Lankans are Sinhalese, who are mostly Buddhist. There are also a large number of Hindus, mostly the Tamils, as well as some Muslims and Christians. But the divisiveness is not so much religious as ethnic and political-economic. One can always hope that diversity will be cherished instead of feared and hated, but that does not seem the way of the world in these times anymore than it ever was.

Sri Lanka: A gigantic Buddhist statue.

Sri Lanka: Detail from a Hindu temple.

≈≈≈

The story of Dhatusena is about more than just his commoner patricidal son. Remember his riches: the greatest water control and irrigation project of its time. He wasn't the only Sri Lankan ruler to care about water. In the twelfth century, the most memorable words of King Parakramabahu I were, "Let not one drop of water reach the sea without first serving man." In the northern area alone, there is evidence of over eleven thousand ancient *wewas*, as the tanks (reservoirs) are called, with their web of irrigation canals.

While there was some trade before the colonists came—especially in crops such as cinnamon—it was the Dutch who expanded the plantation concept with coffee, which grew well there. The coffee plant originated in Ethiopia, but wasn't cultivated until the sixth century in Yemen. It spread rapidly with Islam and Muslim traders, so it grew in what became Ceylon, when the Dutch India Company took over. Being a company, not a government, income and profit were their goals, so forests were denuded and large coffee plantations were established. Production was going well, but the Dutch also had cultivated coffee on Java. To protect the market price, they slowed coffee production on Ceylon, although one Dutch governor was reported to have said, "It [Ceylon's coffee] was superior in quality to the coffee of Java, and approached near to that of Arabia, whence the first coffee plants came."[3]

Enter the British Empire. Nothing small would suffice. Thousands of acres were stripped and planted in coffee, and thousands of coolies (mostly Tamils) from southern India were brought over to work. In 1857 alone, over sixty-seven million pounds of coffee were exported from Ceylon. Exploitation of people and land was rampant—it was the rule of the day. But as with any monoculture, that way was open for disaster, and disaster was what happened—the coffee fungus. But that wouldn't stop the Empire. Out with the dead coffee plants, in with tea bushes. Thus, today we have world-famous Ceylon tea.[4,5]

Not only during the colonial period, but as we traveled through the country, forests were being cut down rapaciously and tea plants terraced into the steep hillsides. Continuing too, the Tamil women tea pluckers carried their large baskets on their backs held by a band across their foreheads. They were paid by the weight of the leaves. With their baskets straining at them, they walked the hillsides plucking two leaves and a bud together for some of the finest tea in the world outside Assam, India.

Sri Lanka: Tamil women tea pluckers.

The Tea Plucker

Damp red socks
lay across deep green tea bush.
The plucker pauses,
briefly confused by this intrusive color.
Fingers quickly resume,
feet plod on, bush to bush,
soon bag is full.

Down past all the tea bushes hovering on the hillside,
down past white-domed stupa
to weigh station for recording.
Then she climbs again,
white stupa remains,
green tea bushes remain,
red socks are gone.

Note: a stupa is a dome-shaped Buddhist shrine.

Sri Lanka: Hillsides covered with tea bushes.

Sri Lanka is more than legend, history, tea, and today's social problems. It is an incredibly mystical and beautiful country. Its steep mountains furled in green and blanketed with early morning mist create a dream-like vision. Sitting on the balcony of our small hotel the second morning of our trip, both Wayne and I were captivated and silenced by the view unfolding before us: the mist, pink from the veiled sun, turned wispy, and, like a magician, lifted to reveal its secret of mountain after mountain into the distance.

Sri Lanka: Mountain view.

Later, our driver took us to Ella, where we caught the train for a day's journey through the high hill country and past tea plantation after tea plantation. On track built by the Brits through over twenty-five tunnels—an engineering marvel to rival the *wewas*—in a charmingly old, wooden car, we wound around and through mountains some seven thousand feet above sea level. We got off near Nuwara Eliya, where our driver met us to continue our journey. Often called "little England," this small city is filled with Victorian-style buildings, once homes and clubs to the British officials and their families, where they went to escape the heat and humidity of the lower areas. Now this architectural stamp of colonialism has become rest houses and restaurants.

The Maldives: Stuck In Between

The wind was undisciplined, coming from the wrong direction, not following its usual pattern, so the anchorage at Uligan in the north end of the Maldives was exceptionally rolly. Because of the conditions, we didn't even put the dinghy in the water for five days. The officials came out to the boat to check us in so it wasn't necessary to go ashore for that. Customs, Immigration, and Health: three neatly uniformed middle-aged men, moustaches carefully trimmed, trouser creases ruler-straight came aboard. Their manner matched their appearance: words politely trimmed, paperwork ruler-straight. Certainly there was no hint at baksheesh or requests for tobacco or alcohol. Many signatures, many lists of our passport numbers, places of birth, yacht documentation, but everything efficiently, pleasantly completed. At that point we'd experienced some twenty-two check-ins; Uligan clearly topped the list as the easiest and most comfortable.

I spent a couple of those rolly days at anchor, scrubbing the boat by hand to remove the grit accumulated from the cement plant next to our earlier anchorage at Galle, Sri Lanka. Because of the wind and the waves it created, I wasn't tempted to go snorkeling at first. When I finally did, I found an abundance of living coral and an equally colorful diversity of reef fish; then I went every day. If I'm not sailing on the water, I would just as soon be in it.

The Maldives, an Islamic country, is most intent on protecting its heritage. Any gifts outsiders might have for anyone on the island must be approved by the Customs official. I did have gifts for the school and made arrangements to visit this official when we went ashore. He readily approved my gifts and my offer to work with the students on their English. In fact, when we departed, he called me on the radio to wish us a safe voyage and to thank me for our visit. While on shore we needed a guide—more like a chaperone—when walking around the village and had to state our intentions if venturing for walks elsewhere. Not that we couldn't go where we wanted, as long as someone knew where and why. We felt like young teenagers again with parents on guard against any waywardness.

Uligan is fairly small—about three miles by one mile—so we couldn't have gone very far anyway. The little village was immaculate. It had a population of about three hundred, and those residents cleaned the island every week. The sand streets were used mostly for walking and a couple of electric carts, and were swept frequently by the women. The sturdy, whitewashed houses were built of coral rock and cement. They had a large wind-generator farm, provided by U.S. aid, that supplied about half their energy needs. Here, unlike Xcalak, it was maintained, probably by neatly dressed men with neatly trimmed beards and neatly organized tools.

Dress was clearly on the more conservative side, a tradition we were familiar with from other Islamic countries, and one we respected. Unlike many other Muslim countries we've visited, the Uligan women and girls were shy when I would meet them in the village. They wore traditional dress, but not veils.

There was a well-equipped school on the island that went through ninth grade and included a small computer lab. I spent about two hours with the ninth-grade English class one day. Rather than a formal lesson we used conversation. They asked many questions about our travels and the United States. One student, whom I nicknamed Mr. Question Man, aspired to be president of his country. Quite bright, he wanted to know how a man gets to become president of the United States. He liked

The Maldives: The class the author spoke to.

to talk as well as question; I thought he would do well in politics.

The girls were shy at first in their spotless white hijabs, but once started, they asked many interesting questions: Why are you sailing around the world? What do girls do in the United States? Where are your children? Except for Mr. Question Man, the boys didn't say much, except the usual fifteen-year-old boy questions: How fast can you go? What is your engine's horsepower?

I left a book about Winston Churchill for Mr. Question Man, which was the closest I could come in my small, ever-changing boat library to anything political. For tenth- through twelfth-grade, the students went to another island. I was able to visit that school also, and it was extremely well-equipped with a large computer lab; biology, physics, and chemistry labs; and a library. Most of the teachers were from India. There was no university in the Maldives, but education was a high priority, and many students went on to university in India.

There was a local business called Sailor's Choice, owned by the judge, but run by young Amaad and his crew, including Hussein, Hussen, and Asad, all of whom were most helpful and courteous. They arranged an excellent local meal for the cruisers, and a day trip to two other islands, including snorkeling and lunch that I enjoyed with some of the other cruisers.

Amaad and his team arranged for laundry and provisions, and if their little store didn't have it, they took us around to try to find whatever we needed elsewhere. They delivered fuel to our boat, gave us a tour of the small town, answered all of our questions, and provided anything else we could think of.

This little island country with its ruler-straight procedures and cleanliness from clothes to streets seemed separate from the rest of the world, not only by water. I had the feeling that this protective net was meant to do just that, insulate them against global tides. With climate change and the height of the oceans increasing, this entire country with its highest point a mere eight feet above sea level will disappear from sight sometime in the future. For me, it was simply not possible to imagine these people integrating into the chaos that is India, their nearest neighbor. What changes will attack this culture, this country, that their protective net cannot withstand?

Wondering what the future held for Uligan was not foremost in our thoughts as we left this charming place that had provided us a respite. Now we were sailing on to Yemen, having to navigate Pirate Alley between Somalia and Yemen, clearly the most dangerous part of our voyage.

The Passage: Magic and Pirates

Across the Indian Ocean from Uligan, Maldives to Aden, Yemen is approximately 2,000 nautical miles, and our passage took us ten days. It started out well with fresh winds. We caught a mahi mahi and saw lots of dolphins.

Passages: Wayne boarding a mahi mahi.

Passing a handful of fishing boats a few days out, one started to follow us. We started the engine and sped up, and they turned away. One night when I was on watch another one started to follow us, but again I started the engine and sped up, and he fell behind. They may

have only wanted to ask for tobacco or alcohol, neither of which we had, but we didn't want to deal with them in rolly seas or take chances that they would take more in a forceful manner.

We passed Socotra, one known pirate base that is about thirty nautical miles offshore of Somalia at the wide mouth of the Gulf of Aden. As advised, we sailed past at night without nav lights, but there was an almost full moon so I'm not sure with our big white sails that it mattered. Nevertheless, we saw no ships, boats, or pirates there.

On watch in the middle of the night as we sailed in the Gulf of Aden, the water looking like black silk, I could imagine its feel against my face. The sky was so hazy it obliterated the horizon, just a melding together of watered-down dark silk in this transition between water and air. A bright glitter of red and diamond flashes—Venus, I thought—shone the way to the sky. But the magic was yet to come.

Suddenly, there were incredible arcs of streaming ribbons sparkling off *Bali Ha'i's* wake; it was the most brilliantly flashing bioluminescence I've ever seen with a color in-between real and imagined, sort of neon blue-green, but not really that. Against our hull, rocks on the shore, the crest of a wave—wherever a bit of salty foam could fly—it became a sparkling emerald and turquoise gem of living light. Each point of light was illuminated for a moment, then taken up by others. I sat in the cockpit my entire watch. These streaming momentary ribbons of phosphorescent light created a space of life separate from our known world.

But then the wind died, and we had to motor. We didn't have enough fuel to motor all the way; Wayne had not expected a lack of wind because high winds were normal in this area. So after motor-sailing a couple of days, we then had to sail with just a little wind and sails slating back and forth. The fourth night out the whisker pole (that holds the headsail out when sailing downwind) broke again. Wayne was able to tie it down on deck for the night and the next morning we fixed it.

We started encountering ships coming down from the Suez Canal and Red Sea. Because we both kept a conscientious and competent watch, there were no problems with them. It became a bit more work the last few days, however, as it was quite hazy and visibility was down to about three miles. There were no incidents as we sailed through the main part of Pirate Alley. The first two local boats we saw were headed the other way and were not the least bit interested in us; all the rest were large ships. Later one or two local fishing boats would occasionally start to follow us, although after we increased our speed, they turned back. But we weren't in Aden yet.

Our last night out, it was exceptionally hazy due to mist, sand, and clouds, even with an almost full moon. We were tacking in close to shore due to our lack of fuel, under sail only, and sailing quite slowly with little wind. During my watch, about 3:00 a.m., I stepped out of the pilot house as usual, looked around, and saw nothing. But less than five minutes later as I was sitting at the nav station, I heard voices just outside. It didn't make sense to me. We were sailing, no one was around. Anyone outside wouldn't have seen me as we didn't have lights on inside the pilot house at night because they destroyed one's night vision (good night vision is essential for keeping watch).

I stepped out into the cockpit to see a man starting to climb aboard alongside. Well, if I was ever going to have a heart attack that would have been the moment, but I didn't. I yelled! I screamed my head off, "We're being boarded, my God, WAYNE, HELP!!" The man attempting to board us was so surprised at my presence and probably my screaming he jumped—or fell—back into his boat, which held two other men. Wayne ran up naked (he had been asleep below off watch). "For God's sake, put some shorts on," I shouted. Fortunately he ignored that, started the engine, and told me to take the wheel and head directly away from them, which I did. In the meantime, they had scooted off about fifty feet and turned their lights on. Because we were so close to shore, Wayne had to check the charts to see where we could go without running into land or a rock.

As I stood at the wheel, my back to the three pirates, who had started to follow us, it did cross my mind that I could be shot in the back. They stopped soon after as our boat is pretty fast under full power, and I was not shot at. Wayne gave me a course and after I got on it, he reset the autopilot.

It was difficult to explain my foolish notion about having him put on shorts. My thought was that we would have to fight and he would be safer partly dressed. It made no sense afterwards. Neither of us slept until we were well anchored in Aden harbor about 6:00 a.m. After anchoring, we took a much deserved rest. Later that day Wayne went ashore to check in, gather some information, and track down the Seaman's Club, the one place where he could buy beer in Aden.

Yemen: The Plastic Bag Tree

Aden harbor is large with many ships coming and going, but the yacht anchorage is a little separate, saving us from the wake, noise, and often dripping fuel tanks of the commercial ships. One day we watched as a large Pakistani war ship arrived with a spit-and-polish welcome by the Yemen Coast Guard.

As everywhere, the people were friendly and welcoming. I was looking at some postcards in a shop at the pier my first day ashore. "Madam, you want?" "No, no, thank you. I am just looking. I don't have any money yet." "No problem, take what you want and pay me later." Also, as everywhere, people ask, "Where're you from?" "No problem, from U.S., no problem." When Wayne went ashore, he was always befriended by some fellow, who often couldn't speak English, but would point out all sorts of things for him in Arabic, smiling, and giving him the thumbs up sign. Aden's local market was a source of delight. That day, I brought back some of the special Yemeni feta cheese, hummus, lamb, yogurt in a clay pot, ambrosial bright red tomatoes, and ripe mangoes. Dinner was going to be superb!

There were pictures of Osama bin Laden and Saddam Hussein in many market stands, little shops, and restaurants. My feeling is that in most of the countries we visited the people have little control of who or what their government is; hence they separate a people from their government. If we are nice people, it doesn't matter that we come from the United States or any other place in which our government may be their enemy.

The area of modern Yemen has an ancient history dating back to at least the twelfth century BCE, with some excavations of early villages dated to about 5000 BCE. Until being conquered by the Romans in the first century BCE, there were three major kingdoms that ruled much of the area, as well as several minor chiefdoms. The mightiest and longest lasting (fourteen centuries) of these was the Sabean kingdom, or, one should say, queendom as this may have been the land of Bilqis, the legendary Queen of Sheba (although historians and archeologists are undecided if she came from Yemen or Ethiopia). The wealth and staying power of this domain were the spice trade and agriculture. Although not quite as extensive as those in Sri Lanka, the Sabeans also had dams, reservoirs, and extensive irrigation systems. The inland area of Yemen was indeed a major center of civilization in those early times.[6]

Its prehistoric importance goes back even earlier, as in 2008 French archeologists found hominid remains from Paleolithic times, the age of Neanderthals.[7]

Occupying the southwest tip of the Arabian Peninsula, the area of Yemen easily became a major trade center, first because of camel caravan routes between India and up through Saudi Arabia to the Mediterranean. Later with the opening of the Suez Canal in 1869, it became the main route connecting East and West. Early camel cargo consisted of myrrh and frankincense. Later the area became known for other crops, including in the fourteenth century the first Arabica coffee.

Its position also made it vulnerable to invasions: Romans, Persians, Ethiopians, Ottoman Turks, Portuguese, Egyptians, and, of course, the Brits. As well, there were many tugs-of-war among the petty chiefdoms. The Ottomans controlled most—but not all—of what is modern Yemen, from 1538 until the Islamic Zaidi wrested control in 1630. But the Ottomans were not ones to forgive and forget, and retook the northern part of their former territory in 1849. By then, the Brits were already established in Aden and part of the south. But this revisiting by the Turks did not go down well with the Yemenis. Between their frequent uprisings and Turkey's loss at the end of World War I, Northern Yemen was once again under Zaidic control.[8]

Fast forward to 1962 when the Zaidic Imam died and during the ascension of his son, the army took control. The North experienced civil war among various factions with one side then another gaining power. Strong outside influences and aid to this side and that by different foreign powers didn't help. In 1967, Britain finally gave South Yemen her independence after a bloody rebellion against colonial rule. Both the North and the South managed reasonably well for a while, but various factors, including external ones, brought turmoil, unrest, and more civil war.[9] The final result was the North took over the South, presumably "reuniting" the country, which had never really been united in the past. From our South Yemeni friends we learned they are biased against the Northerners, whom they find conservative, rural, and unsophisticated.

Ali Abdullah Saleh, a general, took over as president in 1978 and was president until 2011 when members of the democracy movement attacked the palace, wounding Saleh. He left the next day for Saudi Arabia, but returned. During his reign—presumably he was elected, but that was a farce—he amassed great wealth, and maintained a large army and police presence whom he paid well. His picture glared out from billboards and posters in every possible location while we were there in 2008. A South Yemeni friend of ours called him Little Saddam.

Saleh was finally brought down by the Arab reawakening, or "Arab Spring" as the West has labeled it. In February 2012 an election of sorts was held with Abd-Rabbu Mansour Hadi, who served as Saleh's vice president and close confidant, the winner—and only candidate.[10] Whether or not Saleh will be brought to justice for the political crimes for which he was responsible remains to be seen. Although no longer president, his son has been a general with major forces at his disposal. Hakim Almasmari, Editor-in-Chief and Publisher of the *Yemen Post*, wrote in 2012, "Controlling Yemen does not necessarily mean being president, but rather controlling the military and security forces, and this is what Saleh's family has and will die for." In February 2013, Almasmari wrote in the *Yemen Post*, "One year of Hadi rule, and Yemen is still a dangerous time bomb. The country is still in search for its Nelson Mandela." Clearly the U.S. drone strikes, which kill innocent people, along with suspected terrorists, are a major destabilizing force.[11]

With control by the more conservative North, all Yemeni women became ninjas, a term I certainly didn't make up. It was a local South Yemeni joke. Ninjas are the black-burqa-covered women with just their eyes showing, sometimes not even that if they wear veils. Before the country was "united," many South Yemeni women did not wear the conservative Islamic dress, but now all women are required to wear it, although a few do not cover their faces.

While walking with another female cruiser in

Aden and Sana'a, we were often stopped by young ninjas, who giggled and asked where we were from and other typical questions. Also, as a woman I quickly learned to see the smile in their eyes if they looked at me in passing, but they would not, of course, look at or talk to a man. But what they wear at home is quite a different matter. Imagine a gaudy Victoria's Secret. These little risqué garment shops were everywhere, displaying leopard-patterned bikini underwear and more formal long dresses with gold trim, sequins, and low décolletages. It was an ironic picture to see black burqa-covered women eyeing these racy, seductive garments in store windows.

**Yemen: Yemeni women window shopping.
Photograph by Lillian Duckworth, S/V *Tagora*.**

We arrived in Yemen in February 2008. About a month prior to that, in Wadi Dawan, about 180 miles east of Sana'a, two Belgian tourists and their driver were killed by a group of insurgents to embarrass the government. In spite of this, we were determined to go to Sana'a, which may well be the oldest continually inhabited city in the world.

From the sea, the Yemen landscape is dramatic, with sand dunes slipping up toward jagged rocky peaks a few thousand feet higher. Inland the feeling is of an incredibly forceful land with tall, barren rocky mountains, spires, and mesas jutting up from a sandy plain—dust and rock. In the short rainy season, apparently it is green, but that was hard to imagine during our stay when everything was in shades of brown.

The architecture comes from this land with rock and mud bricks creating stair-step meandering buildings wandering up the side of a hill with a fortress on top. Some are relatively new, most are hundreds of years old and in various states of repair, perched along their ridges looking like extensions of the rock. The periodic villages rising up toward ridges and rocky spires were made of the same soil and rock, seeming like a natural extension of the landscape—not really man-made at all, but some other form of this beige landscape, where even the air had a brownish tinge. Many of the older villages with their crumbling forts are remnants of the days of small chiefdoms, falling back to the dust and rock that created them, like the chiefdoms themselves.

It was spectacular scenery, but exhausting to my eyes as I studiously tried to make out details through a sandy haze and the ubiquitous layer of reddish-brown dust. The only contrast was the sharp black burqas of the women as they moved about their outdoor tasks. Only these few women, the occasional neatly arranged terraced rock walls, and a rare glimpse of a small patch of irrigated green in a valley below hinted at any human habitation.

Yemen: Village and landscape.

government wanted no more embarrassment due to dead tourists. I wondered what the police or army would have done if we hadn't turned up at the next roadblock—I suspected it would be nothing. In some cases, local people were made to get out of their vehicles and were patted down. On our drive back we happened on a camel round-up and stopped to talk to the camel "cowboys."

We traveled to Sana'a with another couple, cruisers also, who live in France, although she is from the Netherlands, he from England. Together we hired Abdullah to guide us and make the arrangements for a car and driver. While on our way, we were held at a police roadblock because of a demonstration ahead. They were concerned for our safety and were considering giving us a police escort. However, after an hour, they decided it was safe for us to proceed on our own.

We went through twelve army and police roadblocks going from Aden to Sana'a and eight on the return trip (a different route). Each time Abdullah gave the officials a copy of our tourist passes, which had our names, nationalities, and passport information, and we were waved through. These roadblocks were for our safety to know if we made it from one point to another—the

Yemen: A camel "cowboy."
Photograph by Lillian Duckworth, S/V *Tagora*.

The old walled city of Sana'a is renowned for its architecture. Although rebuilt, renovated, and added to over the eons, it retained the feeling of a centuries-old settlement. The buildings were from five to nine stories tall, starting with stonework, then mounted with clay bricks and decorated with light-colored plaster trimming the windows and doors. It was as if the brown-red land was molded together in tall box-like formations and then extensively decorated with the most intricate, delicate, and graceful white icing accenting various features. This embellishment contained small traditional Arabic details of vines, flowers, and geometric designs.

Yemen: Building detail.
Photograph by Lillian Duckworth, S/V *Tagora*.

Yemen: Old town Sana'a.
Photograph by Lillian Duckworth, S/V *Tagora*.

Yemen: A traditionally dressed gentleman who wanted his picture taken.

**Yemen: A scene from old Sana'a's plaza.
Photograph by Lillian Duckworth, S/V *Tagora*.**

The old city was also fascinating for the glimpse of life lived there. The plazas and walking streets pulsated with activity, conversation, the business of living.

≈≈≈

The national pastime of Yemen has become the chewing of qat, much to the destruction not only of the individuals who chew it, but of the country itself. Qat (pronounced like a cross between gat and got with a bit of a cough thrown in) is a leaf that is chewed until it becomes a golf-ball-size wad inside the cheek, causing one to spit a lot. It is mildly addictive and contains alkaloid stimulants with amphetamine-like properties, and has various possible side effects including digestive disorders, malnutrition, cancer, and insomnia. It isn't illegal, as alcohol is, because qat is natural. It's been around for centuries, but never used to the extent of recent years. Sara Al-Zawqari wrote in the *Yemen Post* in 2013:

> Soldiers in other countries are tall, broad-shouldered, clean, strong, and muscular. Our soldiers? They're very skinny, very young, and you find them at checkpoints each with his cheeks packed to the limit. Our soldiers need to train to build muscles, and muscles are not built with qat.[12]

At one checkpoint, the officer with cheek full of qat, peered into our ramshackle station wagon, "Ah, I see you have five tourists here. Very good."

"No, sir, there are only four here," Abdullah told him.

"What, four? I see five. I count again. See, I am right, five of you, just like your pass says. OK to go. Safe ahead on this road."

We had a laugh about it along with Abdullah, who was quite opposed to qat and expressed to us his worry about the impact on his country. The truth is, it's a tragic situation.

Ahead of us, in the blowing sand we saw a marvelous bare tree decorated, or so it seemed, with many different colors. We couldn't make out what it was until we got closer. My God, it was a plastic bag tree! Caught in its many tiny branches and twigs were multiple colored small bags, the kind qat is sold in. The tree and the ground for miles were littered with green, pink, purple, and clear cheap little bags—qat litter.

Catha edulis grows in the hillside and mountain areas over three thousand feet, and its potency lasts less than forty-eight hours. This creates a qat trail: early in the morning, the leaves of this shrub, sometimes as big as a tree, are picked and loaded into trucks and an assortment of vehicles that then make a mad dash for the cities. Once there, each driver heads to the vendors he supplies in the various public markets. Waiting impatiently, the crush of buyers descends on the small stalls. One day, I almost got knocked down as I was unknowingly in the way between the qat seller and the rush of buyers. Quickly the leaves are gone, and soon most Yemenis have a cheek full of qat.

Yemen: A spice seller with his cheek full of qat.

We met a boy at a small roadside stall, where we had stopped to get a soda and look at some of the local weavings. Although the story of Ahmat is imagined, there were hints to me of how it might have been.

His Name Was Ahmat, a Ballad

He sat at the loom
with cheeks full of qat,
he was only fourteen,
his name was Ahmat.

When he was but nine,
his mama had died;
she was ill a long time.
For a year he had cried.

Then his father had said:
"Enough tears, Ahmat.
I'll listen no longer,
put on your good hat,

It makes you look older."
"Where are we going, Papa?"
"You'll see when we get there."
They wound through the casbah,

Stopping at a rickety shack.
"Abdullah, you old rascal,
Come, I want you to see
my son, he's no criminal,

No pickpocket, no thief,
but he misses his mama,
he needs work to forget.
You know the Sharia.

Abdullah, set him at the loom,
do what you have to do.
He'll work hard, I know,
with me you can't argue.

Remember you're family.
You were related
to his late mama."
The papa then said,

"Good-bye my son,
I'll come see you
when I'm able."
But his visits were long overdue.

He sat at the loom.
He was only fourteen,
his cheeks full of qat,
worked like codeine.

He was numb inside and out
to what he had lost.
So he sat at the loom
with his legs crossed.

He sat at the loom
with cheeks full of qat,
he was only fourteen,
his name was Ahmat.

Mohammed Mahmoud Al-Zoubairi, a poet and revolutionary hero, wrote in 1958 about the evils of qat, which have only multiplied since then:

The devil grew from the earth to consume the nutrients of other innocent plants. He made the Yemeni people lust after Him, and is fighting in their stomachs against valuable nutrients for the human body. Then He runs in their veins like Satan, and enters their pockets to steal their money. Satan can bring them in the morning as far as the mountain peaks but in the evening will not let them sleep, leaving them in the nightmare of their imaginations. The Yemeni people live half of their lives in His magic. He consumes their strength and heroism. He is our governor, this accursed tree.[13]

In earlier days chewing qat was mainly a sociocultural ritual of men getting together, as Brits might have done over a pint and Americans over a beer. Today it is an addiction. More dangerous are its impacts on the economics and agriculture of the country. The growing of qat supplants food crops for local sustenance as well as export. This, in turn, affects the country's overall economy, and the lifestyle and economy of individual families. Men grow qat; men guard the crops; men drive the trucks; men—for the most part—sell qat.

In the past, peasant women traditionally took care of livestock and family crops. Without the crops, the livestock can't survive; without either, the women have no role and are deprived even more. Yemen does not have an honorable record for its women to start with: 71 percent are illiterate; they can be married as young as nine; they are often arrested for "immoral acts" and never tried, just thrown in prison and forgotten; they often die in childbirth as they are given little medical attention; they are the property of men. Ancient tribal laws often govern the way women are treated in rural areas. In many areas these laws have become incorporated into Islamic practices. But women are not the only victims of the widespread use of qat.

Because growing qat is so profitable, those who can afford it use pesticides to keep their crops maximized. Dimethoate seems to be the poison of choice. Although considered only mildly toxic, it has many negative side effects, especially if one is chronically exposed, as so many Yeminis are. Good-quality qat sucks up water and when irrigated can produce three crops a year. So where does the water go? To growing qat, not food.

Sana'a sits at over seven thousand feet; much of the land for growing qat is nearby. Predictions on when Sana'a will run out of water vary from the very near future to 2050. This historic, walled city has been inhabited for over 2,500 years and is a UNESCO World Heritage Site. The plastic bag tree and Ahmat at his loom are the pictures remaining for me of qat in Yemen, and the thought that after all these centuries, this intriguing, historic, resplendent city is to die—for qat.

10

The Red Sea: Combat, Concrete, and Camels

Now my heart turns this way and that, as I think what the people say [and] those who shall see my monuments in years to come and who shall speak of what I have done.
—Hatshepsut, King of Egypt, 1504–1458 BCE

Eritrea: Where Hope Lives in an Alley

*B*efore entering the Red Sea, we had to pass through Bab al-Mandeb, the Gate of Tears, separating Djibouti and Eritrea from Yemen—or Africa from Arabic Asia. Bab al-Mandeb is one of those places in the world where a small distance geographically translates into worlds apart in all other understandings. It separates the Red Sea, Suez Canal, and the Mediterranean from the Gulf of Aden, the Arabian Sea, and the Indian Ocean.

The Gate of Tears was aptly named originally because of its treacherous passage due to frequent high winds and complex currents. Today the name works doubly because of piracy. There are actually two channels divided by an island. The western one is about sixteen miles wide and is the major shipping channel; the eastern channel is two miles wide. This was the one we chose, passing through at midnight with both of us on watch and with nav lights off. We didn't get the high winds there, and had just breathed a collective sigh of relief at

passing that main piracy point and missing the winds when they hit us, but at least it was only wind—and its constant companion, sand.

There was nothing like the high winds on the Red Sea. It was a dust storm on the water and because of the complex currents, the waves were often contradictory creating difficult maneuvering, especially in a sailboat. Everything was coated with sand, including my eyes, nose, ears, and mouth, as well as the winches, the lines, the sails. I really could not always see my hand in front of my face, whether that was because the sand was in my eyes or too thick in the air was hard to say.

Both Goliath Herons and old friends since Panama greeted us as we entered the calm anchorage at Shamma, an uninhabited island belonging to Eritrea. GB and Sarah on S/V *Djarrka* were just leaving but gave us a quick visit. As it turned out, we would anchor with them later as we progressed up the Red Sea and then would have time for dinner and exploring more uninhabited islands together. That night and the next, we were the only cruising boat, along with a local fishing boat, in the anchorage. It made me a bit nervous, as many pirates are part-time fishermen/part-time pirates, depending on what was available. But after the passage here, we both were tired, and it felt refreshing to get a good night's sleep. No trouble from the fishermen, which was the usual case.

Goliath Herons range from about four feet to four feet eight inches tall. Although I'm a little taller, we could see eye to eye; there are not too many birds I can do that with. Also on the island were a few bombed-out ruins, which Wayne went to explore. He thought they might have been used as gunnery sites in the war between Eritrea and Ethiopia. I chose to snorkel and encountered my first Red Sea explosion of diversity and color underwater.

After two nights at Shamma we left for our next stop, Massawa (pronounced Mittsahwah), to check into Eritrea. The entrance to the harbor provided a disturbing view of the remnants of war with bombed-out buildings on all sides, few people, and swirls of dust and sand, as if life had left this place, anything sustainable forced away.

Massawa, Eritrea: A Prose Poem Portrait

Naked, sleepy skeleton of a city, bereft of its young men. Wide, hard-packed dirt and sand streets narrow into old town, smaller still winding behind bombed-out buildings, where life is lived. Once-filled sidewalk cafes mostly shuttered; the few open inhabited by old men on worn, begrimed plastic chairs. It is said the war is over. But a young soldier with his new-born son comes from the border, "Where," he shrugs, "it isn't safe, you know."

A few workers trudge through the port's barbed wire security gate in the dusty mornings, glad for the job. Those young men still alive are on patrol, plowing fields, building, rebuilding, somewhere out in the brown desert country, through their grimy sweat trying to pull this bedeviled country out of its discouraging, benumbed morass.

A sprinkling of children, a smattering of young women, the sporadic older woman with a task outdoors, and the old men sitting. These rheumy-eyed men, who have seen it all, wonder: freedom for what, from what, where is it?

The women know what they have lost: the young, strapping boys-to-be-men, who could have been husbands, fathers; losing shelter and visions of their homes; losing babies and the imagined, unconceived children; losing their future. They carry their exquisitely chiseled, chocolate, sun-burnished faces through their lives of loss. Draped in color, often with turbans bright as tropical flowers glowing against the dusty desert background, they move through these lives of loss with the knowledge of what is. If there is a moment of joy to be found, these women will find it and nurture it as they would a lost child. Some stumble on this path—their hopelessness too much—their eyes show this truth:

This is
one of the heart-breaking places
of the world.

This land, this stretch of coast and the highlands behind, was passed from kingdom to kingdom, empire to empire for centuries, finally ending up as an entity in its own right—albeit a colonial state in 1889–90 under Italy. Like other European countries, Italy had colonial aspirations in northeast Africa, although theirs were dashed in World War II. Before that, for fifty years the Italians had created an economy, an infrastructure, an identity, a country; clearly, though, they did so in colonial fashion with fascist overtones, thus with little improvement in the lives of the Eritreans. With British victory over the Italians in Eritrea in 1941, the colonial state was ever so slightly transformed into a British colonial protectorate and became a major operations base for the Allies during the war.[1]

The rupture and disjoining of like cultures by the colonial powers, as well as the attempt to combine and conjoin dissimilar cultures, tribes, and lives during the all-too-long era of imperialism created bizarre countries. These countries were created in the minds of the powerful with no thought as to what really makes a country: a sense of belonging, of nationalism, of community. Imperialism took a nosedive after World War II, and the world is paying a high price today for the pseudo-countries created and left behind by those powers.[2]

For whatever absurd reason, the United Nations joined Eritrea to Ethiopia in 1950, but with rules for autonomy, some democratic rights, and respect for Eritrea. Sure. Starting with peaceful protests, the differences between Eritrea and Ethiopia escalated into periodic armed conflict between the two. Within Eritrea, the two main groups clashed for power over the country's future. In this context, Eritrea continued the struggle for her own identity.

Finally in 1991, Eritreans gained control of their own land. In 1993, a national referendum turned out some 98.5 percent of the voters, with all but two-tenths of a percent voting for independence. But then how to protect the Eritrean border from its voracious neighbors: Yemen, Sudan, Djibouti, and, of course, Ethiopia? Most were skirmishes of sorts, but the war with Ethiopia was real, if counted by the number of casualties.[3]

≈≈≈

While wandering the back streets of Massawa, I heard children's voices and could tell there was a school nearby. I always enjoyed meeting the children of the countries we visited. Inevitably, they were bursting with questions, and they were fresh and ingenious in their conversations. While looking for those children in the back streets of Massawa, I met Solomon, a soldier, now AWOL, or so I thought, and his family. Pointless fighting at the border ordered by power- and land-hungry rulers had brought him here with his wife and new baby, widowed aunts, younger sisters, someone's little girl. This extended family made do with several other families in a bombed-out skeleton of a building and the dirt alley, where they lived.

War, corruption, disease, poverty beyond Western imagining: I expected desolation. Instead I was invited to join them for tea. One woman wanted her picture taken with her small china tea cup that she pulled out swaddled in rags from a scruffy green plastic bowl. What had she done to preserve this? She then offered me some root drink—I wasn't sure what it was—in her cherished tea cup. It tasted a bit bitter, but I smiled.

Eritrea: An alley where people live.

Tea in a Bombed-out Alley

I stumbled on them in an alley
while looking for a school.
I had heard children's voices, bouncing
over a ten-foot wall.
I never found the school,
instead the Hamera family.

They were splashes of dancing color
in that brown, broken-down, rubble-strewn alley.
Laughing and chattering,
they smiled a welcome to me.
Mrs. Hamera wore henna-painted flowers
winding up her legs like friendly snakes;
the baby was passed from welcoming arm to arm.

They greeted me like a long-lost friend
and offered tea in a cherished china teacup
blue flowers entwined through ivy around its rim,
treasured through bombings, fleeing brutality,
and other horrors survivors suffer.

Despite the dismal, dust-blown alley,
it was an enchanting afternoon.
Like their treasured teacup, I will
carefully cushion this memory
from the shocks of life.

These delightful people surviving and laughing
brought grace and hope
to the art
of living.

Solomon's wife was a beautiful woman with perfect facial bones and deep black eyes. She was covered with artistic henna designs on her arms and legs. They offered more "tea" and something else I didn't know the name of. I refused, but stayed to visit longer.

My experience with Solomon's family nagged at me to explore the quality of hope. What is it that gives us hope? Is it an element of the human condition that is buried deeply in our souls? Is it part of our DNA, a quality that is part of our ever so slowly evolving species? I found hope clawing for survival in that alley in Massawa.

Later on the boat, I printed the photos I had taken of the family and sent them back to shore with Wayne, who insisted we check out of the country and move on as the weather was right. My package with the photos for Solomon's family was to be held at a quay-side store for someone from the family to pick up later. I included a small soft doll, a little toy car, and multicolored beads, which I knew the women would make creative use of. I wanted to send a kilo of rice, but Wayne emphasized we should save it for trading with fishermen.

Sudan's Marsas: Nothing to Give

During the short, one-night passage to Jezirat Durwara, a deserted island in Shubuk Channel, Sudan, I wrote in my calendar/journal: "There's so much sand in the air, the horizon looks like a sandy island." Anchored at Jezirat, we met up with S/V *Djarrka* again and explored some of the other islands nearby.

An odd medical emergency occurred while we were there. Tom, the young crew from another cruising boat anchored nearby, rowed over one night while Sarah and GB were aboard for dinner, requesting our help because their hired captain was seriously ill. The boat owners were an elderly couple trying to make their way back home, to Germany, I believe. With my "extensive" medical background, which consisted only of early lifesaving training and more recent CPR and emergency first aid, I came up with the diagnosis of diabetes. Eric, the hired-captain, had insisted he wasn't diabetic. We gave Tom the information for treating his symptoms from the books in our medical library. Sarah and I emphasized that he should probably be treated as a diabetic in spite of his

insistence to the contrary. Ironically, a few days later, we learned that Eric was in the Port Sudan hospital being treated for a diabetic episode and was to be flown home to Switzerland. So it was to be young Tom who would sail the elderly couple back to the Med.

After a few days in Jezirat, we motor-sailed up the Shubuk Channel to Suakin, another spectral-like town, but for different reasons. Although they looked like they could be centuries old, these ruins were relatively modern. Suakin had been deserted in 1909 when the Brits finished building Port Sudan as their primary port and harbor thirty kilometers to the north, totally ignoring the fate of this historically vibrant, important community. Suakin had been the major Sudanese port for centuries. After the establishment of Port Sudan, it didn't take long for Suakin to become a ghostly town.

It felt odd to be anchored off all these ruined buildings with wild camels and more-or-less domestic goats wandering through, nibbling at the few weeds that were growing in this harsh, windblown climate. A Portuguese captain described Suakin in 1541 as follows:

The water within the haven is so still and runs so imperceptibly, that the ebb and flow of the tides can hardly be detected. The bottom is mud; the anchorage nowhere is less than five or six fathoms and sometimes is seven. Two hundred ships and rowing-boats beyond number can lie moored within the shelter and compass of this haven, and can load by laying a plank from the warehouses to the decks, while the galleys are made fast to the doors and stones of the houses, and rest with their bows overlapping the streets, which serve instead of gangways. There is trade with all parts of India, Arabia, Cairo and Alexandria.[4]

Sudan: Water delivery cart and Suakin street scene.

scooped however much I wanted into a small plastic bag, gave it a twist and there it was—peanut butter! Just a little jam and bread and I would have the standard American fare of pb&j. The market also had barrels of olives, goat meat hanging from hooks, and fish displayed neatly in rows. And, if we needed a shot of caffeine, there was always a coffee seller conveniently wandering through the crowds.

A handful of people still lived in Suakin, and there was a small market open in the mornings. We watched as water was delivered by a donkey hauling a tank on wheels. The water vendor walked along beside, stopping the donkey when someone ran out with a vessel to be filled.

While we were anchored there, I took the local bus with GB and Sarah to Port Sudan, a bustling small city with efficient Internet connections. There was a captivating market with burlap bags of colorful, aromatic spices; bright-hued produce of diverse shapes and sizes; multiple types of grains; and Bedouin women selling ground groundnuts (peanuts in the West)—big slabs of it on wooden boards held shoulder high. One woman

Sudan: The peanut butter seller in the market.

Sudan: The coffee seller.

The bus trip provided a view of the interior we would have missed when sailing along the coast. We passed several Bedouin camps that looked as if they would blow away in the next dust storm. The camps were composed of patched, flimsy-looking tent-like structures stretched between leaning poles; a few dogs, goats, and camels wandered about along with some children. Occasionally, a tall, gaunt-looking man as sere and spare as the landscape in a threadbare, billowing robe walked with long strides as if he could magically glide across the desert. Few women were ever visible to us as we slipped past. In the distance a microwave tower seemed to indicate something was out of place here. Was it the Bedouin or the tower?

We had asked some locals to recommend a place to eat flavorful local food. Following their intricate directions, we finally climbed upstairs to a crowded room with waiters flitting about, shouting, and everyone eating all kinds of exotic- and scrumptious-looking dishes. Our meals included many of the fresh ingredients and abundant spices we had seen in the market. The restaurant lived up to its reputation; a general feeling of camaraderie and being well-fed permeated that engaging place. It's doubtful, though, that I could ever find my way to that specific restaurant again.

Sudan: The Bedouin and the cell tower.

From Suakin we went on to explore some of what became one of my favorite places, the Sudanese marsas. These are fingers of the Red Sea that permeate inland, sometimes quite a distance, wandering this way and that, suddenly ending in a wall of sandstone. Often, off to the side would be salty shallows with flamingos wandering about, beaks bent to the bottom, occasionally raising up their serpentine necks to look around. On shore would be an occasional Egyptian Plover, now rarely found in Egypt, and—odd to us North Americans—a Hoopoe, with its pinkish-brown plumage, long black-barred crest like a headdress too big, and black and white wings. I also saw ospreys, various terns and gulls, hobbies (a small, gray falcon), several species of small wading birds including sandpipers and other species of plovers. And, of course, the camels.

Sudan: *Bali Ha'i* in a marsa with the flamingos.

Sudan: The camels that walk on water.

During our passage up the Red Sea, whenever possible I would go out in my sea kayak to snorkel or, depending on where we were anchored, I snorkeled from the boat. The undersea world was spectacularly colorful with diverse fish, although the coral did not match that of so many places in the South Pacific. Nevertheless, the sea life was captivating. At Juzur Telat, I wrote in my small journal: "Snorkeled. GREAT! I took my sea kayak out across the sand bar and snorkeled both sides. PEACE, JOY!!" In color, the underwater scene was the antithesis of the land—a study of opposites. This could be said of Wayne and me also. I wanted to sail; he wanted to get there and thus the engine was used more often. I wanted to explore with scuba and snorkel gear; he wanted to stay on board. I wanted to invite cruisers and locals to our boat; he wanted privacy. As *Bali Ha'i* sailed or motored on, Wayne and I drifted apart.

At Khor Shinab, one of the longer marsas, two or three other cruisers were anchored also, and everyone wanted to go ashore to climb the highest nearby rocky hill for a better view inland. As far as the horizon there was nothing but sand and rock, with mountains of the same sand and rock to give a three-dimensional shape to it all. Barren was an understatement. This landscape was hardscrabble, wild, arid, parched, but not bleak, not an impoverished view. There was the suggestion of life, a hint at the meaning of infinity as the distance seemed to stretch beyond the horizon, a luminosity that hinted at more, something possibly comprehensible, unambiguous if only we took the risk of journeying into it farther. But we did not.

One experience remains in my mind at another remote and unoccupied anchorage. Wayne and I had gone ashore in the dinghy so I could photograph the flamingoes, hoopoes, and camels better and just to look around. There was nothing human within sight of the horizon. We were both wearing skimpy bathing suits as not only the air, but even the water, was hot. Suddenly, seemingly like a genie out of a spiral of dust, a camel ridden by a father and son in tattered white robes appeared charging our way. "Please to ride our camel, missee, sir." We had no money or anything that might even resemble a gift with us; and, of course, I was totally inappropriately dressed, or mostly undressed just in my bikini. We stumbled over apologies, but they were ever kindly. "Oh, no, no money, just have a ride on our camel, please." Having ridden camels in the past, it wasn't my favorite mode of transportation. Give me an elephant any day, but not a camel. Finally they left. I wanted to leave some sort of package for them on shore, but Wayne refused to let me take anything, arguing that it would be ruined, taken by others, or nibbled by camels. They were so clearly poor and underfed; I felt there was something I could have done, but I didn't. It reminded me of how I felt about the boy running down the hill with the flowers I didn't buy in Sri Lanka. Small incidents, but they weighed on me.

Sudan: Father and son who wanted us to ride their camel.

Egypt: The New Concrete Jungle

Before the new Egypt gripped me in its concrete jaws, I wanted to be transported back to the kingdom of ancient Egypt. The prodigious monuments to the kings of ancient Egypt grabbed my imagination; the sense of mystery, of power, of the antiquity of it all was overwhelming. My son lived in Cairo for four years, and during an earlier visit to him, I had learned much of Egypt's ancient history from museums, historical sites, books, and today's Egyptians.

These multiple dynasties of ancient Egypt lasted from about 3000 BCE until Cleopatra VII lost it all to the Romans in 30 BCE. But even with the occupation of Romans, Byzantines, Arabs, and then Mamluks, Egypt remained something of its former self. It wasn't until the Ottomans took over in 1517 CE that real decay set in. But then hope was resurrected as Egypt became something of its own country in the 1800s—although it was during that period that the Brits and French (with some help from the Americans) sacked ancient Egypt, looting its tombs and artifacts, but also, to be fair, preserving much that would have been lost. Certainly those archeologists working then would not have used the verbs I have to describe their work.

During those three thousand years of royal rule, borders expanded and contracted, religious deities came and went, dynastic lineages were born and died. All the while, power, art, architecture, language, literature, and a culture that cannot be forgotten flourished. Created from the brilliant minds of a few, borrowing from here and there, inspired by the land itself, from the world as it was

then, this sense of Egypt, this sense of place, this sense of history at its rawest and most magical evolved.

The cyclopean testimonials to power and faith forced me to confront this ancient reality. As I stood small in the shadow of Ramesses the Great, or the illumined Luxor temple at night, or basked in the coolness of the tomb of Nefertari surrounded by colorful, decorative, and revealing images of the time, there was no choice.[5] This was the Egypt I wanted to know.

I was drawn to the story of Hatshepsut, the woman who not only would be king, but was—in no uncertain terms. She was the oldest daughter of Thutmose I and his queen, Ahmose. As was the custom of the times, Hatshepsut was married to her half-brother, Thutmose II, who died after ruling for just three years from 1482 to 1479 BCE. His son by a lesser wife, Thutmose III at age seven became king as Thutmose II and Hatshepsut had no son. Thus it was fitting that Hatshepsut, the queen, should become regent. Although it would make history more exciting, according to modern archeological forensics, it appears that Thutmose II actually died of heart disease, not poisoned by his wife, although the rumors persist.

The term *pharaoh* was derived via Hebrew, Greek, Latin, and Old English from words meaning great house or palace in ancient Egypt and wasn't originally used to describe the person until later. Rather, the rulers were called kings.

For a few years, Hatshepsut played by the rules. She was the coregent, while her stepson assimilated his kingly destiny, although there were inklings of what was in her mind as she took the title of God's Wife of Amun, rather than queen. It wasn't too long, however, until she started appearing as a king in public and in monuments and depictions of her. Slowly her image took on more and more kingly, masculine attributes: a false beard, the clothing of a king, even eventually the body of a male. She indicated through writings that she was chosen for her kingly role by her father, Thutmose I. She became king in 1473 BCE, with Thutmose III relegated to a lesser role, even though he was then at least thirteen.

Hatshepsut ruled with her senior advisor for twenty-one years. After a brief skirmish with the Nubians and possibly in Syria and the Levant, she brought peace and prosperity to the New Kingdom. She greatly expanded trade routes and introduced myrrh brought back from a major expedition to Punt—even today, no one is quite sure where Punt existed geographically. Hatshepsut was also responsible for a flurry of building. In fact, one of her obelisks is still the tallest in Egypt today. On the west side of the Nile, after the narrow green strip of fertile Nile sediment, are all the shades of brown imaginable. Within this palette of subtle color shifts stands Hatshepsut's mortuary temple, an example of architectural magnificence with terraces and columns and grandeur abounding.[6]

She died in 1458 BCE, and Thutmose III finally became king. Some twenty years later near the end of his reign, the stone documentation—monuments, statuary, and cartouches—of Hatshepsut's reign as king were defaced. This was not an act of anger by a petulant child deprived of his kingdom upon his immediate ascension to the throne. Rather it was a calculated act that was most likely meant to ensure the hereditary rights of his blood relatives as opposed to Hatshepsut's. Her queenly, coregent, feminine forms were left intact. Archeological forensics denies yet another scandalous tidbit, as she apparently died of an infection from an abscessed tooth and bone cancer, and also possibly diabetes—not poison, as was rumored for centuries.[7]

There is one other aspect of Hatshepsut's story that is touching. The Lapwing, a bird called a *rekhyt* in hieroglyphic texts of ancient Egypt, was quite common, and the term was often used to refer to the common people. Hatshepsut's inscriptions often refer to "my *rekhyt*." As the epigraph for this chapter appears to indicate, she did seem to care for the commoners, a sentiment most uncommon in those times.[8]

But I cannot linger in this Egyptian past for long because the concrete blocks that now fortify Egypt's Red Sea coast strike a discordant blow to the massive remains in Deir el-Bahari, the site of Djeser-Djeseru, Hatshepsut's temple. My impression of this part of modern Egypt was one of size: large, including the tourists, mostly Russian, and concrete blocks forming massive resorts that jostle for space along the coast. Although often colorful, occasionally with a touch of taste and classic Islamic tiles, it was their size that struck me.

Dive boats flitted past like annoying dragonflies. I wondered if anything would be left of these magnificent reefs after all this anchoring and pushing and pulling to see and check this fish and that coral off everyone's lists? However, it wasn't only the dive boats we had to watch out for. Proceeding up the Red Sea took all our attention as ships appeared and disappeared in the sandy haze.

Egypt: Making our way up the Red Sea.

Zamalek is within walking distance over a bridge across the Nile to Tahrir Square and the world-famous Museum of Egyptian Antiquities, but I had spent time there in the past, so prior to my doctor's appointment, I focused on Zamalek itself and discovered the fascinating Museum of Islamic Ceramics. I loved the swirl of colors and patterns of Islamic art, which were visually seductive with their whorls and curves. Islamic artistry with tiles and ceramics is unsurpassed. It seems a gift that they were left with these forms, eschewing human and animal likenesses. This small museum was a treasure in itself.

My appointment was for 6:30 p.m. the day I arrived; the next morning I had an MRI and X-rays, picked them up later that day and met with the surgeon again in the evening. It was clear that I needed surgery with both a torn ACL and torn meniscus. Two days later I reported to the hospital. As it turned out, the surgery was more complicated than expected (that happened to me in the States also) because there was more damage to the knee than showed on the MRI and X-rays. It was not surprising as I'd been clambering around on the boat for months with this pain and exploring on land as well. Two of Chad's graduate students, that he had asked to help me in his absence, arranged a cab. On the way back to Chad's apartment, I asked one of the students who was fluent in Arabic to buy me a cane since it was clear I couldn't walk without one.

Wayne had insisted that I return immediately after the surgery; he didn't want to waste any weather windows to progress up the Red Sea. Neither of us had realized how complicated my injury was. Our next legs presented difficult navigation with frequent headwinds,

The restaurant menus were usually in Arabic and Russian, but some used English also, and often listed borscht. I stuck to local fare, and while I could say a few Arabic words, I could not read it at all. Again, provisioning took on a bit of luck and guesswork and a surprise or two later when I opened a can or package and it was not what I expected.

We anchored off Hurghada, where I had arranged to fly to Cairo for an appointment with an orthopedic surgeon about my increasingly painful right knee. My son Chad, who lived in Cairo at the time, although on sabbatical in the States while I was there, had done the research for me. He arranged for me to stay at his apartment. I had visited there before and loved its location in Zamalek, on Gezira Island in the middle of the Nile, with its parks, restaurants, local shops.

and it was important to take advantage of the right conditions because one never knew when they would recur. Nevertheless, I was not in good shape. I should have insisted that I remain another day to recuperate, but I didn't.

The students had helped me to a taxi in the morning, and in fluent Arabic gave the driver the necessary instructions including what the fare would be. At the domestic airport, a much more casual and smaller version than the international affair, I started to hobble out of the taxi with my bag, when an older fellow jumped forward and took the bag and my free arm. At the counter, I wondered how much he would want, but he refused any payment at all.

The stereotype of people always holding their hand out was so off the mark from my experience around the world. People tended to treat us the way we treated them. Kindness was often extended by perfect strangers. Living in the United States if I watched our horrendous news media, I would have a distortedly negative view of the world, but when I lived in the world, it was quite different. Insularity does not enhance knowledge. While I wouldn't trade my awareness for separatist ignorance, I would find that my renewed sense of the world made my readjustment to life in the United States intellectually and emotionally difficult.

≈≈≈

The day after I returned to Hurghada, we left for an overnight passage to Port Suez. I had no time to rest with two watches that night, but at least they were shorter than my usual five-plus hours, and I was able to keep my leg up much of the time. The next day I took the bus to Cairo and stayed at my son's apartment again for two nights. The following day at my follow-up appointment, the surgeon explained the unexpected difficulties and the condition of my knee, which was recovering well enough. In some ways, I was tough and could almost always heal quickly.

While there, I was able to do a little gift shopping in the Khan el-Khalili, Cairo's famous, historic, and ever-intriguing bazaar. I must have been a sight, limping around with my cane, my backpack, and assorted packages.

The sense of the bazaar was overpowering; it assailed all my senses. My eyes were inundated with color: at times garish and florid; other times harmonious and pleasing, but always blatant and in my face. My ears were saturated with sound in the same tones as color: harsh, grating, discordant, touts wanting me to buy this or that; other times, musical, tinkling, soft like water flowing. My sense of touch felt more than skin deep: jostled, pushed, pulled, grabbed by the arm, "Look missee, look, look, cheep, cheep." Other times, I felt the cool, earthiness of a well-made pottery jar; the incandescence of an alabaster vase; the sensuality of Egyptian textiles, silk and cotton.

There was taste too, not only when I stopped for a classic Egyptian coffee, sweet and bitter at the same time, but also the spices and herbs in the air not only smelled, but I felt as if I could taste them as the flavors seemed to float around my head. And then there was smell. Camels and donkeys were still used to bring goods into the bazaar, plus there was the usual sweat and human smells of a crowded place, and always those spices and herbs. I was sure I distinguished cardamom and turmeric at one point. And then there was the roasted lamb and goat, the hummus, the coffee!

Egypt: Khan el-Khalili, a major Cairo bazaar.

Sometimes when in the bazaar, I stepped to the side of the pulsating crowd, not just to rest my leg, but to savor the whole experience of this place—the sounds, sights, smells, and tastes. This bazaar, Khan el-Khalili, was more than a sensory experience; it felt as if I was surrounded by the sound of the human spirit and all its contradictions. I can close my eyes and be there again. Although it certainly is on the list for tourists to visit, it's more for Egyptians doing their shopping—so much more fun than the West's sterilized, same-same malls and neatly organized supermarkets. Although I wouldn't describe myself as a city person, there are a few cities in the world that I truly love, and Cairo is one of them—especially if I can stay in Zamalek.

≈≈≈

Again, it was over too soon. Returning to Port Suez, I did a little provisioning for soon we were to pick up our pilot (a requirement) for the first half of our Suez Canal transit. It was a boring trip with only sand, dust, and frequent, well-manned guard towers—except for this one amazing experience.

The Bridge Improbable

We are scrabbling up the Red Sea into
the Suez Canal in contrary
winds, sand settling
on the deck, my lips, my eyes.
Even the water has a slick of sand.

Ashore between the dull concrete resorts
the monotonous sand rises and falls
in undulating drifts broken
intermittently
by a string of dun-colored camels,
their splayed hooves produce
sand skirts to hide their ungainly legs.

From time to time, by design, the camouflaged
Egyptian watchtowers emerge
from the dusky landscape,
each with soldier in mufti and machine gun.

Hours of this unbroken, hazy
concrete and camel cycle,
then ahead through the tan, sand-enveloped sky
an iridescent cobweb is strung across the canal.

Such beauty is so improbable,
so startling;

who could have envisioned
this diaphanous sunlit sculpture
of the finest silver,
or so it seems in this bright sun;
this bridge from sand to sand
arched high above the scruffy sea.

What mind could see to make this span
one graceful existence
in this concrete and camel world of sand?

We arrived in Ismailia, but weren't allowed to leave the harbor compound so spent our two days there cleaning some of the sand off and out of everything, ourselves included. Our next pilot boarded *Bali Ha'i* about 5:30 a.m., and we reached the busy harbor of Port Said late that afternoon under gray, cloudy skies. The pilot was picked up offshore by the pilot boat, and, on our own again, we headed out into the Mediterranean. This was to be a different life, and I was not sure I was ready for it.

Egypt: The improbable bridge.

Egypt: Entering the Med.

11

The Eastern Med: Thousand-page Stories

Let all scribes and poets
Write down their wisdom
About the past and the future
Let the whole world learn about it,
Still something will remain understated
The numerous hardships borne by the Cretans.
Because on this island each family
Could write a thousand-page story.
—Saying in Cretan house at Lychnostatis, Cretan Open-Air Museum

Three countries: Cyprus, Turkey, and Greece—or four if one is Turkish and includes Turkish-held Cyprus—have much in common, yet are antitheses of each other; even Greek Cyprus from Greece. There are lessons here, portraits, reflective mirrors, but it requires that we look searchingly and then absorb and learn from these stories, some hidden under and within the very rocks that created these islands—these stories of thousands of pages.

Cyprus: A House Divided

After a two-night passage from Port Said, we arrived early on a sunny, mid-April morning and anchored off Larnaca, Cyprus. In spite of the culture of Egypt and the parade of 5-star pastel-painted concrete resorts spreading like a fungus along the west coast of the Red Sea, it was clear, even after only one trip ashore, that our arrival in Cyprus was entering Western-style civilization. Civilization is relative. Sometimes it merely means a flush toilet and potable water without the side effects of incapacitating diarrhea. Other times it may mean access to the opera and dinner by candlelight—the candlelight by choice, not necessity.

In Cyprus, the women were fashionable, the streets were clean and void of potholes, the toilets were the type I could sit on and there was even toilet paper, the cars were modern and shiny, there were classical music concerts, and a supermarket that deserved the name. This was not something we had seen since Australia, and I'm not sure there are too many Australian women outside the Gold Coast who would consider themselves "fashionable," or want to be, for that matter. In Cyprus, the community of British expats was formidable with their villa communities sprouting like concrete thistles along the coasts and foothills, making English a more accessible language, and, if one desired, English food more available. Was there anything that wasn't served with British chips? No, this was a different world than we had become used to.

Cyprus is a small island, albeit the third-largest in the Med, but only about 150 miles by 60 miles at its widest, yet divided physically, politically, in everyday lives, in beliefs, and ultimately in anger. Herein lie several thousand-page stories, but I will shorten them considerably.

In the old section of the otherwise modern city of Larnaca, I spent time walking around the narrow winding streets. They were lined with well-kept, small, attached stucco homes interspersed occasionally with a stone house, all built to the edge of the little alleyways, but with a small portion of space taken up with five-liter, rusty olive oil tins, terra cotta pots, and whatever else might hold some soil, filled with flowering plants from asters to zinnias. The balconies, some of which overhung the roadway, were also filled with blossoms, and occasionally a few rugs or clothes were thrown over the railings airing or drying in the bright sunshine and sea breeze.

During one of these walks, I met Stella, a Greek Cypriot and ample woman of late middle age. As her hands circled to indicate the totality of her world, she stated forcefully that her family had lost everything in the occupied territory. She, her mother, and one cousin had been able to flee; she did not know what happened to her father, brothers, and other relatives. She wanted me to know, "I have no issue with the Turkish Cypriots,

it is the Turkish military that is the problem." I thought her eyes betrayed her, although it may have only been my impression that their dark brown emitted sparks of hate during her entire statement. I learned from her that many of these little homes had been owned by Turkish Cypriots. Now they were occupied rent-free by Greek Cypriot refugees from the occupied territory with the understanding that they must give them up if the Turkish Cypriots returned.

To recover from the present, I looked to the past. Cyprus's historical memory is complex and multidimensional, as it would be for an island at the crossroads of Africa, Asia, and Europe. Not unlike Sicily, it is primarily a history of occupation. I wanted to learn more about the context for its present-day divided house. Perhaps today's anger covered by civility was created over centuries of life lived under the cultural domain of others. Cyprus represents a microcosm of the history of civilization in many ways. In addition, the island has been subjected to numerous earthquakes and many old settlements were destroyed. Not only occupation, but perceived sociocultural differences and nature's natural acts have shaped the formation of the island physically and culturally.

The earliest excavations are of settlements from the Neolithic age with varying dates from 8500 to 7000 BCE. In the late Bronze age (1650–1050 BCE), life changed considerably: trade took place among the eastern Mediterranean areas, coastal towns were established, a currency was developed. The Greeks started settling here in the thirteenth century BCE.[1]

As humans developed the means for travel, resources, and objects to trade, societies opened themselves up to the conquering spirit that pervades so much of our history. Cyprus was no exception. From about 1050 BCE to 330 CE, Cyprus control was a seesaw among Assyrians, Phoenicians, Persians, Egyptians, Greeks, and Romans. The name Cyprus seems to have come during the period of Roman domination from the Latin *cuprum*, meaning copper, which was a major Cypriot resource.

Zeno, the father of Stoicism (not to be confused with the Zeno of the paradoxes) was born in Larnaca in 324 BCE. I wondered how his Cyprus childhood had influenced his philosophy. Starting in 45 CE, the Christian apostles Paul and Barnabas traveled through Cyprus preaching, and the population for the most part became Christian. According to Christian myth, Lazarus lived here after Jesus raised him from the dead. I wondered too, how he might have spent his "second life" in Cyprus.

An interesting period began when Richard the Lionheart saw Cyprus as a strategic base for his Crusade; in 1191 he took the island and married his fiancée, Berengaria of Navarre, who was crowned Queen of England in Cyprus. Richard decided it was too difficult to control the island, so he sold it to the Knights Templar, who promptly gave it back to him after an uprising of the local inhabitants on the island. He then sold it to Guy de Lusignan, a French nobleman. The de Lusignans established a dynasty that lasted from 1192 until 1489. In 1571, the Ottomans started their takeover of Cyprus, and Islam became the primary religion, although the Greek Orthodox Church was given some religious and political autonomy.

Greek Cypriots became more united after their support of the Greek War of Independence in 1821, and a sense of Cypriot nationalism began to develop. The seed for today's problems was planted then. That seed started to germinate in 1878, when Great Britain signed a secret agreement with the Ottoman Empire that gave Cyprus to the Brits. British colonial rule brought harsh times to the local people both economically and culturally. Uprisings were met with severe restrictions. In January 1950, a referendum was held and 95.7 percent of Greek Cypriots voted in favor of joining Greece, but the Brits changed nothing.

The struggle for independence became a military struggle from 1955 to 1959 as Cypriot nationalists united under the EOKA banner (*Ethniki Organosis Kyprion Agoniston*, translated as the Nationalist Organization of Cypriot Fighters) and used guerilla tactics to gain freedom from British colonialism with the goal of uniting with Greece. Great Britain suppressed them. The British tactics included recruiting Turkish Cypriots to serve in a paramilitary police force, adding to the fissure between the Greek and Turkish Cypriots. In 1959 Britain, Turkey, and Greece signed the Zurich-London Agreements establishing Cyprus as an independent republic as of August 1960, but with a forced constitutionality that was impractical and induced further divisiveness between Greek and Turkish Cypriots.[2]

In 1974, the Greek ruling military junta organized a coup, executed by the Cypriot National Guard (made up primarily of Greek nationals), to overthrow the democratically elected Archbishop Makarios III, president of Cyprus. Taking advantage of this unsettled situation, the Turks attacked Cyprus and took 37 percent of the northern part of the island, although the population of Cyprus was then only 18 percent Turkish. Neither the UN nor any other government recognizes the Turkish-occupied territory.

There is documentation that there was not only discrimination but terrorism against Turkish Cypriots, especially during the EOKA years. Nevertheless, Turkey's excuse for the 1974 invasion was thin at best. The UN patrols the border, and talks for some resolution to the problem continue periodically.

The Cypriots—whether with origins in Greece or Turkey—had lived together peacefully for centuries. It seems animosities started when the external governments of Great Britain, Greece, and Turkey began to interfere. Today, both sides have atrocity museums: the Turkish Cypriots from the EOKA, who attacked Turkish Cypriots as well as the Brits; the Greek Cypriots from the Turkish military during the 1974 invasion. Who knows how many Turkish Cypriots were massacred, made homeless, harassed to despair, and women raped during the EOKA years. Then there was the Turkish invasion, and the same could be said for the Greek Cypriots who were massacred, made homeless, harassed to despair, and women raped in the area taken by the Turks. Perhaps it all goes back to "an eye for an eye"—a grotesque morality we have woven into our cultures.[3]

In 2004 a referendum on reunification had been accepted by the majority of the Turkish-occupied territory, but turned down by the Greek Cypriots reportedly because the Turks—many of whom the Turkish government had transplanted from Turkey to the occupied territory—would be allowed to stay and keep their property, most of which had belonged to Greek Cypriots. It is reminiscent of Israel and their settlements in Palestinian territory, a displacement of people and their lives at the whim of a central alien government. Another well-educated Greek Cypriot told me she expected the West to desert them, and it wouldn't surprise her if Turkey tried to take over the whole country, while the West was occupied elsewhere. A British expat living in the occupied territory for twelve years reiterated the undercurrent of anger, but she was referring to that of the Turkish Cypriots toward their Greek Cypriot neighbors.

I have heard people on both sides say: "reunification—not in my lifetime." Others, mostly outsiders, believe "cooler heads will prevail." I think not, if they are human heads with memories. The seed of discordance has become a full-grown, thorny weed.

≈≈≈

In 2008, when we were in Nicosia, now a divided city but also the capital, the border was quite narrow with carefully maintained UN checkpoints on both sides. The well-maintained walkway was monitored by Cypriot and Turkish troops on their respective borders. Official papers and passports were checked; occasionally a local person was pulled out of line and patted down. We walked through at the Ledra Palace crossing point, our passports and papers examined only cursorily. The Turks have a system whereby they stamp an official paper for us and not our passports, for if they had stamped our passports, the Republic of Cyprus would not have allowed us back in. On the other side is Lefkoşa, formerly part of the city of Nicosia but now the capital for the Turkish occupied part of Cyprus, which they call the Turkish Republic of Northern Cyprus.

The large coils of effective-looking barbed wire, sturdy walls, and other materials designed to keep some people out and others in were symbolic to me of so much that poisons the human spirit. I felt as if I was walking into a prison, then coming out on the other side. Because I knew the history of the disunity of this land plus the visual impact of the separation, the tragedy of such political actions suddenly became personal for me. As I walked this short path through no-man's land, I felt the trauma of families separated, of neighbor against neighbor. I wanted to mourn, not just for Cyprus, but Korea, the Kashmir, so many places.

Cyprus: The UN-patrolled border.

Older Berliners can relate to those living in the divided capital. But what happens in the no-man's land between the Republic of Cyprus in the south and the internationally condemned Turkish occupied territory of the north?

This question may be answered with some certainty by reading Alan Weisman's *The World Without Us*, a thought experiment about what would happen to Earth if *Homo sapiens* suddenly disappeared entirely. Varosha, Cyprus, abandoned by the Greeks in the war and then set off-limits to all by the Turks, has been subject to nature's reclamation since 1974, the model of what might happen in cities all over, if people disappeared. Varosha is now just one part of an involuntary park—the name given areas that are no longer inhabited by humans and that slowly reverts to its wild and natural state, except for the detritus left behind. Checkpoints and leftover land mines keep people from venturing into the Green Line, this involuntary park that marks the UN buffer zone between the Turkish-occupied north and the Cypriot south.

The Green Line is about 112 miles long, and at the widest point a little over four and one-half miles wide. There the returning wildness can be seen more clearly. More than pigeons and rats are having their run of this abandoned human land. Mouflons, native wild mountain sheep that look more like a goat, are making a comeback. What is disappointing is the slow deterioration of the litter of human life left behind: cars, bottles, food tins, and, of course, plastic.

In Nicosia I saw the Venetian walls, walked around the old city, part of which contains the usual Western-world shopping-mall chain stores, providing a cultural disconnect. But the image that stays with me is the UN, Cypriot, and Turkish police monitoring the pedestrian border crossing, as well as the buffer zone and its stretch of venom: knife-like barbed wire, No Admittance signs, thorny weeds, and deserted, broken-glassed, broken-hearted homes. Cyprus is a country divided in its soil, culture, heart, and soul.

≈≈≈

A standard procedure when we arrived via yacht

in many countries was for our passports to be kept by the Immigration authorities and we would be given landing passes, which was the case in Cyprus. To go to the occupied territory, we had to get our passports back, which turned into a hassle-ridden process. The Greek Cypriots unequivocally don't want their visitors to go to the occupied territory. Finally after several visits to Cyprus Immigration and much paperwork, with our passports in hand, we passed through the tense checkpoint/border. Our first stop in occupied Cyprus was the Salamis ruins, which actually date back to the eleventh century BCE, but as the information brochure stated, "[A] prosperous period continued into the Roman era. Most of the ruins unearthed in excavations date from this recent history of the city." Recent meant second to fifth centuries CE. Pieces of the Roman terracotta conduits for water and sewage were everywhere, as were baths and other remnants of their advanced civilization.

From Salamis we drove toward Girne/Kyrenia and stopped first at the magical Saint Hilarion Castle. This was one of those places that I had to see to believe. It is literally perched on craggy cliffs jutting up quickly from a brief coastal plain. I could not tell the castle from the precipice until I was right below it. It is built up along the edge of these jutting rock formations in a succession of structures. There are three such castles on similar cliffs: Saint Hilarion, Buffavento (meaning buffeted by winds; yes, true), and Kantara. They could contact each other by signal lights at night. The highest point at Saint Hilarion is about 2,230 feet above sea level. These castles took my breath away, not just because it was

so steep to get there and so windy, but they just seemed so unbelievable and wizardly. Merlin could have walked out at any moment. The story goes that Walt Disney envisioned the castle in the movie *Snow White* based on the structure of Saint Hilarion. And that is exactly what it looks like.

Cyprus: Saint Hilarion castle.

≈≈≈

I enjoyed my forays into the history of the places we visited. For me, it reinforced George Santayana's famous quote, "Those that cannot remember the past are condemned to repeat it." It wasn't only the facts of the rise and fall of civilizations, of occupation, of war, of trade routes, of imperialism, or of revolt that interested me. Additionally, the curious stories of Hatshepsut of Egypt, the cargo cult of Tanna, King Dhatusena of Sri Lanka, and so many others enhanced my sense of place and added a layer of understanding to the present.

Santayana had another saying: "Only the dead have seen the end of war."[4] What is it about our species that thinks war solves anything, when there is so much evidence to the contrary? That evidence lies at our feet around the world.

≈≈≈

Cyprus has an astonishing geological story. In the Troödos mountains, we hiked around Mt. Olympus, famous because of its ophiolite. In the story of oceanic and continental plate movement, when they collide, usually the oceanic plate is turned down into a subduction trench. As Ron Dutton, PhD, wrote in *Troödos: From Sea to Summit*, "occasionally,...a chunk of oceanic floor beats the customary fate of subduction, survives, and winds up on the edge of a continental plate. Such a stray slab of ocean crust is..." yes, "an ophiolite and... Troödos represents one of the best preserved and exposed examples of this geological wonder."

What's even more amazing about Troödos than the bottom of the ocean now being on the top of the highest mountain in Cyprus, is that its contents are in reverse order to the norm, so that the oldest layer, which had been the deepest—the peridotite-type rocks—are now on top, and the ordinarily top layer of ocean floor debris is on the bottom. If I didn't know what I was walking on and around, it all just looked like lots of rocks, but once I understood its upside-downness, it was quite wondrous. On this same hike, we saw the remnants of the Venetian walls, where the Venetians made their last stand against the invading Ottomans—walls no doubt made up of

ophiolite. So even in its geology, Cyprus is a picture of mismatched cultures.

Unlike Massawa, Eritrea, I can't say this is one of the world's heartbreaking places, especially with all the signs of wealth, but there is a sickness in the soul of Cyprus, and it stems from unresolved issues of neighbor against neighbor.

The Troödos mountains yielded more than their geologic story for me. The following poem is one Cypriot story of a woman I met in the Troödos mountains. Elena is loved and her terminal cancer affects only her and her family, but on another level it represents Cyprus.

Death Sidles Up Through the Trees

She wore black
covering her shriveling body,
the bones of her face
could barely hold the lined skin.
Her husband of more years than they could remember
looked on with love,
her daughter shook her head,
her granddaughter had fled to the city,
her great granddaughter
was old enough to understand.

The old lady
saw Death get on the bus
and head up the mountain.
she saw him get off
down the road and saunter through the trees
toward her.

Sometimes it looked like her mother,
sometimes like the devil.
When it was her mother,
she wanted to close her eyes
and be led away by the old lullabies. When it wasn't,
she crumbled
like the stale, crusty bread she fed the chickens.
She wrapped her arms across her bird-like chest
to hold herself together.
They thought she was cold.
No, she was just disappearing in pieces.
She grabbed at a bone to put it back in place,
but it floated out of reach.

She thought she smelled the priest—
the candle wax and the thyme from his garden.
She heard the coal tit,
its little song over and over
ritty,ritty,ritty...ritty, ritty,ritty
Soon, it too flew out of memory.

Turkey: A Different House Divided

Between Antalya and Fethiye on the southwest coast of Turkey is a magical area referred to as the Lycian coast for the ancient people who lived there. It has a dramatic look with steep, rugged mountains rising above ten thousand feet, impressive ancient ruins, and the Mediterranean Sea clear and turquoise-blue.

Although they also occur elsewhere, there were two types of wind that caught my attention at our Turkish anchorages. The first is what I call "slack wind." During the day the land heats up because land absorbs the heat from the sun more efficiently than water. Because heat rises, the cool air from the sea moves in to fill the void creating an on-shore breeze. Conversely at night, the land loses its heat much more quickly than the sea, so the cool air from the land moves off shore to fill the void created by the warmer air rising off the sea. That's the physical explanation, but there is also the time during the transition when miraculously nothing happens.

I loved this dusk, in-between time, when it was calm between the on-shore and the off-shore breezes. This gentle, soft, barely perceptible wind was not unlike the water when there was a slack tide between the water's rush to get in and then its rush to get out. In this slack-wind time, all was calm, so quiet I could hear my own heartbeat. I imagined I could hear the whispered murmurs of fish beneath the sea, the rocks cooling off after a hot day in the sun, softly droning on to each other. And there in the pine woods were the stones of time, some still standing in ancient agoras, the Roman city walls, the benches of Grecian theaters, quietly breathing their history. But so quiet and hushed. Everything was whispered in this slack wind. It was one of those magical times when only at anchor would I experience this muted sound of life: a time to listen to soft, murmuring sounds of land and sea, of life not usually heard. This way of quiet sound was yet another gift from this voyage.

Then there was the meltemi, this was a wind to drive one mad. It was harsh, full of grit from the land, quick blasts sounding like staccato taxi horns in a traffic jam. I watched it race across the water, wind waves and whitecaps churned up as it came, quickly rushing to me as a new, ardent lover, wanting to grab me and twist me in his arms. But this lover overstayed his welcome and

Turkey: The Greek theater at Phaselis.

soon familiarity became tedious with sand on my tongue, my clothes, and everything I touched. But still it came, occasionally hiding, a tease as it always returned bringing its harsh, pulsating sound and sand.

≈≈≈

Our first anchorage was on the Turkish Lycian coast in the ancient harbor of Phaselis, where we glided over centuries-old Roman columns visible in the clear water beneath our keel. The Lycians were an indigenous Anatolian people who lived in this area before the arrival of the Greeks. It was in early May with blue skies, comfortable temperatures, and a few large white clouds on their usual daytime journey that we went ashore and walked among the pines to the Roman ruins including an excellent aqueduct and intact black and white tile floors lying on the ground where buildings once stood. We found a wonderful Greek theater with perfect acoustics, which we tested as I sat up in the midlevel seats, and Wayne stood on the theater floor, speaking his thoughts of this ancient place in moderate tones. I heard every word.

The view was of a majestic rocky mountain range, pine-covered hillsides, and rocky cliffs falling into the sea. It was a

Turkey: The Roman aqueduct at Phaselis.

dramatic entrance to this fascinating country with its stories and tales of various occupations.

Turkey's early prehistory is similar to that of Cyprus, with prehistoric sites partially uncovered, partially understood. The advent of pottery, basketry, metals; the ability to travel and trade; and then the inevitable grasping of territory, power, control over others shaped history here as well. But the two periods of greatest interest to me were the Ottoman Empire and the much later modern concepts of Ataturk.

The West tends to think of the Ottomans as barbarian conquerors. But the reality is quite the opposite. The creation of the Ottoman Empire is not that of a smooth war machine rolling over new territory, although from a distance that is how it appears. One of the keys to the success of the Ottoman Empire was its inclusion of other cultures in a variety of ways. For example, Sultan Bayezid II welcomed the Jews, expelled from Spain during Queen Isabella's bloody and belligerently intolerant Inquisition, offering them refuge in Istanbul. Almost always, the Ottomans supported religious and cultural diversity—note the *almost*. The Janissaries were one of their exceptions. This corps of brutal, well-trained military troops was made up of young Christian youths who were captured as slaves and—there's no other word for it—brainwashed to became the Ottoman's not-so-secret key to their military success. The Janissaries cut a swathe sword by sword through the expanding Ottoman territory.[5]

Without getting lost in the contours of the development of the Ottoman Empire, I preferred to focus in on Süleyman I, who ruled from 1520 to 1566 CE. He was known to the West as the Magnificent,

and to his people as Kanunî Sultan Süleyman, the Law-giver. His story should be an opera. It has all the ingredients of a great, raging tragic legend. He came to power quite legitimately and controlled the empire at its largest territorially. He was considerably more than the frightening conqueror as Europe viewed him, although his conquest of Hungary certainly supported that view. He initiated many cultural, architectural, and infrastructure projects. Istanbul was the most civilized and resplendent city in the world during his reign. And he was the *Law-giver*, codifying a just and thorough legal system.

Then the story changed for he fell in love with one of his concubines, Roxelana, who became known as Hürrem Sultan; and he actually married her. She was a street-smart, power-hungry, exotically beautiful woman. Originally from a part of the Kingdom of Poland that is in the Ukraine today, she was captured as a slave, sold and resold, ending up in Istanbul, where she was purchased for the sultan's harem. She quickly made her way from there to the sultan's heart. She arranged the death of his closest friend since childhood, Ibrahim Pasha, who had risen to have great influence with Süleyman, thus becoming a perceived threat to Roxelana. She also had his sons by other concubines murdered so as to ensure the ascendance of her son. Roxelana did more than contrive deaths; she was a benefactor to schools and a hospital for women, and was a major influence on her husband to maintain peaceful relations with the Kingdom of Poland and to stop the capturing of slaves in the area from which she had come.

Her son, Selim I, was known as The Sot. Befitting that name, he seems to have been a spoiled profligate and inherited none of his parents' skills in politics or warfare, and was the first in a series of incompetent sultans that weakened the empire and contributed to its ultimate downfall much later. Intrigue, murder, war, peace, and the slave girl who captured the sultan's heart—it all happened during Süleyman and Roxelana's reign.

≈≈≈

From Phaselis, we sailed up to Finike on the southeastern coast of Turkey, where we stayed in a marina as there was not a safe place (in terms of waves and weather) to anchor out. We found Brit cruising friends there whom we had first met in French Polynesia, who showed us the ropes, including wonderful Turkish restaurants with their *mezes* that epitomized the culinary art of the country.

There were cold and hot *mezes*—all mouth-watering. They included: seafood such as tiny grilled octopus, stuffed mussels, or *hamsi* (European anchovies) in garlic and olive oil; grilled eggplant (along with asparagus, peppers, potatoes, or zucchini) and stuffed with nuts, spices, and rice; little yellow lentil fritters or red lentil balls; humus with *pide* (flat bread) or *simit* (sesame seed rings); *köfte* (Turkish meatballs) and small kebabs; goat cheese with tomato and red onion; white or green beans in tomato sauce and spices. Just writing about them, takes me back to so many wonderful Turkish meals from those we enjoyed on *Bali Ha'i* after a trip to the local market; at seaside terraces; small city grills with barely enough room to sit; or countryside village taverns where locals would stare at us briefly, smile, and then start asking friendly questions. We often made a meal of a selection of mezes only, although they were meant to be just the hors d'oeuvres

with a meal to follow. Like the Italians, Spanish, and most Mediterranean people, the Turks spend time at their evening meal. Is it any wonder they are so healthy?

Turkey: A typical market in a souk.

One of the secrets of their delectable national cuisine is that the Ottomans controlled the Spice Route for a few centuries and not only transported and sold exotic spices, but incorporated them into their cuisine. It was not just the spices that made Turkish meals so tasty, it was the freshness of everything and the subtle combinations. And why not fresh? Turkey ranges from desert to snow-covered mountains and everything in between; the Mediterranean, Aegean, and Black Seas lap its shores. It can grow almost anything and does.

It's not only a breadbasket for wheat, corn, and rice, but is bountiful in olives, many vegetables from aubergines to zucchini (courgettes to the rest of the world), fruits from figs to melons, hazelnuts and pine nuts, honey from every wild and domestic flower a bee could be attracted to, as well as tender lamb and goat, not to mention the goat cheeses and yogurt.

But what we saw were huge white, plastic-covered greenhouses growing everything from local tomatoes to tropical bananas. I wasn't a fan of these monstrosities that were sprouting up like goliath mushrooms covering the hillsides. In the past, Turkey has always been able to feed itself and more of the world from its sensible use of land and water. These plastic tents disfigured the landscape and changed the entire agricultural milieu of the country. Food grown under plastic in artificial soil just wasn't the same as that grown in the real Turkish countryside with its luminous sunlight and crisp, fresh air whether blowing in the mountains, plains, or from the sea.

Provisioning continued to be for me so much more than the usual supermarket run in the United States. It was an important way of participating in the local culture, a social exchange as I dealt with the individual stand and shop owners, often bartering, depending on the traditions of the country. I sometimes developed friendships with those I dealt with if we were in a particular anchorage long enough, which often happened. I learned about more than the local cuisine and recipes, but also about the agricultural, farming, and fishing practices of the locale. It was an integral part of the cruising lifestyle—and not just to keep us well fed.

Turkey: A family proud of their produce.

The ecological diversity of the country and control of the Spice Route weren't the only reasons for the development of Turkish cuisine. During the seventeenth century, the Ottoman Empire had some 1,300 kitchen staff living in Topkapi Palace sometimes feeding up to ten thousand people a day. There were numerous specialists in specific menu items from mezes to dessert pastries and everything in between. Pleasing the royal palate has to be added to freshness and spices as a factor in creating Turkish cuisine.

≈≈≈

Turkey eased my entrance back to the Western world. It's the geophysical bridge connecting Europe and Greece—our cradle of Western civilization on its border—to that of the Middle East, with Syria and Iraq to the south; and with what used to be Persia and Armenia, to the east.

Turkey's richness for me was not only one of environments and food. Historically it has excellent ancient Greek and Roman ruins, the epitome being the library façade at Ephesus, or, I must say, all of Ephesus. Ephesus represents a vibrant, exuberant life that fully encompassed body, soul, and mind. Spiritually, it ranged from ancient Greek, Roman, and Egyptian gods and goddesses to Christian saints and Islamic mosques. Architecturally, there were brothels, baths, and conduits through which wine flowed to the homes of the wealthy on the hill as water did for those less opulent; a massive theater, stadium, and, of course, the library façade. Artistically, I saw sensual murals and delicately carved statues of such formidable gods and personages as Zeus and Socrates.

The library was built by the son of Tiberius Julius Celsus Polemaeanus, who was proconsul of the Roman's Asian province of which Ephesus was the capital, between 114 to 117 CE to honor, and as a mausoleum for his father. Inscriptions honor the characteristics of wisdom, intelligence, knowledge, and virtue. But even this rich, diverse civilization was not enough to withstand either barbarians or nature. The value of Ephesus was lost on the Goths, who readily sacked the place in 262 CE, burning scrolls, looting, and raping their way through civilization. We can put the blame for the destruction of the library on their muscular, hairy shoulders, and the city never again regained its splendor. But the Goths weren't the only ones to have a major impact on the city's destruction. In spite of Roman engineering and ingenuity, the harbor kept silting in so that the city actually moved five times before its final destruction by barbaric hands.[6]

Turkey: The library façade at Ephesus.

Ephesus may be the pearl of ancient ruins in the eastern Mediterranean, but it is not alone. In the Cappadocia area there are estimated to be from forty to over two hundred underground communities. A few that have been excavated range from two to eleven stories down. There is some debate about when they were first built and by whom: possibly the Phrygians in the eighth to seventh centuries BCE or by the Persians in the fifth to fourth centuries BCE for refugees. The first known written notation about them is in Xenophon's *Anabasis*, written after his expedition with Cyrus in 401 BCE. Whoever envisioned them, it was a masterful troglodyte brain at work. Some are, indeed, cities. The largest known to date could accommodate up to fifty thousand people. We saw complex systems for ventilation, water, and septic as we made our way single file through the narrow carved walkways. There were stables, wineries, oil presses, storage rooms, schoolrooms, religious chapels, as well as family apartments. Particularly interesting to me was the clever, huge rolling-stone-on-tracks system for closing off entrances to the upper world.[7]

For me, living in the environment of the sea, now stooping, slumping, and shuffling through the light brown stone passages of one of these underground cities with a roof of thousands of tons of heavy stone—while fascinating strictly as an observer—would have been horrifying to live under. I tried to imagine not seeing the sun for days on end and breathing this underground, dirt-rock mustiness, but that only made me want to claw my way out quickly. However, what was on the surface—perhaps an enemy with bow and arrow or mace-like club—might have given me second thoughts. These underground cities were used when the above-ground habitations were under siege.

The Cappadocia region is more than these underground cities. There are many above-ground buildings created in fantastical shapes from monasteries to mausoleums to today's bed and breakfasts. What made both the underground cities and above-ground "buildings" possible is the geology of the place. Its soft volcanic tuff was shaped by erosion and wind into demiurgic shapes. It's a fairytale land best seen with child-like eyes. It is also a center for the ceramics for which Turkey is so well known with their handcrafted detail.

Another part of Turkey that appealed to the child within me was the home of St. Nicholas. Yes, he was the bishop in the ancient city of Myra, now called Kale or Demre on the Lycian coast. There are many legends of how he became the Christmas St. Nick or Santa Claus in the United States. It is known that he was particularly compassionate to the poor and downtrodden. He knew of one family with three daughters with no money for dowries and not enough to feed them. The father was ready to sell them off to that oldest profession for women, when several gold coins were found in their fireplace. Bishop Nicholas, not wanting to embarrass the father and hoping to prevent the sale, easily climbed on the roof and dropped the coins down the chimney while the family was sleeping. This is why the spirit of St. Nick brings gifts down chimneys (when available) at Christmastime. There is a chapel and mausoleum to St. Nicholas.

Turkey: The author and her husband in a Cappadocia underground city hallway.

Turkey: Cappadocia's fairytale world.

Turkey: The hand-painting of detail on a ceramic plate.

Turkey: Ceramics display.

Turkey: The necropolises at Myra.

Myra is primarily known for the ornate necropolises that look like miniature mansions and temples built into the side of the rock cliffs, an interesting place to spend one's afterlife. The inscriptions on the tombs are in the Lycian language, which was banned by Alexander the Great in favor of Greek, so they have to have been created before 323 BCE.[8]

Today, the Turks have their own political meltemi. Do they follow the wisdom of their father, Ataturk, and maintain a secular government, or do they follow the fundamentalist Islamics calling for a religious-based political and social structure? I wondered if given Turkey's present political conundrum the amazing underground cities of Cappadocia might have another use for those hunted and persecuted as in the distant past?

Along the coast, so dependent on a tourist economy for their well-being, there was a growling antagonism, but never in strident voices. This was not cultural. Turks have never been afraid to express their opinions loudly and clearly. As I conversed with a few young men, from whom I had bought some tapestries, I sensed a mist of fear couched in their political complaints. They looked over their shoulders in case someone was listening and they spoke quietly.

But I cannot leave Turkey without remembrances of Istanbul. Like Cairo, Hong Kong, and New York, for me Istanbul was an exuberant, bewitching city that captivated all my senses. The spice market, the bazaar, the calls to prayer, the light on the Blue Mosque, the exquisite tiles in the Rüstem Pasha Mosque with their light-emitting blues and reds of tulips, trees, buds, and leaves, curves and swirls and vines dancing through patterns in dizzying profusion, captured my eyes in a whirlwind meditation. This is how I remember Istanbul.

Turkey: A view of the Istanbul bazaar.

Eastern Greece: Identity Through Memory

We took a six-week sail to the eastern and more southern Greek islands including Kos, Astypalaia, Anaphi, Crete, Karpathos, and Rhodes. Most of those we explored by land, with a four-day drive through Crete. The landscapes were staggeringly spectacular, and the people wore their lives with a sense of endurance.

Our first stop in Crete was the Lychnostatis open-air museum, where I found the epigraph for this chapter. This museum gave us a view of the everyday life in central Crete over time. We enjoyed all of Crete, especially the museums, large and small. Of special interest to us was our visit to Knossos and delving into the Minoan world and to Gortyn, the site of the oldest (and the longest) legal inscription in the Western world.

Greece: Approaching Anaphi.

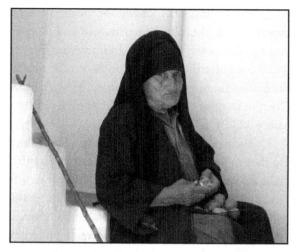

Greece: An older woman in Karpathos.

Greece: Karpathos view, but typical of many of the southern Greek islands.

What struck me most in Knossos was not only the age of what I was seeing, but the color, and the perception that I could actually see life there in the golden age of the Minoans. Knossos was first inhabited in 7000 BCE, the Neolithic period. The cradle of Western civilization via the Minoan culture started about 3500 to 3000 BCE, but came into its own from about 1950 BCE to 1400 BCE, surviving two major natural catastrophes: an extremely earth-shattering earthquake and a monster tsunami in 1730 BCE and 1570 BCE respectively. Before that, there seemed to be a five hundred-year time of peace, a time before people learned to hate each other's religions. Cretans worshipped a mother-goddess, and the Mycenaeans on the Greek mainland were patriarchal, yet they coexisted without wanting to take over the other, or, worse, to convert them.

The impressive complex of buildings on the site wasn't constructed all at one time, so there is no specific date associated with it. My impressions of its realism stemmed from an archeological gaffe made by Sir Arthur Evans, who first discovered the site and excavated it from 1900 to 1905 CE. His contribution was enormous, but he went a step further; he had parts of the palace "re-created." Although his re-creation was based on archeological evidence, this was not an action archeologists were supposed to take. Primarily what he had done was the renewal of the paint and frescoes, but it was exactly this that made the site come alive for me. I found the playful dolphin frescoes in the queen's boudoir so charming that I bought a small vase replica of one of the pieces found there with the same dolphin motif. It sits in my bedroom today. I walked through Knossos accompanied by this queen who loved dolphins as much as I.

Greece: The queen's dolphins at Knossos, Crete.

Evans named it the Minoan culture. His reasons were based on Greek mythology, and Greece being the land of myths, of the many-page stories of the Trojan War and its aftermath in *The Iliad* and *The Odyssey*. What is striking about the early Greek pantheon is their likeness to mankind: Zeus and all his affairs; Hera, the jealous and vengeful wife. They take sides in the affairs of men and argue among themselves. Certainly they have their magic too: their ability to change shape, to appear and disappear, but as concerned as the people might be to please these gods, they were more real than an almighty unknown. Edith Hamilton, the late well-known classicist, called it "A humanized world [where] men were freed from the paralyzing fear of an omnipotent unknown."[9] These wonderfully rich stories are often based on a real event and real people.

The Minoan myth is such an example. In summary, Androgeus, the son of King Minos of Crete, was visiting the King of Athens, Aegeus, who inhospitably sent the youth out to kill a dangerous bull, but the bull killed Androgeus. Needless to say, Minos was quite angry, conquered Athens, and demanded that every nine years they send seven maidens and seven youth for sacrifice to the Minotaur, half man, half bull. The Minotaur was confined in an extreme labyrinth. It was Theseus who killed the Minotaur, but that is another story.

Evans' reason for naming this the Minoan world had to do with the bull theme. He had found many artifacts and art remnants related to the bull including the famous bull leaping. There really was a powerful king on Crete named Minos, whom Homer wrote about, but whether or not some of this myth is based on that king, is not known.[10]

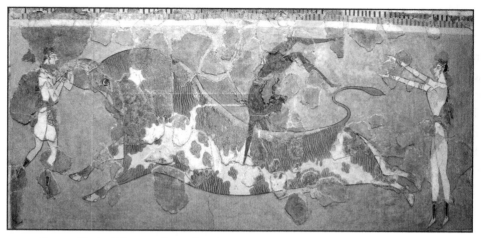

Greece: The bull-leaping fresco from Knossos in the Heraklion Archeological Museum.

Greece: The modern Cretan World War II resistance fighters monument.

I discovered a modern side to Crete's myths and suffering when we came upon a most unusual contemporary sculpture by an isolated stretch of road in the Cretan mountains. This memorial was dedicated to more recent heroes—real ones. The sculpture consisted of a series of modernistic concrete figures with the names of the Cretan resistance fighters killed during the World War II German occupation engraved on them. The first two have fists upraised; the last three appear to be victims of torture or have been hung. It is a dramatic remembrance.

The Cretans are a people who have stridently reacted to the yokes put on them by other, initially more powerful, forces. In World War II, the Battle of Crete was fought by Germans, who were parachuted in near Chania, against British forces. While a technical loss for the Allies, the cruelty of the German troops united most Cretans in direct and indirect resistance to the Germans, requiring the German command to install many more troops on the island than first anticipated, thus depleting their troops elsewhere. The stories of Cretan bravery include both men and women, range from children to old people, involve priests, shepherds, storekeepers, housewives, and many others.

Once the island was lost to German forces, the Brits had their own secret agenda on Crete. They were concerned about the popularity of communism and the number of communists involved in the Greek resistance. Rather than arming and working with a united Greek resistance, British agents undermined it to ensure a fratricidal situation between the moderates and left-wing resistance fighters.

Nothing is black and white in Crete and that's part of what makes the stories one thousand pages long. In a time of chaotic war and its inherent individual bravery and duplicitous actions, there were many stories. Here is one.

George Psychoundakis was born in 1920, the last son of the poorest family in a poor Cretan mountain village. He was twenty when the battle of Crete started, had a head of hair like a black mop, bushy black eyebrows and a mustache to match, and deep-set dark eyes. He had been a shepherd for his family's small herd of goats and sheep since a young age, so he knew the mountains and animal trails well. As soon as the battle started he ran, as he usually did, to Rethymno, about nine miles away—which, as we will see, was nothing to Psychoundakis. He immediately joined the resistance.

In the confusion and difficulty of the Allied abandonment of Crete, many of their troops had been left behind. The Cretans helped by hiding them and sharing their scanty food supplies. Many Cretans lost their lives or were tortured as a result. Psychoundakis helped by guiding remaining Allied troops across the rugged mountains to the sea where they could be rescued. These are dry, scraggly, jagged peaks with deep, rock-scarred ravines and gorges between each ridge one must climb down into and then scramble up to get over the next ridge. I scrambled up and down similar terrain, and still have scarred knees as a result. I'm sure Psychoundakis did too, although I'm equally sure, he never gave scars a thought.

After the war, Psychoundakis wrote *The Cretan Runner* of his experiences during the war. Patrick Leigh Fermor in his introduction to the book wrote:

> When the moon rose [Psychoundakis] got up and threw a last swig of raki [a strong drink like ouzo] down his throat with the words 'Another drop of petrol for the engine,' and loped towards the gap in the bushes...and scuttled through like a rabbit. A few minutes later we could see his small figure a mile away moving across the next moonlit fold of the foothills of the White Mountains, bound for another fifty-mile journey.[11]

Psychoundakis's wartime adventures are best read in his own words. In Crete, I was interested in the man. Ironically, after the war, he was arrested as a deserter; just one of the many insanities of war and its aftermath. Leigh Fermor discovered this quite by accident and was able to secure his release, but after Psychoundakis had already spent sixteen months in a cell. What could he have been thinking at this unbelievable injustice? Yet, this was when he wrote *The Cretan Runner*. Psychoundakis went on to write more books and to translate *The Iliad* and *The Odyssey* into Cretan dialect.

George Psychoundakis with only two or three years of elementary schooling became an author as well as a keen observer and chronicler of the life of the

Cretan mountain people in an anthropological sense, a hero among heroes—a Cretan. When the Brits offered to pay him for his brave service during the war, he refused, reportedly saying, "I work for my country, not for money."[12] Greece could use men like him today—so could the world at large.

Rhodes was another island with thousand-page stories. Like most of the larger Mediterranean islands there was a Neolithic culture there from about 7000 to 2700 BCE. Rhodes experienced the usual Mediterranean historical evolution including various Greek city states, then the Romans, Persians, Arabs, Byzantines (the eastern half of the Roman Empire that survived unto itself), not to mention various sackings by pirates and enemies of whomever the current rulers were. The island also suffered from periodic earthquakes. But for me, although unsympathetic to the Crusades, the Knights were of interest—I think because of the connection, in name only, with King Arthur's Knights of the Round Table. The Knights of the Order of St. John first arrived in 1306. They were made up of knights from seven different nations based on their languages, thus the divisions were known as Tongues: Aragon (later divided into Aragon and Castile), Auvergne, England, France, Germany, Italy, and Provence. Originally this order served charitable functions and were known as the Knights Hospitallers, of the Sovereign Order of Saint John of Jerusalem, Knights of Malta. It was later that they developed a military mission. Each Tongue had its own inn and coat of arms, still visible on the walls of the Street of the Knights, but with a Grand Master over all of them. The Knights were the highest class and of noble families, followed by Chaplains, with religious duties, then sergeants.

Historical records indicate that the Knights were benevolent dictators, encouraging commerce, permitting an autonomous lifestyle for the various nationalities of the citizens. Apparently "Greeks, Latins, Jews, and Armenians coexisted harmoniously, exercised freely their religious duties, and worked together with the Knights."[13]

Eastern Greece is rich in stories, legends, and myths, but its reality can rival them. One must read a thousand books of thousand-page stories to fathom it. And there are those thousand books, and then some: from *The Odyssey* to George Psychoundakis's *The Cretan Runner*. We could learn from them, if we would only then remember.

Greece: A plaque to resistance to fascism in the Ionians.

What are our thousand-page stories? What do we use to explain our times? Our legends seem to be made up of the scandals and duplicitous behavior of the rich and famous. Why are those people even famous? What does that say about us? What richness and texture of life have we lost when so-called heroism is shown in a redundant car chase and bursting flames or armament that can barely be imagined for its destructiveness, as buildings and bodies are blown to bits on TV screens night after night for no meaning, and often enough in real schools, shopping malls, and our streets. George Psychoundakis died at the age of eighty-five in January 2006. We should mourn him and those like him, so many who could tell their thousand-page stories.

12

Greece and Italy: Trials of a Journey

Hold back,...Back from brutal war!
Break off—shed no more blood—make peace at once!
—Homer, *The Odyssey* [Athena commanding Odysseus,
Telemachus, and the unworthy suitors of Penelope]

A Journey of Another Kind

White. Everything seemed white as I softly entered the Intensive Care Unit (ICU) room in the trauma center. The walls, the floor, the multitude of equipment and cables and tubes, the translucent paleness of his skin; even the background hum of the monitors was a white noise creating a Kafkaesque feeling for me. His breathing was so shallow I couldn't hear it. He didn't move; his eyes were closed. I touched a patch of skin that wasn't in a white plaster cast, or wrapped in white gauze bandages leaking blood, or stuck with some albino octopus appendage connected to the machines keeping him alive. There seemed to be a barely perceptible flicker of his eyelids; I may have imagined such movement, making it real because I wanted it to be.

"Pete, it's Mom; I just want you to know I'm here."

Soon I learned what to look for on the monitors and gauges to reassure myself that he was still alive.

Easter Sunday, two days before we were to leave the cabin in the Colorado mountains to return to Turkey to continue our voyage, I received one of those phone calls a parent never wants to get. My son Peter had been in a horrific motorcycle accident and was in the Las Vegas, Nevada Trauma Center ICU. The outcome was perilous. Fortunately, he had been wearing a full helmet and facemask. After closing up the cabin, Wayne and I left together: he to Turkey, I to Las Vegas, where I spent a month.

After a few days, we learned that Pete's brain and spine were intact with no damage, but he had compound fractures of both wrists, a broken pelvis, torn ligaments and other knee damage, broken legs, a torn spleen, and other less severe injuries.

Pete and his wife, Kara, were middle-school teachers, and Pete was a lacrosse coach and was one of a small group of fellows who started the school lacrosse program there. Aside from his family, their dogs, and teaching, Pete lived for lacrosse.

My grandson, Ethan, was thirteen at the time of the accident. He and Kara decided early on that he wouldn't visit his father in the hospital; to see him would be too traumatic. The Las Vegas lacrosse organization dedicated a section of their website to updates on Pete's condition, and the incredible outpouring of support and affection for Pete was overwhelming. The kids at their school put on a benefit concert with the choir, orchestra, guitar group, and jazz band, in which Ethan played trombone. The teachers and staff took turns providing meals.

Kara and I had been spoiled by the care given in the ICU, where each nurse had only two patients, each patient in their own room with an amazing array of technology, equipment, and monitors. There the medical staff was fighting to keep him alive—and they wouldn't stop unless there was nothing more they could do. After a little over a week, it was no longer a life-and-death battle, and he was transferred to the regular hospital. There, it was managing pain and changing bandages. The first night there, he almost choked to death on his vomit as no nurse responded to his pushing the buzzer with the two fingers that he could use, but only if the buzzer was placed in the right position. Fortunately the other patient in the room was able to get a nurse to come. After we heard this, the lacrosse community provided us a cot allowing Kara and me to take turns staying all night, although she ended up doing the brunt of it. Unfortunately after a few nights, in spite of my attempts to stay awake, I would fall asleep and not hear Pete right away. Somehow this night watch was too much for me.

Pete could do nothing for himself, and as pleasant and caring as the nursing staff was, his needs were frequently neglected. We needed to feed him, hold his water glass so he could take his meds, and generally monitor his condition. One of us needed to be there all the time.

I don't remember whose idea it was, but we started keeping a notebook. We listed all the doctors and specialists; descriptions of his wounds and condition; the meds and procedures; the standard temperature, blood pressure, blood count, and other statistics. It seemed important to document this. We were looking for progress, improvement between the lines, interpreting signs and noting them. Our words and numbers showed time passing, life continuing as real. Here, look at this page; on this day he spoke; then his temperature went down, but then the next day it went up again. Without this solid notebook, its lined pages, life could float away.

After a month both his condition and our documentation showed that he was relatively stable, and he was transferred to a long-term, acute-care hospital and then to their rehabilitation wing. Although difficult for me to leave, it was time. His attitude was excellent. Kara and Ethan were managing well and had continuing support from coworkers, the lacrosse community, family, and friends. Wayne was in Turkey, waiting. And so, I left.

Not long after, Pete's condition worsened. At the rehabilitation center, he wasn't able to do the physical therapy necessary to remain there. He still had a monstrous fixator on his leg that looked like an erector set gone haywire, and one of his wrist bones had moved and wasn't healing properly. Worse, he had embolisms in his lungs and was rushed back to the hospital when he couldn't breathe. The process and progress started yet again. Now in Turkey, I was able to speak to him a few times thanks to the improved computer and Internet technology occasionally available. He told me these last developments were just "a bump in the road." Six months later he was back teaching and not too long after that coaching lacrosse, although he will never play again. His wrists never healed properly, and it is painful for me to watch him walk down stairs, but he is alive.

Leaving the Aegean

Back in Turkey, I provisioned, worked on my tasks to prepare the boat for departure, visited with cruising friends, swam, and ate well-spiced Turkish meals. We left for Symi at 7:15 a.m. on a cloudless Sunday morning.

Wayne was drinking more often. Although we continued to sail as a team—albeit with Wayne as captain—ate meals and scrubbed the deck together, more frequently I would do exploring by myself, and my loneliness became embedded in my being.

How I ended up in the Colorado mountains is a result of connections and circumstances, but as much as I love the sea, I am rooted in those mountains too. Once that choice was made so many years ago, it became more and more difficult to leave that land-based sense of place. During the circumnavigation, I had my eye out for land combining sea and mountains, but I never quite found what I was looking for, except in parts of eastern Greece, and the upheaval of relocating there would require more energy than I had. And so I stayed on *Bali Ha'i* and with Wayne—that, too, was my choice. There is a Spanish word, *querencia*, with no real translation into English, that best described means one's "heart place," a place where one's inner strength is nurtured.[1] I'm not sure I've ever found it exactly, unless, somehow I could live in the ocean!

≈≈≈

In Symi, we anchored well because there was a strong meltemi blasting through the anchorage. We found our good friends, Jack and Joanie on S/V *JoanieD* from Canada, were anchored there too. As we were settling down in their cockpit for a welcomed visit, their boat started dragging, so all hands on deck. Our conversation and information sharing had to wait. A few days later we sailed to Vathi lagoon off Astypalaia, where we were anchored alone. This gentle-feeling space and the sea brought me a sense of peace for the first time in what seemed like months.

Vathi Lagoon

Day
I count your blessings by what I cannot
hear: jet skis, discos, motors;
and what I can:
an old fisherman, with his salty, fishy smell,
not unpleasant, singing a Greek tune
older than time. "*Yasas*,"
a smiling welcome in one word.
On the little home-taverna portico
a finch sings
and sings
a melody so intricate and joyful
it's difficult to feel he's caged.
One particular verse
echoes the fisherman's song.
Or is it the other way 'round?

Night
I feel the softened downy feathers
of darkness spread their silent wings
down the mountainside, across
the old, dry stone walls that shiver
with pleasure at the coolness,
slide across the lagoon, enfold the mast,
the deck, my eyes.
Only an occasional goat's bell, a wind dance
to playfully ruffle the water in a duet,
the tiny softened drumbeat of water
on the gently rocking hull.

Bless these sounds
and keep them safe.

From Symi, we wound our way up through what had become my beloved Aegean, anchoring at Kos, Astypalaia, Amorgos, Naxos with side trips to Delos and Mykonos, then Kythnos, Aegina, and finally Piraeus. The meltemi had been strong in several places, but we had anchored well and never dragged anchor. Wayne had always been good at that. From rental cars to local buses, we had explored these islands exhaustively, especially using our own two feet. Although I had been to Evia and Skyros with my children years ago, this was my first time in the southern Aegean, which, for me, lived up to its reputation—even Mykonos. I was prepared to dislike Mykonos heartily for its touristy patina. We were there in early June, so it might have been too early to have acquired that countenance yet, for it had a charming spirit with no falseness about it. There were the colorful pink to scarlet bougainvilleas against the whitewashed walls, brightly painted blue doors and window trim, and little verdant and flowery courtyards partially hidden behind even brighter whitewashed walls up the narrow, winding labyrinth of walkways. The artifacts and crafts on display were of fine quality—no made-in-China tourist gewgaws there.

At Delos, birthplace of Apollo and Artemis, we were returned to ancient Greece. It was called the central shrine or hearth of the Cyclades by Callimachus in the third century BCE—it's too tiny to be a hearth, more like a small beating heart at the center of the flung-out limbs of the Cyclades islands. First settled about 2500 BCE, it reached its spiritual epoch from the seventh to fourth centuries BCE when the Apollonian sanctuary was visited by worshippers from the expanding Hellenic world. But Apollo wasn't the only one worshipped here: there was a temple to the Egyptian deity Isis, a Jewish synagogue, a shrine to Syrian gods, and sanctuaries to Zeus and many lesser Greek deities from Hera to Leto.

I was particularly interested in the parade of the Lions of the Naxians, as astrologically I am a Leo—a double Leo so I've been told. These lions seemed a puny bunch, scoured by wind and crumbled by time, although lined up to be majestic as they once must have been. If the truth be known, these remaining five lions were just replicas. But Delos was not only a place to beseech the gods, but a major free port during Hellenistic as well as Roman times in the third and second centuries BCE. As such, it became a pearl to be taken, or, at least, its riches stolen. After 69 BCE, when the last major pirate attack occurred, the city gradually became abandoned, yet another ancient ghost town, with excavations not started until 1872 CE. We walked around the rocky, dry land, with clumps of wild grasses and wildflowers scattered about, a few small groves of trees, but mostly eroded white to graying pillars and statuary that asked to be remembered.[2]

In calm seas with no wind, we had a long motor to Aegina, with a bright spot of a pod of about thirty dolphins accompanying us for a while. It was the largest pod we were to see in the Med, and re-emphasized why there are dolphin paintings and artifacts from the ancient Minoan civilization on Crete to modern art in Athens.

Sea traffic picked up extensively as we closed in on Aegina with its proximity to the large port of Piraeus. With container ships to small local fishing boats and everything in between, we kept careful watch. The island of Aegina, however, was a pleasant surprise. I found the town quite Italian looking, an indication of what we would see in the Ionian islands, which were under Venetian rule for a few hundred years.

One day we took the bus across the island and were captivated by the landscape of groves of cedars, pistachio and olive orchards, and the vineyards that seemed to float on the hillsides. Our main destination was the temple of Aphaia, a well-preserved Doric structure from about 490 BCE, but worshippers came here as early as the thirteenth century BCE. And no wonder, it was on a hilltop made picturesque by the groves of cedars with bird song and wind whispers the only sounds heard. Reconstruction drawings showed it a brightly colored, impressive, columned building with extensive architectural detail—much of which, like so many of Greece's ancient treasures, can be seen in far-flung museums around the Western world. Some of Aphaia's are in Munich. Because we only saw the deadened white and gray decay of ancient Greece, it was easy to forget that most of these buildings were originally luminous blue and red and gold and crystalline white Naxos marble shimmering in the clear Mediterranean sunlight and crisp sea air.

One of the intriguing aspects of Greece was the constant reminder of old and new juxtaposed—whether the use of wind energy, transportation, or villages and buildings.

Greece: Wind energy old and new.

Greece: Modes of transportation from donkey to fast motorcycles.

Déjà Vu Doesn't Work at the Acropolis

Both Wayne and I had visited the Acropolis, he in the 1960s, I in 1972 with my children in tow. I remembered that I had been particularly taken with the Caryatids, those stalwart women posing as columns for the Erechtheion. Each Caryatid is draped in stone cloth of similar, but not identical, design; one leg is bent at the knee to enable her to stand in such a position for centuries, I suppose. Their expressions were steadfast; they

knew their responsibilities could not be shirked—like women the world over.

Greece: The Caryatids at the Acropolis.

Part of the Acropolis was built in the sixth century BCE with the Parthenon constructed in 447–438 BCE as a temple to Athena, the patron goddess of Athens. It had survived extremely well over the centuries until 1687 when the Turks chose to use it as storage for gunpowder. The Venetians were attacking the city, but they ordered that the Acropolis not be shelled. Nevertheless, a young

French (allegedly) lieutenant fired into it, and it exploded.

On our earlier Acropolis visits, we both had been impressed by its grandeur, its connection with the whole of Western civilization, its very age and majesty. But this time, neither of us could resurrect those previous feelings. It may have been the pushing and shoving tour groups, the scaffolding everywhere (certainly useful for the structures themselves), the lack of mystery, but something didn't work. On the contrary, we were entranced by our decades-later re-visit to the National Archeological Museum. Classical sculpture was my undoing. I wanted to shout encouragement to the little jockey, and then after he had won—for surely he would have won—run my sun-browned, arthritic fingers over the juxtaposed exquisitely fine lines of his horse, as well as the classic Greek heads, the innumerable folds of a woman's marble dress, the curly beard of one of their gods. I didn't really, of course, although today many are casts with the originals squirreled away to protect them from pollution, human insanity, and other horrors we might think of to inflict on these gifts from the past.

Greece: Detail from The Horse and Little Jockey, an example of classical Greek sculpture.

So unlike the beauty contained in the museum, I had quite forgotten the profligate ugliness of graffiti. Although in some quarters considered an art form—which, in fact, it can be—the graffiti in and around Piraeus was grotesque. Perhaps it was a bold and blatant foreboding of the troubles Greece was trying to sweep under the rug that later became a blistering economic wound.

The Spirit of Odysseus

I re-read *The Odyssey* as we traveled Odysseus's "wine-dark seas." Helen, Paris, the Trojan Horse, Odysseus, *The Iliad* and *The Odyssey*—are all well known. But not so widely remembered is that Odysseus didn't even want to go. His home was Ithaca. When summoned, he feigned madness plowing his fields erratically and sowing salt, not seed. Palamedes, who had come to fetch him, was as cunning as Odysseus and put young Telemachus in front of the plow. Odysseus swerved to avoid his young son, and thus the king of Ithaca became part of the army to avenge Helen, but against his wishes. He may have had a premonition of what was in store for him.[3]

But how did it all start? I don't mean Helen's affair with Paris, the gods' interference, and the pledge that forced the Achaean chiefs to go with King Menelaus to win her back—but before that.

Zeus was the god, unrivaled among the assembly of Greek gods and goddesses—the almighty in the Greek pantheon. There's no question about that. When someone—be it god, goddess, human, or other entity—

had a major complaint, they went straight to Zeus. Earth had a major complaint, so Earth went to Zeus and explained that mankind was too numerous and arrogant and asked Zeus to do something about them. Zeus came up with war—the Trojan War.

≈≈≈

Before we could reach Ithaca, Odysseus's kingdom, we transited the Corinth Canal, which first opened in 1893. Although Nero started to have a canal dug, his interests got taken up with insurrection in Gaul, and it wasn't finished. It's quite narrow and the side cliffs go up 250 feet. It has no locks and is only about four miles long, but what a difference in time and distance for passing between the Aegean and the Ionian Seas. It's reputedly the most expensive canal in the world per mile. It cost us about US$600 for our 63-foot boat. The Panama Canal was only twice that price and much longer with locks at both ends. The Greeks and Romans used a *diolkos*, a wooden tramway by which their ancient ships were pulled across on rollers still visible in places. Octavian used the *diolkos* to pull his ships across when pursuing Antony after the Battle of Actium.

Ithaca was the home of Odysseus and the end of his odyssey. As Odysseus said, "It is a rough land, but nurtures fine men. And I, for one, know no sweeter sight for a man's eyes than his own country."[4] It was here that I searched for his spirit.

I had a map of the island and had made notes from various sources, including *The Odyssey* itself, about the location of such places, particularly where, on his return disguised as a beggar by Athena, Odysseus met Eumaeus, his old swineherd. It was "by Raven's Crag and the spring called Arethusa." We had rented a car to explore, and after a drive up torturous mountain roads around multiple tight curves and between rows of olive trees branching overhead with black cloths spread below to catch the ripening crop, we arrived at a small, one-room museum with a curator—both the museum and the curator dedicated to the memory of Odysseus.

Greece: Transiting the Corinth Canal.

An Italian archeologist, the only other visitor to that well-hidden place, explained to us some of the finds there. Its prize possession to my eye was a piece of clay fragment with the distinct words in ancient Greek "Dedicated to Odysseus." His palace was clearly near here. The curator gave us directions. The way was more like a wide goat trail than a road, so we parked and walked around, Wayne was impatient to be on, but I needed to feel this ground that belonged to Odysseus.

The sky was clear, the sun bright; there were wild grasses, a few flowers—no doubt they could be considered weeds—and several boulders piled up at one end of a small open area that seemed like an old gravel pit. It was not an attractive place, and a small weathered, hand-painted, wooden sign was all that indicated it as the site of Odysseus's home, and the sign didn't seem as if it would last another year or two. Yet, he stood here, growing up under his father's, Laertes, watchful eye and benign rule, becoming king himself, and finally returning after twenty years—ten in battle against Troy, ten on his odyssey to return to Penelope and Telemachus and his dearly beloved land. This is sacred land to the literature and tradition of Western civilization. I breathed in not just the sun-warmed, sea air of this Greek island, but time, age-old time. I closed my eyes and floated on Homer's "wine-dark sea"; watched his "rosy-fingered dawn"; saw the young, "thoughtful Telemachus," and Athena, too, always bright-eyed, eyes ablaze and flashing when settling on her favorite, "the nimble-witted, noble, much-enduring Odysseus." In my mind's eye, I also saw Penelope, no longer having to pluck out the stitches of the shroud she pretended to make for Laertes to keep the ravenous suitors at bay while Odysseus was away. They were all here.[5]

≈≈≈

On our way to Corfu, we anchored in Preveza, where the Battle of Actium in 31 BCE was fought between the armies and navies of Gaius Julius Caesar Octavianus (the name Gaius Octavius took after Caesar's assassination) and Antony and Cleopatra VII for control of the Roman Empire. After Caesar's assassination in 44 BCE, a jostling for power took place. In the process,

Antony married Octavianus's sister, Octavia, more or less cementing their dual powers. However, Antony then started cavorting with Cleopatra, not the first politician to become undone by a blatant affair. The Romans didn't like this at all. One thing led to another, and eventually the battle of Actium occurred. Cleopatra and Antony's generals were at odds. Antony and Cleopatra's fleets were inside the Gulf of Ambracia. Octavianus was outside with ships and land forces guarding the entrance. A few battles were fought, but mostly it was a waiting game. Then on September 2, on Cleopatra's advice, or, some think, a plan conceived by the two of them, and against Antony's generals' wishes, they made a break for it, and for several hours the Battle of Actium was fought at sea. It was an odd sort of battle for the times. Usually, the idea was to ram the opponents' ships and sink them, but Antony had quinqueremes protected with bronze plates, quite difficult to ram and sink. Octavianus had smaller, very maneuverable liburnian ships; they, too, were difficult to ram and sink.

Late in the day, possibly to take advantage of the oncoming night, Cleopatra and her sixty ships suddenly made a dash for the open sea—and Egypt. Antony, whether as the lovesick fool or the cunning escape artist, left his command ship, took a few ships and followed her.[6] The rest is history and a movie.

We sailed through the battle area and anchored inside the bay where Antony and Cleopatra had been. Just as when I was at the site of Odysseus's palace on Ithaca, I took in the smells, the taste, the background sounds, the feel of the place; it was a time machine of the mind. The literature, the historical facts helped, but it was an intense sense of place that was the transport.

The next day in fierce winds with gusts over 50 knots we sailed past the stone boat and its crew that Poseidon turned the Phaeacians into after they kindly returned Odysseus to Ithaca. This is Corfu, or Kerkyra, thought to be Phaeacia in *The Odyssey*. Poseidon was angry at Odysseus, but Zeus, thanks in large part to Athena's influence, wanted Odysseus to live and return home. Thus Poseidon couldn't kill Odysseus outright, but what Poseidon could do to Odysseus's helpers was another story, which led to the Phaeacians and their boat being turned into stone.

I had seen Corfu in 1972, when my children and I took a ferry from Brindisi, Italy to Piraeus, Greece. Corfu had fascinated me at the time; we arrived at night, and I went up on deck and saw a huge, mysterious, and seductive mountain outlined in the moonlight. I wanted to return and see more of it, and so I did.

On Corfu, we rented a car and drove up Mt. Pantokrator, meaning in Greek *all strength* or *all-powerful*. In the Orthodox Christian churches it is used as a descriptor for Christ when the Bible was translated from Hebrew to Greek. The traditional icon showed Christ facing us with a stern, judgmental look, long hair touching his shoulders, one hand raised. To me, this was not the Christ of "Suffer the little children to come unto me." This was a hell-and-damnation Christ. And the mountain was well-named.

There is a monastery at the top, first built in the 1300s, with frescoes and icons from the seventeenth and eighteenth centuries; various repairs and rebuilding of the original structure having occurred since then. During the military junta, a huge radio tower was built over part of the monastery—communication and control

meaning more to the Greek military than religion. When we were there, it was just one of twenty or so radio, TV, and mobile phone towers complicating the view with an invasive modernity. But in places along its steep flanks, I found that Pantokrator spirit and sense of place I had felt so many years before, but now in a wild olive orchard that provided an open shelf with a view across to Albania and a panorama of the sea surrounding Corfu itself.

≈≈≈

Before we set sail for Italy, I considered some of the lessons of ancient Greece. During the Golden Age of Greece, from about 478 to 338 BCE, Greece invented and developed most of the concepts upon which Western civilization is based. From democracy—a true paradigm shift from tyrants, chiefs, and kings—to history; from geometry to architecture; from tragedy and comedy in literature to Socratic logic; from cultural anthropology to philosophy; from medicine to competitive sports. The list goes on; it was an exceptional time of radically creative thinking. It is thought that the Greek panoply of gods and goddesses set the stage for some of this creativity. As noted earlier, the Greek gods were somewhat human-like and had their human foibles. The Greek depiction of their gods even made them look human—the statues of Zeus and so many of the other gods demonstrate that concept. Although Zeus was the most powerful, there was no single totalitarian, omnipotent being. Certainly the gods had their magic and could become other shapes and cause all sorts of trouble to humans, as well as bring them benefits, but basically it was a world that was humanized. Democracy could only develop from such seeds, but it should be remembered that it wasn't perfect. There were slaves, women were not recognized as full citizens with the same rights as men, and it was not a particularly compassionate culture.

Although there were also wars—mainly the Peloponnesian Wars between the Athens and Sparta city-states, as well as many other skirmishes and much shifting of alliances—nevertheless, the main intellectual and conceptual accomplishments happened during times of peace. Relative prosperity based on sound agriculture and extensive trade were other characteristics of the times that provided a foundation for such achievements. If their resources hadn't gone into war, the Golden Age of Greece might still be going on. Instead Philip II of Macedon defeated the Greeks in 338 BCE and was succeeded by his son, Alexander the Great, in 336. After defeating the Macedonians in 168 BCE, Rome made Greece a Roman province in 146 BCE. Roman nobility sent their sons to Athens to be educated at the great schools there, founded during Greece's Golden Age by such luminaries as Plato. About 529 CE, these schools were closed by the Christians, who banned the Olympic games as well, which were not to start again until 1896. It's not until 1821 and the start of the Greek War of Liberation from the Ottomans that Greece becomes an independent country once again.

Interestingly, the other great period from this area was the Minoan culture on Crete. It, too, was a time of peace, extensive and sustainable agriculture, and trade. These are lessons for today and re-emphasize Santayana's paraphrased adage if we don't learn from our historical mistakes we are bound to repeat them. It appears that peace, sustainable food supplies, and international, equitable trade are the basis for prosperity and intellectual development.

≈≈≈

From Corfu, we had a two-night passage to Siracusa, which went well. Wayne had a new piece of equipment that was helpful and served as an incredible safety device. It was an AIS system and was newly required on all commercial ships. Since *Bali Ha'i* is a boat (or yacht), not a ship, it was not required for us, yet it was extremely useful. The display told us what ships were in the area, their name, speed, direction, bearing, how close they would come to us, and when. During my watch, one ship was going to run us over if we both stayed on the same course. I was able to call the ship by name, and the officer in charge and I were able to discuss the options, and they changed course. Although sailing vessels have the right of way when under sail, large ships cannot change course quickly, nor do many of them want to. In their case, speed is money. However, if we're under sail, we can't always change course easily either. It depends how much wind there is, how closely we're sailing into the wind, what the currents are, and what other obstacles there might be. That was why it was so important to keep watch and be able to judge the distance, bearing, speed, and closest point of arrival of other vessels long before that occurred, making Wayne's new "toy," the AIS, a splendid addition to our nav station.

Umbria as a Dream; Sicily as a Nightmare

Umbria: silvery green olive orchards as their leaves quivered in the breeze, luminous lavender fields, splashes of bright yellow sunflowers marching to the same drummer, darker green of the draping vineyards drifting along the hillsides, all topped by lovely, stone-built villages. The best olive oil in the world comes from Umbria—they actually have olive oil tastings—it's supremely sublime. Also, the wine is superb. Umbria is enough off the main tourist routes to feel natural, at ease, life lived as it has been and should be. I came into Umbria a stranger, but I felt that my presence didn't damage the natural rough linen feel of life there.

≈≈≈

My visit to Umbria happened in a circuitous way. My son Chad and his wife, Yasmin, were the first American Fulbright Scholars to be allowed in Pakistan since 9-11. Chad's PhD was in cultural anthropology with specific expertise in Pakistan, and Yasmin's PhD was in South Asian history with specific expertise in Bangladesh, India, and Pakistan. At the end of their fellowships in Pakistan, they spent two weeks in Umbria where I was able to visit them for six days in the small villa they had rented, and we toured extensively there. Then they came to visit us on the boat in Siracusa, Sicily.

My favorite of the Umbrian perching hillside villages was Bevagna. It was there that I had the best gourmet local food ever at Osteria Il Podesta. The dishes were provocative: a local specialty of snails in tomato sauce, veal with capers in olive oil, beef with an artichoke sauce, fresh, warm, home-baked bread, and a salad of crispy fresh young greens. It was a meal that lasted for hours; everything fit: the ambiance, the company, the restaurateur family, the sunlight, the sunflowers on the table, the wine, not to mention the superlative cuisine. The whole essence of Umbria was captured in that one experience. Not only food, but the art of eating has always been a part of the Italian experience. We weren't about to be exceptions.

One day Chad drove us to Florence. Although I had loved *Firenze* when there some thirty-six years ago, this time the city seemed quite shabby and down-at-heels to me, and the Duomo thoroughly overdone. Perhaps Florence was another "déjà vu doesn't work."

I returned to the boat in Siracusa via the night train from Rome. Going to Umbria I had a compartment—called *la donna comfort* set up for four women—all to myself, so it was quite restful and quiet, but on the return there were three more *donnas*, all Italian; I made what conversation I could, and we enjoyed a bit of camaraderie. The seats made up into four bunks, and a sheet and pillow were provided. It was affordable and comfortable, provided one was either a heavy sleeper or didn't have a cabin mate who snored.

≈≈≈

Chad and Yasmin had come to the boat as planned two days after I had returned. The next day Chad developed a high fever, terrible headache, and general weakness. We thought it might be a recurrence of the falciparum malaria—the worst kind that goes to the brain—that he had twice while in the Peace Corps in Mali, and that Wayne and I had in Honiara, Solomon Islands, although recurrences are rare. Because we were used to fending for ourselves medically, we treated him with the Chinese herbal medicine that does, in fact, cure it (but is not available in the Western world). We knew it worked since we had used it ourselves successfully.

But Chad got worse and worse. We took him to the emergency room at the hospital, but not one person spoke any English, and my Italian was not up to the complexity of the situation. They diagnosed him with swine flu and quarantined all of us immediately. We knew that wasn't it, and after frustratingly futile attempts at communication, we left with Chad. But Chad continued to get worse. Yasmin and I ran around old Siracusa in search of a doctor we had learned of who spoke English, but we had just missed him. We took Chad back to the emergency room. They kept him, but we had to leave. Later he reported it was the worst night of his life. Yasmin and I were both determined women. The next day, at the hospital we got the chief surgeon of infectious diseases to examine Chad. We followed the gurney as they took him down for a CAT scan; at least they would find out what it was. We both thought the right antibiotic would work and all would be well. Yasmin and I waited in the anteroom, painted the ugliest brown I had ever seen, and sat on the cracked brown vinyl chairs.

And then the doctor emerged.

"He's crying," Yasmin grabbed my arm, her fingers digging into my skin. "The doctor's crying."

With no effort to control his tears, in his broken English, he said, "It's serious; it's very, very, very serious." He pointed to the cracked, brown vinyl chairs we had just left. We sat again, reluctantly.

"Liver," he said. "Grande infection en liver." Then he said a word I didn't understand. I pulled out my Italian-English dictionary. He took it, skimming pages rapidly, he pointed. *Parassita:* Parasite.

I remembered the story Yasmin had told me years ago. Chad had returned from his first prolonged stay in Pakistan, a country and people that he loves. She had said, "I opened the door, and saw a stick standing there." He'd had dysentery, or maybe the parasite had started then.

My son was dying, and I couldn't speak enough Italian to stop it, to help, to do something, anything.

This was unbelievable. I have two sons and within three months they are both facing death?

Chad was diagnosed with amebiasas, a parasitical disease that had attacked his liver, causing numerous complications. He received multiple surgeries, procedures, and meds there, but didn't get better. It was touch and go with constant crises. First he was placed in a ward room with three other patients whose families brought food, tended them, nodded and commiserated with us, and, being not only Italian, but Sicilian, spoke loudly and often to everyone. Chad was miserable; we were exhausted.

At our repeated requests and because of the surgeons' concerns, Chad was transferred to another building for infectious disease; there it was much quieter and there were fewer patients. Yasmin politely insisted Chad be given a private room. "I will stay here," she declared, "but please bring me a thermos of tea." So I became the *chai walli*. I bought Yasmin an expensive cot because it was the only one available. I learned many useful Italian phrases, such as "*Lui ha intermittent forte mal di testa, la temperature fluttazione a trenta nove gradi centigrade, e dolore toracico. Lui ha grave dolore acuto al petto, quello che che lei pensa che sta causando? Capisco, anche ha pericardite.*" [He still has intermittent severe headache, temperature fluctuation up to 39 degrees C, and chest pain. He has severe chest pain; what do you think is causing that? I understand, he also has pericarditis.]

The assistant surgeon spoke excellent English and downloaded and printed two medical journal papers on this type of infection. They were not encouraging, but at least we knew what we were dealing with. Dr. S. L. Stanley, Jr., in a paper published in the medical journal, *The Lancet*, wrote, "Few pathogens are more aptly named than *Entamoeba histolytica....* Think of this parasite as a macrophage on steroids with pumped-up...capabilities invading human colonic mucosa, and occasionally... reaching the liver and causing fatal abscesses."

With the exception of the emergency room staff—and that because they thought we were about to infect them with a viral plague—everyone was caring and helpful. Yasmin made friends with a lovely lady who had lived in the United States and spoke excellent English and helped translate for us while Chad was in the ward. Her aged mother was a patient; we visited her as she lay curled up like a little bird in a nest of white sheets. Her small withered hands grasped ours and in breathless Italian she expressed her concern for Chad. What a beautiful language Italian is, no matter what is said, except the word *parassita.*

The Gift

Tiny, fragile birds,
little, brittle bones
that could break in a gust
of wind, curled up in your
small, carefully twisted
white nests of sheets
and lace handkerchiefs.

Your dry, raspy hands clasp mine
like a child taking her first steps,
but you are taking your last.

No, you're not even walking.
Soon you'll be flying; you could
you know, you're so feather-light.

Sometimes you're here; other times,
your eyes see a place
I will not know for some time.

Your words float out oddly,
feathers flittering about,
and soon you leave us this gift:
a pillow of wisdom
to sleep on.

After several days, one morning when Chad had seemed stable, we decided to rent a car and go with Jack and Joanie from S/V *JoanieD,* to Mt. Etna. Halfway there, I got an emergency call from Yasmin. With a thirty-minute warning, Yasmin had been told they were airlifting Chad to Palermo, and they had told her she could not go in the helicopter. Wayne did a quick u-turn, and we headed back for Siracusa. Once there, I jumped out of the car, ran up to their room, only to find no one there. Some of their things were lying about, some seemed as if they had been packed. The English-speaking surgeon was out. The Italian nurse told me "donna-aeroplano." But Yasmin had told me she couldn't go on the plane, so I was perplexed. I packed up their things, and after Wayne took Jack and Joanie back to the dinghy dock, we loaded everything into the little car.

Eventually, Yasmin called. It turned out there is a hospital in Palermo, ISMETT, that specializes in liver and cardiac disease and organ transplants and was associated with the University of Pittsburgh Medical Center in the United States. She was able to fly with Chad after the surgeon intervened and insisted the air medic unit take her too. The doctors had told her there was nothing more they could do for Chad in Siracusa and he needed more specialized care.

Wayne drove me to Palermo the next day and Jack and Joanie came along for the ride—not quite Mt. Etna, but a cross-island view of the countryside. I was relieved. ISMETT was a seriously real hospital. Chad was in the ICU, and it looked just like the ICU Pete had been in. Most of the professional medical staff spoke English, and there was actually an interpreter's office twenty-four hours a day, and an interpreter assigned to us during regular hours.

After a few days Chad had yet another procedure, the surgeons thought possibly the last. Then he could start to recover—and so could we. For the first time in over two weeks, we believed—not just hoped—that Chad would live. He was not yet well, but we thought now it was not just possible, but probable, although we were still not quite sure. Again, I thought, how strange that in a period of three months my two sons would be close to death.

≈≈≈

Because of Chad's illness, we had been anchored in Siracusa so long that the bottom of *Bali Ha'i* had so much of what we call *grass* (various forms of algae and seaweed) and barnacles that had grown on it, we could have started a fish hatchery or maybe a marsh.

While Chad was still in the Siracusa hospital, before being transferred to ISMETT, I had worn a

path between where we took the dinghy ashore and the hospital, passing stacks of deep purple mussels being transported from fishing boats to trucks. The fish stalls in the public market had more varieties of seafood than most aquariums, and the hawkers outshouted each other (as only Sicilians can do) with the value of their fresh-from-the-sea wares from anchovies to tuna and so many others including some rather odd-looking species. During these walks I had time to remember my last trip to Sicily.

Italy: The view from our boat at anchor of Ortigia, the *Città Vecchia* (Old City), an island that is part of Siracusa.

In 2004, rather than return to New Zealand with Wayne, I remained in the States for three months because there was to be a family reunion and celebration for my father who was ninety-five and starting to fail. During that time I had completed some contract editing and indexing, which I do on a part-time basis, visited friends, and took a trip to Sicily with my long-time friend, Liz, who had been my roommate in college. Wayne had been furious that I went to Sicily rather than return to New Zealand with him, but one US-Italy round-trip was infinitely less wearing than the multiple times I would have had to make the US-New Zealand, and US-Fiji trip. I supposed I also needed to not hear the sound of pop tops being torn off beer cans all day and to spend some time with other friends and family. I loved Sicily then and learned much about its history.

Sicily is the largest island in the Med and a veritable crossroads of conquerors and civilizations. The Phoenicians were the first recorded colonizers, but it was the Greeks who really put Sicily on the map. Siracusa was the most important Greek city-state outside of Greece itself, and Sicily has excellent well-preserved Greek ruins. Fortunately I saw most of them in 2004 as there was no time while we were anchored there because I was preoccupied with Chad's illness and then with Wayne's impatience to get on to Sardinia.

One day during the 2004 trip, Liz and I drove up to the hill village, Montalbano Elicona, from which my grandfather, Francisco Aliquo'—until he got to Ellis Island, where he became Frank Alico—had emigrated to the United States when he was fourteen. Montalbano Elicona is famous for Emperor Frederic II's castle built in 1233, which stands like some sturdy decoration lifting the village to new heights. My first task was to find relatives.

My father and stepmother had been there in the 1970s. My father was sure the cousins he met then were Mafioso. "They drove the biggest, blackest American car I've ever seen. How they got it around those damn narrow streets, I have no idea. They owned the movie theater, a few restaurants, the pool hall, and God knows what else. Of course they wined and dined us and insisted we stay, but I thought we should get the hell out of there as soon as possible."

Italy: An example of Sicily's well-preserved ancient ruins; this one at Agrigento.

I had no names, just the original spelling of Aliquo', but if they were proprietors of so much, someone should know them. I located one Aliquo' family who owned a café and restaurant side by side, but that was all. They did serve us a tasty lunch, and the adult son, who also sold cars in Messina, took us to the cemetery to look at family graves. I took pictures and made notes for the genealogical-minded in my family. If they had been Mafioso, which I doubted, it seemed to me they were now retired. Later my brother and I determined we were related through our great grandfathers, who had been brothers.

After returning from Sicily to New England and my family reunion—in fact, the last time I saw my father alive—I took that long flight back to the western South Pacific and all the rest that wound me up in Siracusa... again.

≈≈≈

My days in Palermo consisted of long hospital visits and sending emails from the hotel about Chad to his uncle, who was a doctor in Kansas and was most helpful in translating medical terms for us into layman's English and communicating with the Italian doctors on treatment. After five days in Palermo, Yasmin and I met again with the chief surgeon and the hospital's American coordinator. They were encouraging about Chad's prognosis. Then I visited with Chad, lunched with Yasmin at what had become our favorite trattoria across the street, visited with Chad again. Finally I was off to the bus station to return to Siracusa.

I turned sixty-nine that day, although there were times during the past weeks that I had felt like ninety-nine. Back on *Bali Ha'i*, my birthday dinner consisted of take-away lasagna and pistachio gelato, which I had insisted on, although it was fairly well melted by the time we got back to the boat. In my small journal, I had written, "Not a memorable birthday." On the contrary, it may not have been a happy one, but it was not one I'm likely to forget.

Wayne and I planned to sail around the south coast of Sicily to an anchorage near Agrigento, and I would return to Palermo from there, dependent on Chad's situation. Chad and Yasmin's insurance company was sending a medic to travel with Chad when he was stable enough to return to the United States, but we didn't know yet when that would be.

I still had to provision, and enjoyed my time in the markets for that. In addition to all the seafood, there were the creamy white and yellow cheeses, the dark green fresh basil, the bright purple aubergines, the red and green peppers, the various types of tomatoes, not to mention the sundried tomatoes soaked in flavorful olive oil and basil, earthy wild mushrooms, and numerous types of black and green olives, all mouth-watering. The wine was as cheap as bottled water, cheaper than beer, and very palatable. Yes, eating was a major activity for Sicilians and visitors alike, and what one wants to take time for.

Two days later, Wayne and I were up at 5:00 a.m. to leave for Cape Passero at the southeast tip of Sicily. The same time the next day, we set sail for Licata, where we had a calm anchorage. Except for a few boxy, ugly, high-rise apartments, Licata was a charming town with an interesting Sicilian version of Italianate architecture incorporating hints of Byzantine, Romanesque, Baroque, Gothic, and Classical styles. One building I particularly liked had thirty-six balcony balusters, each one different alternating between a gargoyle-type face and a cherubic one. We spent three nights there for a little R&R, then on to Porto Empedocle, birthplace of Pirandello, and from where I planned to return to Palermo. As in much of Sicily, no one spoke English. We inquired about the bus schedule to Palermo, where I would stay until Chad was well enough to return to the United States. With much gesturing, smatterings of Italian on my side, smatterings of English from the Italian gentleman who took it upon himself to help us, we determined that a bus was leaving the next morning at 6:50 a.m. It turned out to be a comfortable and easy trip.

Italy: In Licata, Sicily, the alternating balusters.

bit of space taken up, like most European cities. This section of Palermo was a busy place except for Sundays when everyone was at church, presumably, and every day between about 1:30 to 4:00 p.m. when they were eating and resting.

Although most of my time in Palermo was spent in a triangle from the hospital, my comfortable little hotel, and the trattoria, where I would get carryout to take back to the hospital, I did venture forth to do some errands for Chad and get a wedding gift for one of my nieces. My walks enabled me to see once again the interesting incorporation of Islamic architecture into Norman churches and public buildings. To me, the Duomo, founded in 1184, seemed to incorporate all those architectural styles I mentioned for Licata in one building! A slight exaggeration, but it does encompass Gothic, Catalan, Norman, and Islamic design elements. In Palermo, even in the newer areas where the streets were built to accommodate cars, I found vehicles parked willy-nilly on sidewalks, double-parked, every

Italy: The Palermo Duomo and its mixture of styles.

Finally it was agreed that Chad could be released, and a few days later the medic arrived and familiarized Chad and Yasmin with the procedures for their travel. Chad remained weak, but clearly improving. His entourage from his hospital room to the airport van included a hospital nurse pushing his wheelchair, the medic, Yasmin, me, our so helpful ISMETT interpreter, and a fellow carrying several suitcases and packages— quite a procession. At the airport, the medic, who does this sort of transport all the time, was most efficient at getting Chad an airport wheelchair, checking their luggage, obtaining their boarding passes, before whisking them through security where I said my good-byes.

Meanwhile, a continent away, Pete had just been released from the rehabilitation facility. His wrists were still not healed, and he had continuing physical therapy to do, but was recovering and had a great attitude. Chad was going to the hospital in Chapel Hill, North Carolina, where he and Yasmin lived, and all would be well in my world. But part of me was empty, wounded. I made my way to the main bus station to return to Wayne and *Bali Ha'i*. Standing in the shade of a building waiting for what I hoped was the right bus, a pigeon shat on me, a drop on my head and much more on the back of my blouse, which I couldn't reach to clean off. It was not the only shit to happen to me that day. Wayne met me at Porto Empedocle quite drunk.

"God damn it; how could you do this to me?" I yelled at him. I was emotionally and physically exhausted. Now that the crisis with Chad was over, I perceived Wayne's behavior as personal desertion, although I knew intellectually that it was his own issue.

He went into lock-down mode. The sparkle in his blue eyes turned to ice, his face impassive. No answer. Nothing. We returned to *Bali Ha'i*.

The next morning, I provisioned, and after getting everything stored on the boat, we went ashore for lunch. We got shanghaied into a trattoria by Mama, the well-proportioned proprietor and cook, who tempted us with a *piatti di mare* (fish cake) that was *deliciozo*. After a satisfying lunch of spaghetti *vongole*, one of Wayne's favorites, and a conch and shrimp salad, we returned to the boat and hauled the dinghy on deck. After I tied the bow down and was hurrying back to the cockpit, I tripped over the jackline, flew over the cockpit coaming (the side wall of the cockpit), hitting my ribs on the way, ending in a crumpled heap on the cockpit sole (floor). I screamed for Wayne.

"Just get up," he said.

"I can't," I cried. "I think my leg is broken, and maybe a rib or two."

"Your leg doesn't look broken and ribs aren't serious. Here give me your hand, I'll help you up."

I stood; clearly my leg wasn't broken. I was broken.

Fragments

Our parents die
before us, but not
our children.

That's the way it's supposed to be.
When the cycle is broken,
we are too.

Our lives are torn asunder; we become verses
in the Old Testament. Beliefs support or fail,
we alone choose.

Integration, coordination, harmony:
these are not words
we can understand.

We jangle discordantly, a cacophony
of bells keeps us awake,
we grasp at meaning.

We are the glass half empty.
Tears fill our cheeks,
we have a winter full of sobs to release

It is said that time
heals all wounds;
we know
that is a lie.

My sons didn't die, but I knew this emotion.

≈≈≈

The next morning we were up at 2:25 a.m. to
motor-sail on to the Egadi Islands off the northwest
corner of Sicily. First we went to Favignana and an
anchorage not even listed in our cruising guide. Wayne
had thought it would work well after looking at our
electronic charts. He was right, but half the boating
public of Sicily also thought so. If I thought cars were all
over the place in Palermo, here yachts were all over the
place, every size and shape crammed into the anchorage
absolutely chock-a-block so most of the boats had their
fenders on. It was Times Square on New Year's Eve,

but with boats instead of people. After moving a few
times, trying to find a safe place, we finally picked up
anchor at 6:00 p.m. and left for Levanzo, another smaller
island, where we anchored for the night. No sooner
were we there when another boat came up and anchored
quite close, but it was infinitely more comfortable than
Favignana. We call such action the *herd instinct*. We can
be the only boat in a large anchorage and the next boat
(unless experienced cruisers) will anchor nearby.

There was some interesting exploring to be done on
Levanzo, but the winds were right so we left early for an
overnight passage to Sardinia. The winds were not only
from the right direction for a change, but quite strong so
we had an excellent sail with our headsail alone for several
hours and no motor! Our mainsail had been incapacitated
when our boom had fallen off the mast in Siracusa (for
the second time; the first, in Thailand). The system,
recommended by the builders of our boat, had been a
constant problem. Leisure Furl (the manufacturers of
the system in which the mainsail furls inside the boom)
provided an inadequate piece for repairs the first time we
had this problem. Wayne had made arrangements to have
it fixed yet again in Palma, Mallorca.

The wind, the sailing, the sea comforted me. This
time, I was quite relieved to watch the Sicilian islands
disappear in the horizon behind us.

Italy: Along the coast of Sardinia, an ancient watchtower, like those seen frequently sailing in the Med.

Sardinia and the Nuragic Mysteries

Our first anchorage was at Porto Malfatano, a pleasant area with no town, but a popular beach. We climbed up to an ancient watchtower like the ones we had seen all over the Med; many were Venetian, some earlier.

I actually found some decent snorkeling and saw several different species of fish, some even slightly colorful, as well as a black eel with yellow spots and an orange starfish. The seascape consisted of rocks covered with various forms of algae, nothing like the Red Sea or the South Pacific with their infinitely variable, fascinating, and colorful coral reefs.

After three nights we moved on to Calasetta on the island of Sant'Antioco in the southwest corner of Sardinia. One day we took the ferry over to Carloforte on Isola di San Pietro, an upscale town reminding me of Capri, exceptionally clean and pretty with fancy, expensive shops and many tourists. The little I saw of Sardinia was much cleaner than Sicily. Both islands are nothing like the Italian mainland nor each other and could be separate countries in terms of culture and even their dialects.

Sardinia has a fascinating prehistoric culture called the Nuragic. We rented a car and drove to the largest, most excavated site, Su Nuraxi di Barumini in southern Sardinia. There was no written record of these people, but many building sites were left. The only mention of them by name was from a section of a Roman clay tablet stating how difficult it was to fight against these Nuragic people in their stone towers. Some of these buildings were at least three stories high with each floor having a conical roof, all built of stone, and clearly required engineering skills to construct. There are about seven thousand known sites, but archeologists think there were over thirty thousand of these complexes on Sardinia of this Bronze Age culture, which dates from at least 1500 BCE.

Sardinia, like Sicily, Cyprus, and the Balearics, was invaded by Phoenicians, Carthaginians, Romans, Arabs, Byzantines, Normans, and Spaniards, and I'm probably leaving a few out. Nevertheless, the inner mountainous regions, to which the indigenous population fled when attacked, were never subjugated by any of those forces. Today, it remains an area of isolated villages, shepherds, and its own distinctive customs.

We left Sardinia on August 24 for an overnight passage to Menorca in Spain's Balearic Islands. It was an end as well as a beginning.

Italy: The author standing just inside a structure at Su Nuraxi to give a sense of its height.

13

The Western Med: Entrance as an Exit

This Arabic-Islamic science and technology, reaching Europe 'via Sicily and Spain' awoke her from the Dark Ages in which she was slumbering.
—Stanford Cobb, *Islamic Contributions to Civilization*

Spain: Rewritten Stories

I would love to rewrite the story of my life; wouldn't most of us? But we can't. Why then, can nations, historians, the keepers of a country's culture rewrite theirs as they so often do? I bring up Spain, not because she was unique, but it was happening before my eyes.

In Ponsa, Mallorca, a noisy, several-hour dramatization with boats, cardboard swords, and a hundred or so costumed kids reenacted the Spanish expelling the Moors in 1492. This pseudo-historic pageant took place in and around our anchorage. Actually the Spaniards didn't so much kick out the Moors as killed many and made the others slaves, which they also did to the Jews. The Spaniards conveniently forgot that the Moors had brought civilization to the Iberian peninsula after conquering the Visigoths and contributed art, science, commerce, and culture, and had lived in peace with their Christian neighbors for centuries.

The use of children convinced me that the Spanish perception of the Moors (and other non-

Catholic Spaniards) was a misplaced conviction that would be carried on for generations to their unrelieved deprivation—ignorance is not bliss. It requires extensive imagination and rewriting of history to consider the Moors and Arabs as infidels. As Europe emerged from the Dark Ages, cities were materializing, crafts were developing, guilds were forming, but the Roman Catholic Church still held great power, and literacy and learning were confined to the clerical hierarchy. Ancient Greek and Roman literature and knowledge were considered pagan and were destroyed. Whereas for Islam, education was a key for all the people. Mosques and madrassas (schools) were built together. Mohammad understood from Allah that "Seeking of knowledge is incumbent upon every Muslim."[1] One of the five questions that "a man shall be asked...on the day of resurrection" includes "what was it that he did with the knowledge that he had."[2]

Islam was always a religion of knowledge and incorporated what Muslims learned from other cultures,

including China, India, and other areas. They had been extensive traders and incorporated into their culture much that the Greeks had discovered centuries before. Historic Islam, even its militant side, never destroyed libraries, learning, scrolls, knowledge. Islamic learning included medicine, astronomy, chemistry, geography, navigation, and mathematics, among other fields, and diverse innovations such as the use of paper, the determination of latitude and longitude, the use of coffee, the water mill and windmill, and so much else we take for granted today as Western. Europe's emergence from the Dark Ages was, in fact, thanks to their inheritance from the Arab world. This was a gift from the Moors, before they were victims of Queen Isabella's ethnic and religious cleansing. Charlemagne may not have been doing France such a favor when he defeated them centuries before. Ironically, today's fundamentalist Muslims have turned their backs on one of the basic tenets of Islam—education, as well as several other principles of that faith.

Menorca, our first Spanish landfall, is the eastern-most Balearic island, separated from mainland Spain by not only water, but language, customs, and the choice of alcohol—the latter being gin, not the wine for which Spain is famous. Like Sardinia, Menorca has an interesting Bronze Age culture found nowhere else. First was the Pre-Talayotic era from about 2500 to 1500 BCE, a simple culture with stone huts like inverted rowboats, communal burials, and basic pottery.

About 1500 BCE, increased population, complex structures, villages, hierarchical society, water systems including cisterns and canals, and trading relationships with other Mediterranean societies appeared. For example, a statue of Imhotep from Egypt was found, as well as Greek, Phoenician, and Iberian artifacts. This era is called the Talayotic for the *talayots*, which are cone-shaped, stone tower structures that exemplify the period. In one site we visited, Torre d'en Galmés, there were three *talayots* on a hill in the midst of a large settlement. They provided a view of that village, and of several other Talayotic sites in the area.

The Talayotic society had *taulas*, which archeologists today conjecture may have been worship areas. These *taulas* have a huge stone *T*—at one site the upright stone is ten feet tall—which archeologists think was possibly an altar. The individual houses had multiple rooms and stone ceilings with large stones resting on a central stone column. Some were quite complex. There was also a public area, possibly for markets, meetings, or maybe the local café where the men could hang out and talk, like today. The Talayotic culture lasted until the Roman conquest in 123 BCE; then the people, their structures, and their culture were enveloped by Rome.

Jumping some seventeen hundred years to the eighteenth century, when from a poor, backwater, remote island, frequently looted by pirates, Menorca changed radically as the Brits dominated the island. Menorca was well-positioned for all the wars among the Brits, Dutch, Holy Roman Empire, French, and Spanish, and all those pirates and privateers. The city of Mao (or Mahon), now the capital of Menorca, is located within a huge, well-protected natural harbor. The British built Fort Marlborough at the entrance to the harbor between 1710 and 1726. It was a fascinating place to visit with well-developed presentations as we wandered through its labyrinth. Among other techniques, the Brits built tunnels with countermines, which they could blow up if enemies tried to dig their way in. The fort came under siege twice—once by the French and once by the Spanish—but was never taken. Spain gained the island in the Treaty of Amiens in 1802.

Spain: The author by a Talayotic *taula* in Menorca.

The Brits also built a large hospital and quarantine area on an island in the harbor, which was being restored when we were there. As we dinghied into the main harbor, we noticed across from the hospital island a small graveyard; we spun over to take a look. It was surrounded by a brightly whitewashed wall with graves of American naval personnel and one for the wife of an American seaman dating from the 1820s through the 1870s. It was interesting to speculate about how and why they were there. It appeared to be well maintained, we guessed by

American expats and the U.S. consular office.

A huge fortress, named for Isabella II, opposite Fort Montgomery, was built by the Spanish in 1848 as both the French and the Brits used the harbor to take on water and provisions, and the Spanish were concerned that they may want more than that. It took twenty-five years to complete, and like many war-related projects today, by the time it was finished it was outdated.

The Spanish Civil War started when the elected government was overthrown by the generals in 1936, who declared General Francisco Franco y Bahamonde the country's new leader. The Republicans fought back with help from the International Brigade. In April 1937, Hitler bombed Guernica on market day killing hundreds of civilians intentionally and providing the subject matter for Picasso's famous painting. He used his support of Franco as a training ground for his air force and military armaments and strategies. It is unlikely Franco would have won without Hitler's help. It all went downhill after Guernica until the Republicans surrendered in April 1939, most of them slaughtered or jailed in usual fascist form. No one talks about it today. Franco died in 1975, and free elections returned in 1977.

As I wandered through this historical site, what I thought about was how Franco had used it for political prisoners. Menorca had been a Republican stronghold. No doubt, Franco rounded up many who were tortured and killed on the grounds on which I walked. How did the countries that became the Allies in World War II let such a fascist come to power with help from Hitler and Mussolini, is a question for contemplation. If we had confronted Hitler in Spain, would there have been a World War II?

≈≈≈

As much as the history, cultures, and cuisines of the Med entranced me, sailing there was a nightmare. Although certainly there was ship traffic, it was the monster yachts that dominated. There are many people with much money, and many have yachts with excessive chrome and numerous crew to keep it polished. It seemed a competition of ostentation, bad taste, and pretension. The waste and misuse of resources was appalling to me.

While this bothered me philosophically, personally I was still recovering from the stress of Peter and Chad's near-death experiences. Wayne's remoteness was a visceral problem that I was unable to deal with in any successful way. To add to this, anchorages continued to be crowded, and with our 63-foot yacht and 7-foot draft (how far her keel extends below the waterline), being able to anchor successfully and safely was increasingly problematic. I loved sailing and I loved Wayne, the person he used to be, who had been fun and affectionate. I had enjoyed his dry, subtle sense of humor, and engagement in life. At some level, I was reliving my thousand-page story of childhood abuse at the hands of my father, attempts to hold life together, as the oldest child caring for and protecting my younger siblings and my mother. At this point, I couldn't change anything, not Wayne, not even myself, the only one I really did have control over.

The Museum of History and Art

The days float along
each one a separate room in the museum
of historical events and periods of art.
I remember the Dark Ages,

that's when you started shouting.
I used to yell when I was angry;
you never did, until then.

Of course, the Middle Ages, that's—
well, this is a bit personal—but when
we stopped making love all the time.

I think the Impressionist period was when
you were drunk every day.
There was a haze about you, a cloudiness,
but not nearly as attractive as Giverny
or even Mont Saint-Victoire
with its rocks and cypress trees
or were they cedars?

The Surreal period is when life really fell apart.
The days were in blocks, mostly cubes,
which led to the Cubists, of course,
but also squares and rectangles,
and even some bridge-shaped blocks,
they led me ashore and were green, as I remember.

After all that, I may return to the prehistoric,
perhaps the Talayotic on Menorca. I would sit
in the top story
of one of their conical roofed structures
by the stone-arched opening facing west. There,
I would write poetry on a clay tablet, but then
it wouldn't be prehistoric anymore. I would record
in odes and villanelles,
although they hadn't been invented yet,
all the important events—births, deaths,
and who made that fanciful bronze figurine

that would be found a few thousand years later. It will all end when the Romans come in 123 BCE. And then we move on again.

The days float along
each one a separate room in the museum
of historical events and periods of art.

And so we floated on to Mallorca, where we anchored in Pollensa, Porto Soller, and Ponsa before heading into Palma for repairs. Nevertheless, I could still enjoy well-prepared local cuisine and out-of-the-way explorations. Highlights included a great Mallorcan meal at The Cellar in Pollensa and a fun old-fashioned train ride from Porto Soller to Soller (all of about six kilometers away) where I visited their free museum in the old train station with works by Joan Miró and several of Picasso's ceramics.

In Palma, yachts have to go to a marina, so we went first to Real Club Nautico, which had many amenities including a gym and large pool, although it was a long walk to get there, or to anywhere for that matter. We hated going to marinas in the Med because we had to back tie, that is, back into a berth with no finger piers on the side. We did not have a bow thruster, and we did have a folding prop; the lack of the first and the existence of the second made it difficult to back our boat in tight quarters, although, of course, Wayne was quite adept at steering *Bali Ha'i*. Also, we needed a passerelle (like a gangplank). Wayne had bought a used one in Turkey, but it was difficult to put up and not always quite long enough. In addition, one needed deep pockets.

Spain: Welcome aboard *Bali Ha'i* via the passerelle.

I quickly learned my way around Palma and found the usual excellent public market with an olive seller and fifty different kinds of olives. There was very acceptable wine I could buy from a barrel, decanted into whatever jar I wanted to bring, cheaper than bottled water, not that I would buy bottled water anyway after witnessing so much plastic trash everywhere on land and sea. I also found the fresh produce I had come to expect since Turkey, as well as fresh eggs, cuttlefish, and chicken that tasted like chicken (rarely found in the United States in my experience).

My days were spent doing laundry, errands, sightseeing, swimming, and working out. Fancy marinas have lots of amenities! But it turned out we were not allowed to have the mast worked on there because we couldn't have any external sanding or painting done—it might mess up the chrome and paint jobs of the monster yachts nearby. After six days we had to move to a dock that was more like a boatyard. From there it was easier to get to the market, to the center of Palma, to take great walks along the quay, and we had a beautiful view of Palma's amazing cathedral. I had kept my swimming pool and gym pass so I had the best of both worlds. Of all the places we'd been holed up for repairs—Pago Pago in American Samoa and Honiara in the Solomon Islands come to mind—this was by far the most pleasant; in fact Palma shouldn't be mentioned in the same breath as those particular horrendous anchorages.

The architecture in Palma was fascinating to me. The Spanish may have kicked the Moors out, but many buildings, both old and new, bore the recognizable Moorish imprint of arches; flower, leaf, and vine motifs; and the use of interior patios. Also visible were examples of Romanesque, Gothic, Renaissance with its classical Italianate look, Baroque, and Modern with the work of Antoni Gaudi and his disciples. I found it a lovely city, particularly the old town. There were many parks, separate bicycle and walking paths, diverse public sculpture including pieces by Alexander Calder and Joan Miró, and numerous art galleries. Palma's artists celebrated their annual Night of Art our last week there, during which all the art galleries hosted open houses, many with the artists. I thoroughly enjoyed it and met two intriguing artists.

One day, I took a public bus to Miró's museum, housed on the grounds of his studio. I wandered around expecting him to come back at any moment as it is just as he left it with half-finished paintings and sculptures, brushes and paints on various work surfaces. It seemed to me he had just stepped out for a cup of café. I found his sketches on the walls of the studio about the sculpture he was designing particularly enchanting. Mallorca wears its art on its sleeve, but it comes from its heart.

Spain: Miró's studio on Mallorca.

Palma's pièce de résistance is its cathedral. Located just above a lovely park with a large pond and fountain, I often walked around it and toured the interior. It's remarkable. There are sixty-one stained glass windows. One, from the 1300s, is thirty-six feet wide, and represents the morning star, which, they say, is the symbol of Christ risen. It and the window at the opposite end above the main door looked Islamic in their design and could just as easily have been in Istanbul. One of the smaller windows, which is not to say it's small, was so suffused with light, it was impossible to accept the colors as real; they were figuratively heavenly.

The most amazing aspect of this cathedral for me was the Gaudi centerpiece suspended above the altar. He worked on it from 1904 to 1914. Bear in mind that the ceiling is 144 feet high. The centerpiece is a colossal, spiral mobile of lights with a three-dimensional scene at the top of Christ on the cross, but not bleeding profusely like most Catholic crucifixes. Although on the cross, it is as if he really is ascending to heaven. Below him are two women, probably Mary and Mary Magdalene, standing among reeds. There is a tapestry suspended behind. The cathedral was one of those rare places that fed my spiritual soul, although I'm not Catholic.

Spain: Palma's cathedral.

Spain: Gaudi's ethereal hanging sculpture of the Crucifixion in the Palma cathedral.

The work on *Bali Ha'i* was finally done, and we left Palma on October 1 after almost four weeks there. We stopped at some of the other Balearics for about a week. I had heard about mud baths on S'Espalmador near the island of Formentera, and after a long walk, which turned out to be the wrong way around, we found them. We slathered on the mud wearing next to nothing. We let the mud dry as we walked back to the beach, and then went into the sea to wash it off. Our skin was like a baby's. Wayne even liked it. Not any old mud will do; it has to be a special kind. The results are amazing, but it doesn't last forever. We met up for a couple of days with Steve and Karyn, old friends from Florida, who had been sailing around the British Isles and the Med, and we took them to the mud baths too. It was a wonderful visit with them, and I hated to say good-bye. I think it reminded me of how many people I'd said good-bye to in these almost ten years, many of whom had become dear friends whom I will probably never see again.

Gibraltar: The Rock Incarnate

Entrance/Exit. For me, this was stepping off the flat earth, not geographically, but, emotionally, into the unknown. It was one ending. Another ocean wasn't the issue. The approaching conclusion was the issue. Ten years. How could I adjust to life on land, not rocking to sleep at night at sea, not learning some necessary words in a new language every few months or weeks, not figuring out where to buy whatever we needed. Not moving on. Not sailing. Not being at sea in the middle of the night

with nothing of humanness around, just that pure, silent, special place, some flashing bioluminescence in our wake. But first we had to pass the Rock. It was a final grace, a symbolic, iconic achievement, given that we had come to it from the west, some 36,500 nautical miles.

The Rock was impressive, no matter how we viewed it: from the sea as we sailed past, from our anchorage off La Linea, Spain, from walking across the tarmac of the airport as we exited Spain and entered Gibraltar looking up, from its very top looking out at the flat expanse of the Spanish countryside or the sea to North Africa, or from within its internal tunnels built for defense and protection.

Gibraltar: The Rock as we sail around it.

Gibraltar: View from the top of the Rock.

and winding around the curved streets, we found the cable car site, and rode it up, then hiked across the top of the Rock and into the caves and tunnels, contemplated the view, photographed the macaques, then wound our way back down along trails.

The Rock dominated the scene. We couldn't step up into our cockpit at anchor without commenting, "The Rock is covered by clouds today." "Now we can see the peak!" "Quickly look, the light is reflecting off the cliffs." "Wow, we can see the tunnel cannon stands!"

It is incredibly fortressed, with British names—Montagu Bastion, Wellington Front—emblazoned on various components of this citadel. It is a city of massive gray walls, cannon, and over thirty-three miles of tunnels carved inside the Rock with periodic embrasures for cannon.

It was an odd place. There was the customary British supermarket, Morrison's—thank heavens, with its Dijon mustard, muesli, biscuits, and tea. Most of the population speaks Spanish first, then English. The word *gibberish* is allegedly derived from the multiplicity of languages used in Gibraltar, where we heard English, Castilian, and Catalonian words in one sentence. Many Spaniards crossed the border every day to work in Gibraltar, but many also live on Gibraltar itself. The border was closed from 1969 to 1975 because of disagreements between Spain and Great Britain. Families were separated, jobs were lost. The reality in personal suffering must have been a thousand-fold greater than the diplomatic swaggering of the two nations involved. To me, it didn't feel Brit at all. It feels like the Rock—the people seem incidental. The Barbary apes, which are not

The sheer size of the Rock is majestic and imposing as it rises some 1,475 feet from the sea on three sides and from land only a few feet higher than the sea on the north. Its position at the northern Mediterranean Sea side of the Straits of Gibraltar is nothing short of immensely strategic. Its size and shape, its geological composition (mostly limestone), and its guardian role were the characteristics that still define it.

To get to Gibraltar, we walked past Spanish and British Immigration and Customs, flashed our passports, then headed across the airport tarmac, which stands on reclaimed ground just north of the Rock, but within Gibraltar. When planes arrived or departed, the gates went down, the sirens started, and the police kept everyone behind the barricades. After crossing the tarmac apes at all, but tailless macaques, may be the most at home. Nothing is as it seems, except the Rock itself.

Wandering about, reading plaques and local history, and talking to locals, it was easy to gain an understanding of its history. The Romans fortified the Rock, but didn't settle there. With the waning of Roman civilization about 400 CE, the Vandals and Goths (Visigoths) swept down from the north, destroying most everything in their path. Then in 711, the Muslim Berber, Tarik ibn Ziyad, landed at the Rock and used it strategically to commence his takeover of Iberia. The name Gibraltar is derived from *Jebel Tarik* (the mountain of Tarik). From then until 1462—with a short break from 1309 to 1333, when the Kingdom of Castile took it—the Moors controlled Gibraltar and much of Iberia. The castle built in 1160 by the Moorish ruler still stands.

It was a Spanish fight for succession that led to the Brits controlling Gibraltar. In the spirit of the usual European free-for-all, the Brits and Dutch sided with the Austrian Charles III vying for the Spanish kingship versus Philip of Anjou. A British-Dutch force took Gibraltar ostensibly for Charles, but as that war drew to a close in 1713, Great Britain saw the strategic potential of the Rock and in the Treaty of Utrecht gave up Menorca for Gibraltar in perpetuity. They immediately started to fortify it. There were fourteen sieges against the Rock altogether; the last one being the Great Siege, from 1779–1803. It was a remarkable feat requiring cunning, bravery, and the characteristic British perseverance that saved Gibraltar for them. It was during this siege that the tunnels were started and used to aim the guns not only farther out, but down. In the United States during World War II, we were encouraged to grow victory gardens—I remember my mother's—to supplement food supplies. The commander at Gibraltar had done this 140 years earlier.

Among other inventions of warfare, the Brits' *hot potatoes* were a clever addition. The Spanish had developed some barges using several feet of wood, then packed them with straw and wet sand so cannon balls couldn't penetrate them. The hot potatoes were cannon balls heated until red hot, then fired onto the barges, which set them on fire. The Brits destroyed all the special Spanish barges this way. The Rock has never been taken since 1704.

Additional tunnel space and room for an underground—more accurately under-rock—hospital and small city were developed during World War II, although Gibraltar was never directly attacked. Standing in that area and listening to the guide's stories reminded me somewhat of the underground cities of Cappadocia, but this was more like an amphitheater, an unusually large cave-like space. Gibraltar was extremely important in keeping the Straits open for the Allies and as a preparation center for the attack on German Field Marshall Erwin Rommel and his forces in North Africa. Slowly but surely after that war, Gibraltar was given more autonomy and democratic rights. The Spanish continue to make a claim for it.

We were told the story that the Brits will leave when the apes leave—in spite of all the graffiti telling them to leave now—so the local Brit officials continue to make sure there are plenty of apes. We saw these Barbary macaques hanging around in certain areas on top of the Rock, begging for food—and sometimes attacking if the food was visible, but not forthcoming—although they looked quite well fed. They used their leisure time to search for lice and fleas on each other.

Wayne had found a marvelous small family-run café in La Linea with terrific food. We returned so often, the owners greeted us like old friends. Wayne even learned a few more words of Spanish to use there. He was a menu reader. As we walked down a street, he had to stop and check out the selections and prices of every café we passed. I kept walking. Whatever he picked was where we would go. He was adept—almost always, but I still remember the turkey tails in Pago Pago and the rubber octopus in the San Blas—at finding small hole-in-the-wall type restaurants with cheap, but delicious, local food.

≈≈≈

When we sailed away, it felt like the last hurrah. We entered the Atlantic—our last ocean. Although we hadn't sailed across the Atlantic before, it seemed nothing compared to the Pacific, the Indian, the Red Sea, the Andaman Sea, the Gulf of Carpentaria also known as the Washing Machine, even parts of the Caribbean, such as Kick-'em Jenny Passage. I knew the Atlantic. As a child I swam in it almost every summer. We had sailed in its coastal waters in our previous boats. It was just a place to get through to finish. Like all bodies of water, it could be nasty for sailing, although it is called the Pond by sailors. It was the final act. And Gibraltar represented all that for me. It was so solid, so there. This circumnavigation felt like my Gibraltar. It was almost too real, too intense at times, too voluminous. It was not easily categorized. It couldn't be pigeonholed in a mental, multidrawer rolltop desk.

Gibraltar was the passage point. It felt over. My conflicting emotions battled for supremacy, but nothing won. My feelings were a confused sea: joy and grief, pride of accomplishment and anxiety about what next on land, something gained and something lost. We sailed on through the Straits of Gibraltar into the Atlantic Ocean. The Romans had left us with sound advice as we clawed our way through the Straits in *Bali Ha'i*, *Ne plus ultra* (nothing further beyond, i.e., go at your own peril).[3]

14

Entering the Atlantic: A Multitude of Drops

"And only as you gasp your dying breath shall you understand your life amounted to no more than one drop in a limitless ocean!"

"Yet, what is any ocean but a multitude of drops?"
—David Mitchell, *Cloud Atlas*

Morocco: Kindness and Calligraphy

Rabat is the King's city and the capital, and the only place for a yacht is at the King's marina, but not tied up to the King's dock—that's only for the King's boats. There are no natural harbors on that part of Morocco's west coast, so we had to choose an entrance time wisely. The process involved surfing over not one, but two, sandbars; passing the kasbah in the old medina; motoring a little way up a narrow, dredged channel in the Bou Regreg River; turning left, and then we had arrived at the King's marina.

If the swell was too high or the tide too low, we could not have entered and would have to keep going. Wayne had checked the weather and thought we would be able to get in. We called the marina as we approached the river, and their pilot appeared promptly in a large inflatable. He instructed us to follow him exactly, which we did. As we surfed through the entrance to the river,

we never saw less than fourteen feet for a depth and since *Bali Ha'i* draws a little over 7 feet, it was no problem. But the previous day, a yacht, which had been through the entrance before, didn't get an answer from the marina, so attempted it themselves, broached, and almost capsized. All four family members were thrown into the water. One son managed to get back on the boat and turn it around; the others were rescued, the mother sustaining some injuries. Our entrance, while slightly exciting for us, was nothing for the cruiser gossip mill.

We were side-tied to the end of the dock next to the King's pier, as *Bali Ha'i* was too long for a slip. This side of the river is actually in Salé, now a suburb of Rabat, but originally a Phoenician colony in the sixth century BCE. Long before that, it was at least a stopping-off place for someone, as archeologists found fossilized hominoid bones dating to four hundred thousand years ago. The Berber tribes became a force about 2000 BCE. They were taken over later by the Romans then the Germanic Vandals tribe, and in the early 700s CE the Arabs with their predominant religion, Islam. In spite of all these changing cultures, the Berbers maintained their own tribal customs, and continue to do so. The isolation of many Berber villages in the Atlas Mountains, which are still difficult to access in many areas, has enabled the maintenance of their culture, much like the Sardinians who were able to escape assimilation in their rugged mountains.

Morocco: Entering the Bou Regreg River, past the kasbah in Rabat.

For me, finding these serendipitous parallels in history was not only like solving puzzles, but part of my uncovering of this complex world we have inherited from so many before us. The main tapestry of both human and

Earth's histories are readily accessible, but the individual threads are more obscure and less easily uncovered, yet add layers of understanding and awareness.

In 1777, the progressive Sultan Sidi Muhammad recognized the independence of the United States of America, one of the first countries to do so. He wanted to shift from an economy of a paid army collecting taxes from the people to maritime trade, so he gave U.S. ships—and those from a few other specific countries—the right to stop in Moroccan ports and to not be harassed by Moroccan corsairs, that is, government-sponsored pirates. A little over one hundred years later, in the shifting point/counterpoint of European power, France ended up with the majority of what is Morocco today as a protectorate, with Spain controlling a few isolated areas as part of the carving up of Africa by foreign powers. The only visible—actually audible—remnant is the French language. In 1956, Morocco finally regained its independence as a constitutional monarchy.

≈≈≈

Casablanca is one of my favorite movies of all time. It is the epitome of what a movie should be. I had to go there, and, of course, to Rick's Café. I knew the movie was shot on a back lot in Burbank, California and that Rick's was based on a dive in Tangier, but Casablanca was what the movie said. Casablanca, as the movie indicated, was a stop on the contorted path from France and Eastern Europe to Lisbon and from there to the Americas to escape the horrors of World War II. There is a Rick's Café now, created by a former U.S. diplomat, somewhat loosely adapted from the film set. Frankly, I would have done it exactly. In the lounge where we were seated before a large screen, the movie unfolded before us. Unfortunately we didn't hear Sam play it again; nevertheless, we thoroughly enjoyed ourselves.

Morocco: The author, her husband, and cruising friends enjoy a visit to Rick's Café in Casablanca.

us all, although rarely acknowledged as such, especially by organized religions.

Morocco: A peaceful interior courtyard at the Hassan II Mosque.

We and another cruising couple had taken the train from Salé to Casablanca and first visited the Hassan II Mosque—the only one in Morocco that non-Muslims are allowed to enter. It is a newly built, huge, elegant temple to Allah, who is the same God revered by Jews and Christians. Although the third largest in the world, the mosque radiates a sense of spirituality and beauty, rather than size. While I am not Muslim, Catholic, or of another specific faith, I have found a sense of spirituality in certain religious shrines. Although I don't participate in their belief systems, this mosque; the cathedral in Palma; and a small, hand-built stone, simple chapel in a remote area of the Bahamas, exude a peacefulness to me. It makes me feel there is a universal spiritual unity that is part of

After our day trip to Casablanca, I spent a few frustrating days on the Internet arranging a land trip to Fes and Chefchaouen. My French was better than my Spanish, but after coming from Italy and Spain and not using French for several years, I was rusty and confusing my languages. Moroccans speak Arabic, French, and in many places, various Berber dialects. My funny mixture of French, Spanish, and English wasn't facilitating immediate comprehension. Although presumably the off-season, many places were full. Finally I arranged it all and bought our train tickets. We packed and left the next day. Our itinerary included a night in Fes, a four-hour bus trip to Chefchaouen for a few days, then return to Fes for a few days before taking the train back to Salé.

In Fes, I had agreed to pay extra to have someone meet us at the train station, drive us to the medina walls, then walk us through the tiny, confusing jumble of alleyways dodging donkey carts, hand carts, and motor scooters, while wending our way through masses of people who all seemed to be going the other way. Our guide efficiently led us to our *riad*, a small bed and breakfast in an old building—not that there is any other kind of building in the medina—built around a central courtyard.

Morocco: A not-too-busy walkway in the Fes medina.

I think we would still be wandering around that labyrinth if not for the guide. After two days, I could find my way around parts of the old medina, but surprised myself when I came upon a museum I wanted to visit, but not at all where I thought it was. The Moroccan medinas

are the old medieval walled cities with narrow maze-like alleyways running this way and that, with buildings two to three stories high on each side, some with balconies extending out from the upper floor so the alleyway becomes tunnel-like, much like the old section of Larnaca, Cyprus. The kasbah was the fortified area where the royal family lived; it also served as a fort, usually located within the medina. Both the medina and kasbah were designed to repel invaders in the past, and today this centuries-old design works effectively to require tourists to hire guides. Whether past or present, the medina and kasbah throbbed with life.

The medina was for me a symbol of Morocco: old; hidden, yet public at the same time, for life seemed to be lived in view. Patterned like an Arabic tapestry, it held many curves and twists then a surprise of color; movement, but with corners of peacefulness—a wandering sort of place. Like most cultures, there were contradictions, but here they satisfied; they fit like two pieces that belonged together, opposing as they might be.

We left the next morning, traveling via bus to Chefchaouen in the Rif Mountains in northern Morocco. A particularly interesting Berber-dominated town, most of Chef's buildings are painted a luminous blue and the trim on many doors and windows a bright blue, somewhat like Mykonos in Greece. I noted that most of the Berber women wore a traditional dress with long vertically striped skirts often with red stripes, wrapped outside their tunics that was different from most rural Moroccan women. I quickly learned that these women did not want their picture taken. I asked Wayne to photograph a passageway in the medina that included an older woman sitting on a wooden box with two large bags of greens at her feet, and he got more than a dirty look. After that I had to take the photos and be careful where I aimed my little camera.

Chef felt open and airy once we were out of the inner medina. Like so many Greek villages and some in Turkey, it was crawling up a mountainside so that when we were on one street we were almost above the buildings on the street below. We hiked in the mountains—dry, dusty, with stands of pine, cactus, some wildflowers I didn't know. On our way out of the town, we passed the public laundry, which seemed like a sociable way to get that chore done. Occasionally we passed an older man leading his overladen donkey down to the market, although on some of the steeper parts I wasn't sure if the donkey wasn't in the lead. I bought some Berber weavings older than I was, and we learned something of the area in the small museum and the kasbah within the medina.

Morocco: Chefchaouen public laundry.

Between Chef and Fes, once we left the mountains, there were miles and miles of plowed undulating hills waiting for seed, then they would be waiting for the rains, then waiting for growth, then the harvest, then another cycle of seasons would begin. Occasionally an olive orchard broke up the view.

We spent a few more days in Fes. I spent most of my time wandering the medina, where there were literally a hundred or more small shops selling the Moroccan leather slipper-shoes in a variety of colors from bright yellows and pinks to rust and umber. Although many Moroccans wear them, I didn't see how there were enough people to buy all those shoes.

The tanneries in one section of the medina were alluring with their multicolored vats for dyeing the camel and goat leather, but also grim as I pondered the health effects on the workers who stomped on the leather, working the dye in with their feet, with their loose white trousers tied up around their thighs. The first are the white vats with a solution of lime and pigeon poop used to prepare the hides, then many other vats with natural dye colors, some were bright, dazzling colors, others with subtler shades—not just red, but rose, magenta, burgundy, pink. The job of dyeing the hides is handed down from father to son. I wondered what the age of the father was when it became time for his son to inherit the job.

I meandered through the tiny walkways up a hill, around corners, down even smaller alleyways leading off in all directions, some dark and silent, others as bustling as the main walkway. I saw a camel's head hanging from a butcher stall, sacks of varied smelling and colored spices, Moroccan women in dress from Western garb to full veils and one women led by her son with just the barest slit for her eyes to peek out. Hawkers of fish, shoes, meals, fabric, clothes, radios, satellite dishes, camel meat, olives, dates on branches piled next to dried figs and apricots all vied for customers as the flood of people waxed and waned past their small stalls. Cats, mostly lean and stalking, were everywhere. Men yelled "*Balak*!" which meant "Get out of the way or my donkey cart will run you over!"

caravansaries are everywhere in North Africa and the Middle East. They were places were the camel caravans would stop for the night or longer. The camels were kept in the center courtyard with storerooms for the different merchants' goods around that. The Moors were noted for their fine woodwork and other crafts and the exquisite detail in their work. The flowing Arabic calligraphy chiseled into wood and stone invoked a response beyond seeing—I recognized two words: peace and Allah, in a section above a doorway. For me, this presentation of words was not merely writing, nor art, but faith itself. I could worship here, worship this way of bringing words to light. It was not the language translated that created this effect for me, it was the Arabic calligraphy itself that brought me to my knees.

Morocco: The tannery in Fes.

One unusual building I found interesting was the woodcraft museum in an old, restored caravansary. These

Morocco: Example of detailed Arabic building art.

Morocco: Arabic calligraphy on a building wall.

While in Fes, I took an individual lesson in Arabic calligraphy as I wanted to create the saying, "Peace to all who enter this home," for my new-home-to-be. I was terrible, absolutely hopeless, at calligraphy. The young man who made an attempt to teach me told me the history of Arabic calligraphy and presented me with the saying beautifully wrought by him. It hangs in my entranceway today.

Morocco: The author's gift from her calligraphy teacher.

Morocco: The calligrapher at work.

The Calligraphy Lesson

Before writing,
there were drunk poets.
They loved wine
almost as much as words.

It was a great honor
to be chosen the best poet
of your clan.
You competed with all the best poets
in ninety- to one hundred-line odysseys
of local history. You recited

these from memory, also improvised
in a poetic duel. Someone won.

Then God entered the picture.
He didn't like lazy people,
especially lazy, drunk people.
So He said, "See, Learn, Read!"
Thus calligraphy was invented
to entice a reader by beauty
into the beauty of God's Revelations,
and to enable people to learn—
sober people.

He had three revelations about drinking.
One, leave wine, gambling, belief in evil spirits
behind to succeed in life.

Two, don't approach prayer after drinking
(and since you pray five times a day,
there's not time left for drink).
Finally, He said, "Are you finished?"

I don't know what he revealed
about sober poets;
I do know that the prayer "Oh Allah,
make it easy, don't make it difficult,
and show me the good" displays
all calligraphy's geometric rules:
the circle, the human body, measuring dots—
all techniques and tools to record
in Arabic, Allah's revelations.

Pens are cut from Iranian bamboo,
honed to a perfect slant edge;

the width of the other end one-third
exactly.
The ink is collected on the end
of the pen by light jabs
onto a silk cloth soaking
in its blackness
at the bottom of the ink jar.

You breathe,
you breathe the beauty.
The calligraphy flows
drawn from pen, ink, hand, soul
by belief, breath, and endless practice.

In beauty
the words of Allah are
revealed.

En'shallah.

We took the train back to Salé, and that night after we had returned to *Bali Ha'i,* I was extremely sick and was basically bedridden for the next week with gastroenteritis. Although still weak, I was finally able to get up, and we made plans to leave Morocco, but not before I had finished my Christmas shopping. The marina launch took me across the river to the steps of the Rabat medina, and I proceeded to wander through the silk merchants' and woodcraft shops. Being the King's city, Rabat is fairly clean and in some areas modern looking, but with the old medina and kasbah well preserved.

The next morning, minutes before we were to leave, Wayne in his rush to get away, tripped over our dock line and hit his head on the metal toe rail of our boat. I found him bellowing my name, sitting on the dock, his head in his hands with blood everywhere. After helping him onto the boat, I covered him because by then he was in minor shock and hurried to the office to get medical assistance. It looked to me like he needed stitches; Wayne said no, of course. The marina staff came to our aid immediately. A medic was on site, took one look and said "Hospital, stitches." They quickly summoned an ambulance and shepherded us through the whole emergency room scene. (I could have used them when Chad was so sick!) Wayne wasn't even given a local anesthesia. Later we concluded that was because they have such a high volume of work, they don't take the time. They gave him a tetanus shot, and the marina assistant saw us back to our boat. Wayne even agreed we couldn't leave that day. He appeared to have a mild concussion, but we did leave the next day without incident. Wayne's cut was diagonally above and to the side of his left eye and the whole area was bright purple and swollen for a few days.

The Moroccan people on the whole were friendly, helpful, and kind. It was something I noticed—not just that people were helpful, but they were kind. For whatever reasons, we had several experiences in Morocco in which we needed help—some informational, some physical, some just a need for understanding, and, of course, assistance after Wayne's accident—and it was all forthcoming in a gentle and thoughtful way. Kindness was not a quality that I have observed before so extensively on a national level. Of course, there were exceptions, but it was a predominant characteristic of the many interactions we had.

Morocco seemed a world apart from most of Africa. I was surprised at how many cars there were. In most developing countries, the primary mode of public transportation besides chicken buses, are mopeds, bicycles, *tut-tuts*, and depending on the country, elephants and camels. Certainly we saw those in Morocco too along with the donkey carts, but also a large number of cars.

It was always dusty. There was major construction going on near the marina along the river creating dust almost as bad as the Red Sea sand. Throughout the country there was a dustiness from the endless miles of not-yet-planted, plowed fields in the northeast and, of course, sand from the Sahara. The trash lining roads and walkways wasn't as bad as Indonesia or Yemen, but all the plastic litter is truly a world-wide problem. (I swear we are going to suffocate ourselves in plastic!)

≈≈≈

We were on our way again, headed for the Canary Islands, doing our usual motor-sailing so "we can get anchored at x by x," as the captain says. Wayne couldn't forget the pilot in him, and schedules—even if we made them up arbitrarily ourselves—had to be met. I certainly looked forward to sailing; at least Wayne couldn't motor all the way across the Atlantic! During our passage to the Canaries, in the process of moving the whisker pole (a pole attached perpendicular to the mast to hold the headsail out when sailing downwind) from one side to the other, the pole broke off the mast...again. Before it happened, I heard something that didn't sound right and told Wayne, but he didn't hear anything. A few seconds later, Boom! there went the pole. At least the seas weren't too rolly, and with our safety harnesses on we were able to get the pole tied down on the deck, and, for a change, it happened during daylight. This was one of the items just recently fixed in Palma, and several other places prior to that. Wayne's hearing had really deteriorated. He could still differentiate engine noises quite well, which I was never good at, but I could pick up other sounds that indicated something wasn't right.

The Canaries: Cactus Gardens and Christmas

Canary Islands: Lanzaraote from the sea.

Lanzarote, a bare bones volcanic island in the northeast Canary chain, is about space. Its whitewashed towns cling like barnacles to its spare coppery sides along the meeting of sea and land. Its hero and icon is César Manrique, who was an artist, sculptor, eco-architect, designer of space. I found his spaces at once whimsical and grounded. They rose up from the place that birthed them, whether a restaurant, cactus garden, or massive public sculpture. His spaces intrigued, but also extended. As the viewer, I was within and without. Manrique was a conjurer of space that enchanted and beckoned a closer involvement as well as the distant view: the forest and the trees, if there were any. I was taken by this sense of space—but we moved on.

≈≈≈

Las Palmas on Gran Canaria became for me a place of corkscrew tight emotions and waiting, waiting, waiting. With Wayne's increased drinking, I had said, "No way am I crossing the Atlantic with you, without a third person." "I don't want crew, but it's your choice," Wayne told me. I didn't really want crew either; we'd never had crew before. We had sailed safely and successfully so very far already. Wayne didn't drink as much when other people were around, and I thought a little more sleep for both of us, which a third person would bring, might help.

Canary Islands: A scene of Manrique's cactus garden.

Later, I wondered if it was his confusion, like mine, about returning to life back on land that led to his behavior. I escaped thinking about it by retreating into books, the water, my poetry. The life we had been living for the past ten years was so different, so challenging, so fulfilling. How could we ever adjust to land life? It was a frightening prospect. I suppose we both were finding our own ways to handle our reentry and the myriad feelings and issues that encompassed our return.

After it was clear my cousin Scott, who had asked to do this passage with us before we even started ten years ago, wouldn't be able to come because of the uncertainty about dates and the holiday season, I asked Jane. Scott was young, strong, a proven racing sailor, and would have been ideal. This was the only leg Jane hadn't done to complete her personal circumnavigation, and because she was free, she jumped at the chance. Wayne had met Jane briefly before, and I had known her since Turkey, but not well.

Tensions increased after she arrived from the United Kingdom. Wayne didn't like her before she even came, only because she was crew and he didn't want crew. Little did any of us know we would be sitting in Las Palmas for a month before setting sail because of contrary winds and adverse sailing conditions.

I would slap on my headphones and bury myself in the sounds of Yo-Yo Ma, the Los Angeles Guitar Trio, and the Three Tenors or escape by taking the bus to the Vegueta quarter, founded in 1478, where many of the original buildings remain. There I wandered through Casa de Colón, the home of Columbus while he waited for the right winds, just as we did.

Canary Islands: A scene in Vegueta, the old city of Las Palmas.

Jane tried to be accommodating and would disappear most days to explore and leave us to our privacy. I had provisioned well as needed for a two-week passage: precooked our meals and frozen them; had plenty of snacks and tea and coffee for whoever was on watch; easy meals if it was too rough to cook; the right amount of produce that wouldn't go bad, but would keep us going. Yet as we kept getting delayed because of the conditions, we ate up our stores, so I provisioned a little more, and a little more, and a little more. I must have done this about five times. I cleaned and prepared for passage including storing everything we had been currently using, but wouldn't need on passage, then took them out again, only to repeat the process over and over.

We all just wanted to leave, but the winds were absolutely against us, right from the direction we needed to go. The seas were between thirteen and seventeen feet and would be on our beam (side) coming from storms in the north. It was an impossible situation.

In the marina, there were about twelve cruising boats left, all of us waiting, waiting, waiting. Occasionally we would meet for dinner or the ladies would get together for coffee. Jack and Joanie, who had been with us during our Siracusa ordeal, were there, and another couple from the United Kingdom became good friends, but neither knew the full extent of my dilemma and the tension on our boat. Once on passage, I thought it would be easier.

When it became clear we all would be spending Christmas in Las Palmas, we made holiday plans. A group of us went to a Christmas concert; I dug out a tiny fake Christmas tree that had been stored at the bottom of a locker; a Brit couple invited all the cruisers to be ready to be picked up by dinghy at a set time on Christmas Eve. We crowded into three dinghies rafted together, drinking sangria, snacking on hors d'oeuvres, and putted round the large marina singing Christmas carols. The women organized a Christmas dinner pot luck; another woman, who presumably spoke Spanish (but as it turned out, not the Canarian dialect), and I went to see the port commandant about a place where we could meet. He referred us to the yacht club (of sorts) where the young sailors had their little duck boats. We called them duck boats because all over the Med there were kids' sailing clubs, and they looked like little ducklings following their mother (their coach in a large inflatable) out to sea to practice or race.

After a few hurdles, we had a place under a large tin roof with some tables and chairs and a fellow we were required to hire to help us to clean up and to restore everything as it was, but we couldn't have our dinner until he was finished with his family celebration. Jane and several others worked to make the place as festive as possible. With cruising boats from Australia, Canada, New Zealand, Spain, the United Kingdom, the United States, and points east and west, we had our Christmas dinner that included roast turkey courtesy of Jack and Joanie on S/V *JoanieD*.

We finally left on December 30, 2009, almost a new year.

The Atlantic: The Passage from Hell

We have a friend who's crossed the Pond (the Atlantic) about twelve times. It should have been our easiest sail. Ironically, it was the most challenging and unpleasant.

Someone once described sailing as driving a car on ice, but it's much more complicated than that. Imagine... imagine what? There is no metaphor I can come up with that parallels the experience of moving a boat via constantly moving and changing wind, waves, and current. It's not that it is intensely difficult, but it requires a skill-set and knowledge of the impact of these varying conditions, plus the ability to ascertain these conditions as they change, as well as knowing how the boat reacts.

Our crossing was 2,898 nautical miles. The seas were confused with the exception of one half-day that was reasonably comfortable; otherwise it was an eight- to eighteen-foot swell from one direction and wind waves from another direction. The second day out, the vang (the hydraulic arm that supports and positions the height of the boom for the main sail) broke off the mast. We would not have an effective main sail for the duration. The wind was strong enough, generally in the vicinity of 25 knots (about 29 mph), often higher, very occasionally lower, but from all directions for the first 900 nautical miles. We spent about 200 nautical miles tacking back and forth so we could go the direction the wind was coming from, then it turned directly behind us, which was only slightly better than directly in front of us. It meant we had to carefully control the autopilot to keep the wind off the beam enough to avoid an accidental gybe (when the wind changes to the other side and the sail suddenly slaps across the deck jarring everything including everyone). Plus we had several intentional, controlled gybes so as not to get too far off course. We had the whisker pole to keep the headsail out, which was needed in downwind sailing, but after a few days it too broke off the mast with a wham-bang-crash-clatter, further damaging the mast and the deck—the third time this had happened since Wayne bought it in Australia.

Without the pole, it was even more critical—as well as difficult—to keep the wind in the headsail just right. Jane was a skilled cook, but, unfortunately I had all those frozen meals, so her culinary skills weren't much needed. She was also excellent at washing up and polishing the brightwork, which she did before we left the Canaries and after we arrived in Barbados. But her sailing skills were equivalent to that of a landlubber who had never even seen a sailboat. We couldn't believe it as her sailing résumé was quite long, and when I had originally met her, she was crewing for a fellow she had sailed with extensively. Wayne and I all too quickly realized her previous sailing responsibilities had been confined to the galley and cleaning detail. This totally defeated our purpose of having crew, for the whole point was to have someone else to keep watch so each of us would have a longer sleep period.

The crossing saga continued: the rugged conditions created a couple of rips in our headsail. During our watches we could only watch helplessly as those initial rips became bigger and bigger. Finally, when the sail was almost useless, we brought it down on deck, and Jane and I spent the better part of a day on the foredeck, waves sloshing over the bow, rocking side to side, repairing it with sail tape. We didn't have enough fuel to motor all the way, so we had to be able to sail. We got the sail mended and back up, but that night while Jane was on watch she had an accidental gybe that literally bounced me off the settee where I was trying to sleep. That was the end of the headsail.

Before we left Las Palmas, I had told Wayne we should have all our sails available in the sail locker. He said our two spinnakers were, but the storm staysail was under the two dinghy motors: a 5-horsepower (hp) and a 25-hp. I thought that while we were in the marina, he should move it to be more accessible for if we needed it, it would be in difficult conditions and not at a time when he could easily move a 25-hp engine in a small space. He ignored me. He eventually did have to wrestle the motors around in a confused sea to dig that sail out. There was too much wind for either of our spinnakers, so we sailed with the small storm staysail and motored when we could the rest of the way. It took us twenty days. I no longer remember the sequence of all the other horrors, but one autopilot packed it up early on and the generator broke again. We had crossed the longest leg of the Pacific, which is about 500 nautical miles longer, in fifteen days.

The most pleasant highlight happened when two Minke whales came to play alongside us for over two hours one day. They would get behind us, surf down a wave just under the surface in a smooth glissade, go under our boat, and surface on the other side. Then they would do it all over again. They provided a pleasurable and amusing divertissement for us.

Landfall Barbados: Recovery

The last night of the passage, I was on watch for seven hours. I had woken Jane for her normal watch time, but the conditions were unsettled. Because I knew she wouldn't be able to keep the boat on track, I sent her back below. By the time Wayne awakened, I was getting drained from sleep deprivation, frustration, and my own rotten attitude.

Finally, we made landfall under a sultry, hazy, brownish-gray polluted sky. We were tired: of each other, of the boat, of broken parts and systems. I was tired of not sailing—not really sailing, not slightly heeled over slicing through water with no mechanical noise. I was tired of jury-rigged parts that kept breaking, I was tired of Wayne's behavior, I was tired of Jane's chirping, I was tired of my own grouchiness. And that was all I could escape, but it would take meditative work and sleep.

Basically, the voyage was almost over. An overnight sail to Grenada in a few days and then up the island chain, which we had been up and down before. Technically we were only missing the short run from Martinique to Dominica for us to complete our personal circumnavigation, but *Bali Ha'i III* had to return to Ft. Lauderdale for it to be official in this boat. No problem, so I thought then.

I have been in Barbados a few times, but by plane. Only a couple of friends were in Barbados when we arrived from the Canaries, as others had made different landfalls or moved on north, south, west. We got the scoop from the cruisers who were there, and Wayne checked us in. Jane got sorted out and prepared to leave, which I was sure she was anxious to do. It was a sluggish time: the sultry weather, our disappointments, the brokenness of our last little dreams—they all contributed. *Bali Ha'i* had become recalcitrant too, I thought. She was probably tired just as we were. Wayne found a pleasant little local café for us with a friendly waitress. A good meal helped, sleep helped, and there was still more sailing to do in an area we knew well.

15

Eastern Caribbean and Bahamas: Sorrow Hides in Nostalgia

Certainly, travel is more than the seeing of sights; it is a change that goes on, deep and permanent, in the ideas of living.
—Miriam Beard

Grenada: Encountering Grace

Unfortunately the wind was howling; fortunately the temperature was 85°F; unfortunately the humidity was 87 percent; fortunately the water temperature was 80°F and swimming every day was a pleasure; unfortunately our generator didn't work—again; fortunately after a few weeks of Wayne's mechanical band-aids, there was now a professional mechanic working on it. Unfortunately we didn't have any sails; fortunately there was a sail loft here; unfortunately our sails were too big for them to work on; fortunately (presumably) they could be made in Guadeloupe only about two hundred miles north; unfortunately we learned our sails were in South Africa because the Guadeloupe loft couldn't make them either; fortunately they were to be shipped to London and then to us in Grenada; unfortunately British Air (how the sails would be sent) employees planned a strike during this period, also unfortunately the sail loft in South Africa forgot to order

enough material for the head sail so they hadn't started work on them yet. The sails were apparently like the Emperor's new clothes.

In 1987, the last time we were here, it was richly green, and St. George's was charming with its waterfront buildings reminiscent of Copenhagen. During that earlier trip, we found graves from the 1500s in the cemetery on the hill, old for this New World, with inscriptions ranging from poignant to picaresque.

This time, the landscape was brown, burning up—sometimes literally with brush fires—from a prolonged drought; St. George's seemed littered and grungy, but the people were still smiling and saying "good afternoon" to everyone whenever they squeezed into the little van buses that zipped around. Little girls still had their hair braided into dozens of little pigtails and bunches with colorful barrettes and ties and ribbons. Buses still slowed down for goats and children crossing the road, but not much else.

The cruising community in Grenada was more of a semipermanent one than any other place we had been with the exception of the Rio Dulce in Guatemala. There were the occasional circumnavigators, like us, but most sailors anchored in Grenada didn't sail much. Some left their boats there and returned whenever, like a second home; others seemed to live mainly there. Some sailed around the Caribbean periodically, and a few sailed back and forth to the east coast of the United States or Canada annually.

What such semipermanence allowed for was a closer relationship with the Grenadian community. When we arrived, the primary outreach program was Saturday sessions, tutoring Grenadian kids in reading, writing, and arithmetic. It was begun in 2006 by a resourceful Grenadian woman, Mrs. Jeanne Pascal, who had moved back to her home country with her husband after retiring in Canada. As their home was being built, a young boy in their Mt. Airy neighborhood took to throwing rocks at the construction and breaking windows. The neighbors said, "Oh dat boy; he no good; a'ways de trouble in school; jus' a bad boy." Jeanne went to his family, "This boy has damaged our home and needs to be punished. I will take him every Saturday morning, and he will study his schoolwork with me." She fetched him that Saturday and worked with him.

After a few Saturdays, other kids turned up for help, and then more and more appeared until Jeanne and her husband couldn't work with them all. A U.S. Peace Corps volunteer suggested the cruising community. A local person volunteered to drive his small bus to transport the cruiser volunteers from two of the main anchorages. A local funky bar offered its room as it wasn't open on Saturday mornings. Chairs and tables were found, and the Mt. Airy Young Readers program continues its success. Sometimes up to thirty-five students attended and fifteen or so volunteer tutors—all this in just one small hillside Grenadian neighborhood, with kids thirsty to learn and parents who cared about their children's education.

Grenada: The author tutors two interested young girls for the Mt. Airy program.

We had our usual cruiser beach parties and saw old friends and made new ones. One Friday night we went to the fish fry in Gouyave, a small town up the coast.

There they closed off a few streets and the local cooks set up stands to grill melt-in-your-mouth fresh lobster and shrimp! Three new cruising friends and I created a make-up-your-own island tour by local bus. We thought we had far more fun and interesting experiences than those who did the tour with a professional guide. The little van-type buses were privately owned and most drivers had an assistant who leaned precariously out the side door looking for potential passengers. As they added up, he helped jam them in. At one point I was on a small cushion suspended between two seats, but so squeezed in, I couldn't have fallen in any direction.

I swam almost every day, although the water was not clear. In fact, I got a severe ear infection, probably from the polluted water. I actually found a small coral head behind our boat with some fish around it, and there was always a variety of fish under our boat. *Bali Ha'i's* bottom was once again rapidly collecting *grass* (algae and seaweed) and barnacles from staying at one anchorage too long, like Siracusa!

Cruising life was definitely not over. Without the generator, our freezer didn't work, nor the watermaker. Wayne finally jerry-jugged some water to the boat before the tanks went completely dry, but we washed in saltwater and rinsed with a little fresh water. When we had an intermittent squall, I collected water in buckets for cleaning. I tried to keep the deck clean by washing it in saltwater so Wayne could open the water tanks after the deck got rinsed off with fresh rainwater for several minutes. We'd done this all during the circumnavigation as Wayne had the deck designed to serve as a water catchment system. He had to run the engine to charge the batteries, although some days there was enough wind

for me to charge my computer with the output from the wind generator. This was classic cruising.

We had sailed to Grenada not just for the start of our nostalgia cruise of the Lesser Antilles, where we had been so many years earlier, but because we needed new sails, and there was a sail loft there. As with the fortunately/unfortunately conditions above, new sails became problematic. Since we were delayed in Grenada for a while, I made a quick trip back to the States. During my time to Colorado, I had an adjustment dealing with a few feet of snow after the hot, humid Caribbean, but I finished up my visits and work and rushed back anxious to take off. Five weeks later we were still in Grenada! This time it was the generator, but finally that was fixed too. Three months after they were ordered, the new sails found their way back to our boat, but they didn't fit properly. We made our way up the eastern Caribbean chain from one North Sails loft to another. This was not the relaxed, nostalgia trip we had planned, but eventually a sail loft in the British Virgins, pronounced the sails unfixable, a fact we already knew, but which North Sails had been reluctant to face.

Often I had offered to play a project-manager role for boat repairs because I had extensive experience in project management as a consultant and then as CEO of my own technical writing company. Wayne would have none of that. He was the owner, the captain, and knew more about the systems—all true. But he was also a retired airline pilot and a captain for twenty-four of his thirty-seven-year career. During that time, he gave orders, and assumed they would be executed competently. In the airline industry of the past, that was true. Crews knew their jobs, did them well and in a timely manner—

otherwise they were gone. Boat repair didn't usually work that way. In fact, it never worked that way. This time, first it was sail delays, then generator repair delays. Finally Wayne found someone who seemed as if he really could fix the generator. Everyone else just did what Wayne had already done, and it didn't work for the long-term.

I didn't actually meet Jamie until he emerged from our engine room through the dark tunnel of the so-called workroom, in which no one could ever actually work. It was filled with a hodgepodge of boat parts—some even workable—on shelves along with a collection of batteries, the vacuum cleaner with its various tubes and parts, a rusty machete, a plastic tub filled with shock cords and duct tape, a box of latex gloves, and fluorescent light bulbs for a light that had broken long before. On the narrow cabin sole (floor) there was usually an opened case of beer or two along with Wayne's tool bag and a jumble of tools on top.

Earlier I had passed Jamie a bottle of water after asking if he wanted anything. He had been in there for hours and never even came out for a bite to eat, to pee, or a drink of water. He said, "I told myself, I wasn't leaving here until I got dis part of de work done." And he didn't. Because we still had several Frisbees left with our boat name and logo on them that we had given to kids around the world (and some older people too), I asked him if he had young children.

"How young?" he replied. I explained about the Frisbees.

"Well, I've adopted some children. You see dere is dis centre here, de Dorothy Hopkin Centre for de Disabled, and I am sort of a sponsor for dem. Dese are children with many problems. Some cannot walk, others

are blind, some have Down's syndrome, and dere parents take dem dere and dump dem and never look back. Dey are abandoned dere, so I help as I can. Dere are thirty-five or so. Last year, I started putting all my change into a can when I got home from work and by de end of de year, I actually had $3,000 ECD for dem. I couldn't believe it!"

"Would they like visitors," I asked, thinking I could read to some of them or take someone in a wheelchair for a little walk.

"Oh yes, I tink so, I tink so," Jamie's Trinidad accent was faint, but every once in a while audible. Compared to local Grenadians, he was easy to understand, probably because of the mechanical work he did and the clients he had to talk to. "I will give you de director's number."

A few days later I called her to explain. She agreed to meet with two of us from the cruising community on Saturday when Jamie was off and could drive us there. I easily found Sharon, another cruiser interested in helping at the center. Our appointment was on a blue-sky day, not hazy or cloudy, and we had a lovely drive up into the hills with an occasional vista down to the water where we could see a few sailboats coming and going. On the way Jamie told us his story of how he became a mechanic.

"You see, I knew from a young age, I didn't want ta stay in poverty. We were poor, yes, so poor. I was de oldest of fourteen children; I learned ta fix sewing machines, yes, sewing machines. Dey were very old, but some of de women had dem ta make crafts and clothes and tings like dat. But at age fourteen, I left home. I had a little money saved, and I took de bus ta a town about twenty-five kilometers away. Dere I walked aroun' and aroun' and found parts ta build a bicycle; a nice lady gave me a place ta stay and one meal a day, but I needed a job quickly ta pay her. So I stopped a garbage truck and asked if dey had any mechanic jobs; de driver said 'Yea, mon, you in luck, here's ta place ta go.' So I got on my bicycle and I went fas' down ta da place. De boss, he looks me over and I tink he wonders how can dis scrawny lil' kid be a mechanic, so he gives me an engine ta fix. Well, I tried, a' course, but I didn't really know how ta do it. So, de boss says ta me, 'I can see you're not a mechanic, but you are very bold. I will teach you.' We spent de next t'ree days and most of de nights rebuilding de engine. So dat's how I became a mechanic."

I noticed how his Trinidadian accent came to the fore as he progressed in his story, then disappeared again as he finished with a flourish.

"After dat, I knew I had ta get more information, so I went ta de library and read many books so I could be successful. You know Trinidadians are smarter than Grenadians; it is a fact. Even many Grenadians will admit dat."

"So why did you come to Grenada?"

"My sister was here, and dere are more jobs here. I tink it's because the Grenadian boys don't want ta work ta be successful. I tink so. I said ta the boys at the bus company, 'You have ta read books; you have ta learn more, but de jus' laugh at me and go on slouchin' aroun'." His dark face breaks into a shy grin, "But, you know, I have a race car. Yes, I race. I work on dat car; oh, I put in de hours on dat car. But dose boys, where are de? De still be slouchin' aroun'."

When we arrived at the center, we saw that the grounds were well cared for with colorful bougainvillea and hibiscus in brilliant flower and a small vegetable garden above a stone wall. We met with Mrs. Shawn in her tiny office, thankful that it was only two of us—there wouldn't have been room for anyone else—while she told us the history of the center and her philosophy about it. The idea was to give the children love, feed them, keep them clean, and allow them to develop within their abilities, not try to teach them or push them. It was for children, but the center had been open since the 1960s, so many of the residents were well into adulthood. Originally it was called the JFK Centre, named by Dorothy Hopkin, the founder, as she admired President Kennedy so much and wanted to honor him after his assassination. After she died, it was renamed for her.

Mrs. Shawn took us on a tour. She had emphasized to us that no photos were allowed because they did not want to exploit the children. The residents' dorm rooms were immaculate with each bed well made and most having a stuffed animal or two sitting on the pillow. A few of the residents were in their beds: one woman with cystic fibrosis had had a stroke; a young blind child sleeping; another child unable to walk also sleeping; a teen-age girl who looked about six and couldn't move except for one arm. The rest of the residents, it turned out, were downstairs waiting to entertain us and hoping it would be soon since it was their lunchtime. Finally Mrs. Shawn led us into the community room, and we were regaled with songs accompanied by small drums, tambourines, and sticks, some held with a partial arm, or resting on the arm of a wheelchair, or in one case held under a chin and beaten with the stump of an arm. Sharon and I were amazed and close to tears. Although the term physically challenged is politically correct now, these souls were more than challenged. They were severely disabled, many with multiple problems. But there were smiles galore and a clear joy in being able to do this performance for us, even by those who were just there, not able to sing or play anything. Sharon and I each spoke a few words to them, and they sang a good-bye song as Mrs. Shawn led us away.

Sharon and I were impressed with the center, but realized our simple idea of help wasn't going to work. We both were volunteers at the tutoring program; clearly the center was a different situation. We talked about how the cruising community might help, and after our visit I wrote up a detailed public relations campaign plan, which we had discussed in general terms, and sent it to Mrs. Shawn. I found someone to take my place as liaison, as surely someday we would be leaving Grenada! We were now well into our third month there and needed to be in Florida before the start of hurricane season in July, which, as it turned out, we didn't quite make. We also arranged for the marina and one of the local restaurants, De Big Fish, to accept donations of items for the center. And to top it off, we found there was a fund of about US$1,500 that could be given to the center from the sale of donated charts and a dinghy by a thoughtful South African cruiser and earmarked for deserving Grenadian charities. Included in the plan I sent to Mrs. Shawn were many other ideas for raising money and expanding consciousness about the center and its work. It was some time before I heard back with an email from Mrs. Shawn with grateful thanks for our first visit and my plan. Later, she called, and we arranged a visit to present the donation of $1,500. In the meantime, Uli, a talented German cruiser, created the perfect logo for the center, which they had expressed a need for, and I sent on.

Several days later, we had arranged another visit, and Jamie drove my liaison replacement and me to the center. There we met Barbara Cross, the Chairwoman of the Board of Directors, a well-organized, no-nonsense person, who, along with Mrs. Shawn, gracefully accepted our donation, and then introduced us to the Prime Minister's wife who visited once a week and worked with three or four of the more capable patients on craft projects. This week she had brought several old magazines for them to cut pictures from, but we could see the challenge even in that. Her patience was obvious as it rippled gently over the small hands she guided to cut through the brightly colored shiny magazine pages.

Barbara Cross, with well-managed pride, gave us a tour. Although I had done this before, my heart lurched as a four-year-old boy with a paralyzing disease, who weighed less than ten pounds when first brought here, clutched my finger and waved my hand back and forth in front of his deformed eyes and smiled as I stroked and cooed to him. My instincts were to gently climb into his crib and wrap him in love, but as a guest not only of the center, but the country, I dutifully followed Barbara as we continued our tour. As I softly pulled my hand away, his little smile faded, and he wrapped his arm under his frail, tiny body.

Encountering Grace in Grenada

The modern director wants Physically Challenged
not disabled. The challenge here is in a breath,
a smile, a small song to be sung.
Your mangled, misshapen bodies; you
are more than challenged,
more than disabled; few voices
can say words; few feet

can take steps, few eyes
can focus, few hands can hold
anything. You were the rejected, the forgotten.

This small boy,
asleep, half-blind, crippled, but clean and loved.
Four-years-old, less than ten pounds
when he was found.
He half awakes, I hold his tiny black hand; he smiles,
for a moment, we two are cloaked in grace.

The shy caregiver
with her black and gray cornrow braids
neatly balancing her lovely brown face
wants me to know,
"I have worked here for twenty-four years."
She smiles and grace flows through the room;
she has a gift; she *is* a gift.

I can't even imagine how she does it.
I smile back as some of these children sing for me,
but my heart is broken for them, by them.
There is nothing I could do to change their lives.
They were abandoned by families unable to care;
found love here,
love that cannot be demanded
or contrived.
Love is
or
it isn't.

The last day in Grenada my friend Elaine and I
were two of a handful of Mt. Airy tutors to help with
their senior students' field trip around the island. It
seemed a fitting good-bye to my connection here: a land
circumnavigation of this island where I had spent so
much time; a day with local kids and with Elaine, who
was a new friend made there, from Australia, and whom
I will probably never see again; a visit to Grand Etang, a
national park in the mountains with its monkeys, then to
the beach—the two extremes of Grenada, and so much in
between.

Like the extremes of Grenada, I was struck by
the contradictions of cruising: getting involved, making
friends, enjoying the land and sea of a particular place—
then the good-byes, the disconnection, the pulling up of
the anchor, the leaving to start it all over again. And, of
course, so much in between: the passage. I loved passages
because they provided a transition, a time in which spaces
were separated. During a passage, I was pulled to the
past and what was left behind, then pushed to the future
and what might be next. Thoughts and experiences of
the previous anchorage settled into memories; and the
expectations of a new one came to the surface.

The Lesser Antilles: Croissants and Dancing Fish

Mayreau, Bequia, Martinique, Îles des Saintes,
Guadeloupe, the British Virgin Islands, U.S. Virgin
Islands: all places we had been before holding a sprinkling
of memories from anchorages to beaches to favorite
restaurants. With a sail bag full of inadequate sails and
a duffle full of emotional issues, could we create some
wonderful new memories in some of these places we used
to love?

It happened quickly.

In Mayreau at Saline Bay many years and two sailboats ago, we were anchored alone when a local, engineless, trading sailboat with homemade mast and boom sailed into the bay at sunset, and the two lithe, dark brown men in tattered shorts lowered their sails at just the right moment and anchored neatly just off shore, close enough for them to wade in, no words or signals between them.

Few, if any, of those boats are left in the Lesser Antilles, but we both remembered the flawless execution of superb seamanship that could have been a ballet in an age-old legend of this fragment of the Caribbean. This time our memories were made by Wayne's cooked-to-perfection lobster that he had bought in town. We sat in the cockpit enjoying every mouth-watering bite and sharing reminiscences of our earlier sails and adventures in this area. It was a brief slice of how our intertwined lives used to be.

Mayreau: The author enjoying excellent local lobster in the cockpit of *Bali Ha'i*.

In Bequia, after scrubbing the deck with Wayne's help—he hauled up buckets of saltwater and I scrubbed—I rented a bike and rode up and down hills to the Old Hegg Turtle Sanctuary I had heard about that protected the endangered Hawksbill turtles. The turtle caregiver was a dedicated middle-aged fellow who carefully explained what he did there. Less than one percent of the eggs a female turtle lays ever make it to adulthood. Most are wiped out as hatchlings racing for the sea by both predators and human habitat destruction, including lights that confuse the tiny turtles about which way to go when they emerge from their eggs buried in the sand. Raising them in tanks until they are a year old increases their chances to about 10 percent.

At Old Hegg, they were kept until about five years old which greatly increased their chance of survival. The little ones were separated into different tanks as they grew. They swam around and raced and butted up against each other like children of many species, including *Homo sapiens*. The turtle caregiver had one turtle that was old and blind, which he planned to keep as it wouldn't survive back in the ocean. This turtle liked being petted. I didn't know how a turtle could tell it was being petted through that shell, but maybe his other senses became even more attuned with the loss of sight, and he could sense the movement. The turtle seemed a sweet old guy, and I wished him and his caregiver well—another joyful memory to hold on to. Another day I took the dinghy to Devil's Table to snorkel and saw a particularly beautiful cowrie shell well-protected by two black, exceptionally well-named Long-spined sea urchins and a Spotted snake eel. Hopefully, the cowrie is still there.

Bequia: The author and the turtles' caregiver at the Old Hegg Turtle Sanctuary.

In Martinique, a new memory was of a particularly excellent meal—what else could it be, it's a French island—with the best octopus I've had since eastern Greece. We ate ashore because we waited six hours for the sail guy, who kept promising "*Bientôt, bientôt.*" Soon, soon. We were Americans, but having traveled the world our sense of time was more relaxed, although six hours still did not constitute *bientôt*. Later, we still didn't have sails that worked.

On the passage from St. Pierre at the north end of Martinique to Îles des Saintes, we saw Red-billed Tropicbirds perform their straight bombing dives plunging into the water for fish, their long graceful tail streamers floating behind them, and three small whales. Just before Îles des Saintes, which has always been one of my favorite places in the Lesser Antilles, we maneuvered through a minefield of fish traps—déjà vu Malaysia—to a crowded anchorage. No, I couldn't go home again, especially after so many years away, but I snorkeled every

day, and we ate epicurean French food (is there any other kind?). The best part was calling on the radio the night before to order two fresh croissants to be delivered to the boat the next morning. Ooh la la, sitting in the cockpit in the pink sheen of early morning light with fresh-brewed coffee and its wonderful aroma and a just-baked croissant, as only the French can make them. It was an indulgence to have at least once.

Îles des Saintes: Fresh croissant delivered to the boat.

All through the chain of the Windwards and Leewards that make up the Lesser Antilles, we had 30- to 40-knot winds frequently, but with continuing sail problems couldn't sail as much as we would have liked, although we were able to get up to 8.9 knots for a while one day. Normally, *Bali Ha'i* can easily sail over 9 knots in winds like these.

Guadeloupe was hot and buggy. At Pointe-à-Pitre, where we had anchored, it was too polluted to swim. Reality crowded in. Throughout the Caribbean, the lack of hard corals where I snorkeled, which was everywhere I could, was depressing, as was the large number of motorboats, both trawlers and yachts. Of course, it was more crowded; that was to be expected; but I felt fortunate to have been there years earlier, when it was quite a different scene. Not only had it been quieter, but there was a more pronounced feeling of locale, with emphasis on the *local* part of that word.

I was looking forward to the British Virgin Islands (BVI), where we had sailed frequently in *Bali Ha'i II* and earlier in charter boats, and had some favorite anchorages. At the same time, we were both reacting to the impending close of our circumnavigation in our own ways.

≈≈≈

My youngest son, Pete, and his family were to visit us in the Bahamas, something I had been really looking forward to, but I learned while in the BVI that they weren't coming. I was deflated and almost defeated in spirit. So I went snorkeling.

It was in the BVI that I saw the dancing fish that inspired the poem of that name. Although I had seen them many times before all around the world, this particular troupe seemed even more spectacular, coordinated, and acrobatic.

Dancing Fish

Almost dusk, the silver fish dance
in front of the rainbow
taking on its colors.
This must be a painting by Chagall.

It's fanciful enough, but this is real.

This kaleidoscope of fish
dances so exquisitely,
their choreographer must be Nureyev;
though there's something of the Busby Berkeley
in their dance, it's so theatrical,
so timed, so coordinated.

We have these questions to resolve:
Who taught these fish to dance this way?
Did Chagall paint this or not?
Finally,
what is real?

Coral reefs are a gift not only to those of us who snorkel or dive on them; they are nurseries for much of the ocean's fishes; they are a vital part of the oceans that cover the majority of our planet; they are home to diverse species beyond our imagining. And they are dying; victims of global warming, pollution, and direct human destruction. This is an unfathomable loss. Seeing the dancing fish brings home the message that saving our oceans, coral reefs, and their diversity and inexplicable beauty must be a priority.

The Deep: The Puerto Rican Trench

We left the BVI for the fuel dock in St. Thomas in the U.S. Virgin Islands, and departed there at 10:30 a.m. for our last real passage—four days to Great Inagua, Bahamas. We sailed briefly through a squall with 30- to 40-knot winds, but the rest of the time it was motor-sailing with winds usually less than 10 knots and generally from aft. Not the one last hurrah I had hoped for. We skirted Culebra and could barely see its outline through the rain and haze, then rounded the north coast of Puerto Rico.

We had had a wonderful cruise in *Bali Ha'i II* along the south coast of Puerto Rico, Vieques, and Culebra on our way to St. Thomas in 1993. Hmm, "wonderful"? That part of it was, but the passage from the Abacos in the northern Bahamas to Boquerón, Puerto Rico had been a nightmare. We needed a cold front to get east, which meant lots of wind. We also had large swells from the north, and our auto pilot gave out the second day, so the two of us had two-hour shifts of hand steering over fourteen-foot swells, augmented by wind waves. In the two hours off, we had to sleep, eat, and take care of personal needs. When at the wheel, I had to work hard to keep the boat from broaching. Broaching—similar to a car skidding and being turned sideways—is caused by large, steep following seas hitting the rear quarter or stern (yawing) resulting in the boat being thrown broadside into the trough of the sea, which can cause a knockdown or capsize. We surfed down a few waves at over 13 knots in our boat whose hull speed was about 9 knots.

I remember enough to tell the story, but my real memories are of the three whales that greeted us as we entered the Mona Passage and the pod of dolphins that escorted us part of the way toward Boquerón in the last few weary hours. I remember the comfortable anchorages along the southern coast and the young taxi driver/guide in Ponce taking us to the baseball museum and proudly showing us a picture of his grandfather, who was on a championship team many years ago. Once Puerto Rico was freed of its colonial U.S. fetters, baseball became a passion for Puerto Ricans.

But now I was on my last passage on *Bali Ha'i III*; it was my watch and the lights of San Juan faded behind me as the moon came up. For the first time in several days there were a few stars visible. The AIS showed a ship, the *Stella Orion*, 12.9 nautical miles away, but basically not moving and not under command. The data displayed indicated it was a 338-foot tanker and the destination was international waters. I guessed it was just drifting waiting to get into San Juan harbor. I trusted there really was someone on watch on board, but I was, for sure.

Technology had certainly changed since I started cruising in 1986, but we still did a 360-degree visual check every ten minutes. I wore prescription glasses not just for reading. Ironically when I was on watch at night, I saw better and more clearly without them when I did my visual scan. It was not true during the daytime. I was sure there was a scientific explanation; mine was more visceral: these night watches were my time, and I could see.

Later in my watch, the chart showed we were in a depth of 21,488 feet, but I knew the Puerto Rican Trench was at least 27,560 feet.[1] Our depth finder went off soundings somewhere around four hundred feet. I wondered how long it would take a penny dropped to reach the bottom? What was down there? Was it one of those thermal vents with all kinds of surprising life forms, grotesquely designed for that unearthly environment? On land I've been a little over 14,200 feet up, in the sea 1,000 feet down in a submersible and about 185 feet using scuba, but 21,000 feet down? The thought took my breath away, and would, of course, literally, long before I had progressed very far.

A few days later, a large pod of dolphins came to play in our bow wake. Although this had happened often around the world, it was always a treat. We tried trolling, but never caught anything. I missed the delectable mahi-mahi and tuna we used to catch on passages. We arrived off Great Inagua at the southern end of the Bahamas about midnight of our fourth day and anchored out.

The Bahamas: The Crush of Change

We stayed in Great Inagua a few days, just long enough to check in, eat some cracked conch ashore, and for me to take a trip out to see the Caribbean Flamingoes, which I always enjoyed. As well, there were White-cheeked Pintail ducks, Royal Terns, cormorants (I think they were Double-crested), American Oystercatchers, which are so funny with their carrot-like beaks, and several other species. The day after my birding outing, we were up bright and early for an overnight passage to Raccoon Cay in the 100-mile-long Jumentos archipelago in the southwestern part of the Bahamas.

We had had a special experience finding a new route, getting to, and cruising in the Jumentos many years ago. At various times, we had kept both *Bali Ha'i I* and *II* in Marsh Harbour, Abaco at the northwestern end of the Bahamas. Wayne had been sailing in the Bahamas since 1976, and sailing through the Abacos was the first cruise we did together in 1986. In those days, we made a point of exploring the less-sailed parts of the Bahamas. We pioneered a route through the Tongue of the Ocean and across the banks to the Jumento Cays. From studying the charts, Wayne had thought there might be a possible

route that way, but there was no published information about it. We learned more about the possibility of such a route from a black Bahamian supply-boat captain whom we had searched out in Marsh Harbour. He invited us into his well-used pilot house to show us his hand-marked charts. When I went to buy charts for the area, the salesman at Bluewater Books in Fort Lauderdale said, "You're either crazy or very courageous!" We weren't either, just analytical and a little adventurous.

When we were last in the Jumentos, the conch and lobster were plentiful. This time we managed enough conch, but only a few lobster. The professional fishing boats from Spanish Wells were anchored nearby and working from their multiple skiffs every day. We dinghied over to say hello and inquire about what they were fishing for, and they nicely gave us a ten-pound package of fresh grouper. I thought, however, that it wouldn't be long before this area was overfished also.

I remembered the abandoned salt pans I had found years ago on Raccoon Cay and found them again. Salt pans are low-lying areas—not that there's much else in the Bahamas—where channels are dug to allow the saltwater in, then closed until it evaporates off and what is left are huge sheets of crystallized salt. Duncan Town on Ragged Island, the only settlement in the Jumentos with a population then of about forty, at the southernmost end of the chain, used to have a salt-producing industry. It must be the water in this part of the Bahamas as Morton Salt has a huge salt operation on Great Inagua. Part of the reason there are so many flamingoes there is because of the shallow man-made lagoons.

On Raccoon, it was incredibly hot, and the bright, white crystallized salt covering the reddish sand made it even hotter. Wayne lost his sandal in the gook under the salt and actually burned his bare foot in the process of getting it out. I went back later with my buckets and collected lots of salt, which I lugged back to the boat, cleaned, and set out to dry on the deck in every appropriate shallow container I could find. Once dry I checked it again for tidbits of sand and whatnot, washed and dried it again, wrapped it up, and stored it away. My very own sea salt! I used to not use salt much at all, but this salt had flavor—as well as memories.

the boat, what was to be shipped, what was needed for the next month. What, what, what? Decisions, decisions, decisions. Whispers from the past, disheartenment, in the doldrums.

Bahamas: The author's salt drying project.

Bahamas: Abandoned salt pans.

I started sorting and packing in the Jumentos. There was so much to do before Florida: deciding what was mine, what was Wayne's, what was to be thrown away, given away, what went to the cabin, what stayed on

So much change was about to happen. I was building a home near Salida, Colorado, a town that had classical music concerts and poets—two necessities for me. Wayne and I had not mentioned divorce nor any sort of permanent separation, but it was clear he was going to live at the cabin, and I was going to live in my new home when it was finished.

I still snorkeled every day and one day picked up

ten conch, which we heartily ate the next few days in a variety of ways. One of our favorites after the usual conch in red sauce, cracked conch, and conch chowder was conch with spaghetti and conch in scrambled eggs. I wondered if I'd ever have fresh conch again.

We spent a long day going up to the Exumas from the Jumentos and crossed some particularly skinny water over the banks, but made it without going aground. Our 7-foot keel wasn't designed for the Bahamas, which we well knew. We stopped at what the charts call Osprey Cay. Lynton Riggs, who first cruised here in the 1940s and 1950s wrote a cruising guide for the area, calling this cay Little Bell, and so did we. In his guide, he described an osprey nest on a rock outcropping that we first saw in the 1980s and it was still there! At Warderick Wells, we visited the park headquarters, which we had helped build in the 1980s. Today it is larger, well-staffed, and with many accoutrements. Wayne and I sorted through our gear, and I took a dinghy load of items to donate to the headquarters in the process of raising our waterline and getting *Bali Ha'i* ready to sell in Florida. We hiked around the island. Now there are trails, some of which we had helped build. On our first trip there, we had bushwhacked.

As we sailed north, once out of the national park I collected more conch. Then we were in the Abacos. This truly had been our old stomping grounds as we kept our previous boats in Marsh Harbour for several years. The Bahamas were an infinitely better cruising area than Florida. We could fly over instead of sailing across no matter what the Gulf Stream conditions were, as it could be uncomfortable and took considerably longer.

Bahamas: The osprey nest on Little Bell.

That time in the Abacos, nothing seemed right. I couldn't get Internet service in Marsh Harbour until finally I was able to in a casino (they never had casinos before); I had my chronic digestive syndrome; snorkeling at Powell Cay was awful with few fish, lots of algae, poor visibility; then to top it off, we ran aground outside Manjack! We couldn't get off right away as the tide was going down. We put out the anchor and stayed. At 2:00 a.m. with the lowest tide, we were so heeled over, everything was falling, including us—it was hard to stay in the bunk. In the morning two boats tried to pull us off, but we were hard packed into sand and clay, and they had no luck. We had to wait for high tide. I spent as much time as I could in the water since I could barely stand or do anything on the boat because of the extreme heel. I even found a few more conch—I was always successful at finding conch if there were any to be found! Finally about 10:00 p.m. with a high tide, we were able to get off ourselves and headed out for deeper water to anchor for the night. Well, it was one way to clean off the keel. Someone has said, "A sailor who says they've never been aground either has never left the marina or is a liar."

The next day we motored to Hopetown on Elbow Cay, although we had to anchor quite far out because of our keel depth. There's a strikingly special place on this cay where the ocean and the bay are separated by a small spit of land. There's an old lodge and restaurant there, first started by two Northwest pilots as I recall. It's a particularly special place to sit and watch the sunset. Wayne had taken me there on our first cruise; it was the perfect romantic idyll then.

What seemed like years ago, I had done a ten-day cruise on *Bali Ha'i II* with three women friends on my own—that is, without Wayne, when I was really the captain. We had spent a lovely evening there also watching the sunset and chatting as women friends can do. I had done that cruise as I wanted to be sure I could handle a sailboat on my own if anything happened to Wayne during the planned circumnavigation. Of course, I had to learn *Bali Ha'i III's* systems and idiosyncrasies, but those I could do with Wayne around. Being a captain, even temporarily to practice, when he was present, was not possible. He would always second-guess me before I had a chance to trim the sails or set a new course.

This time in the Abacos, I packed, snorkeled, and wandered on shore. I alternated between anger and the deepest sadness at losing the love of my life.

We had been away from the Bahamas for about thirteen years so the changes were particularly evident to us as they weren't incremental from year to year. What we first noticed was the dearth of sailboats, and in their place motor yachts and trawlers. In the Lesser Antilles motor yachts might be expected, but in the out islands of the Bahamas, we weren't ready for that. We were horrified at the number of small cays now in private hands with large, often pretentious, residences and outbuildings, closed up while we were there (it was July and was hot and humid). We wondered how often they were used and what the tearing up of so much fragile land was doing to the area. The results became obvious all too quickly. I snorkeled at every anchorage so had first-hand visual confirmation of my findings. The runoff from development as well as the heating of the ocean due to climate change had created what I called the *algaefication* of the Bahamas (and the entire eastern Caribbean from the same causes). In many places the water was so warm, it wasn't even refreshing to swim. There is documentation that the water temperatures are higher, particularly in the past ten years. In fact the news in Fort Lauderdale one day reported the sea temperature at 87 degrees F!

There was very little hard coral left in the Bahamas; soft corals and sponges continued to struggle on, but even the fire coral, which isn't a true coral, has been bleached by the hotter temperatures. There were still plenty of barracuda, nurse sharks, damselfish, and several other species of coral reef and pelagic fish, but there wasn't the diversity I used to see; and everything, even the turtle grass, was covered with algae. Of course, there was always some of this, it was just the expanded extent of the algaefication this time, and the boring, faded look of previously exciting reefs. In the entire length of the Bahamas from Great Inagua in the south to the Abacos in the north, I saw only one edible-size grouper!

I couldn't believe my eyes when snorkeling at Great Inagua: a lionfish, a South Pacific and Indian Ocean species! What was it doing here? They are magical-looking fish and adept predators. In this environment, other fish were not used to them, thus not hiding from them, not escaping their beautiful, flowing, but poisonous tentacles. The lionfish were a menace to native species and, as a result, to the fragile coral reefs already under assault from other causes in Florida, the Bahamas, and the Caribbean.

Later I learned that some Florida aquarium owners either tired of their hobby or moving and not wanting the difficulties of transporting fish, have released them randomly into the Atlantic. The first one was caught in 1985 off Ft. Lauderdale. As more and more were periodically released, a breeding population developed and with no predators of their own—being an unknown species in the area—they rapidly spread so that now they are along the eastern United States coast as far as New York and spreading down the coast of South America. Marine biologist and author, Carl Safina calls them, "the worst marine alien invasion."[2] I would see more as we moved up the Bahamas archipelago. I was not adept with a pole spear, our only weapon against them, and Wayne rarely snorkeled, so we were no help in controlling them. Later I learned from Safina's *Saving the Ocean* DVD that

they can easily be caught with nets and that diving clubs sponsor Lionfish derbies to at least keep them off some reefs.

Grouper and conch used to be mainstays of the Bahamian diet. Now, only the large fishing boats from Spanish Wells and a few other larger islands catch grouper miles offshore on the Bahama banks or in very remote areas: a clear case of overfishing. I wondered how the diet of the less affluent locals was being forced to change. The previously beautiful azure water was now mostly green and lonely without its usual denizens.

Since Pete and family weren't coming, I had invited my daughter, Daya, as she hadn't been to the boat before. She and a business partner had bought my company from me. I had always wanted her to have it, but it was a decision that cost me in many ways. Nevertheless, we both were trying to get past that. She could only come on a certain date, and Wayne wanted to push on. I was caught in the middle, but somehow we worked it out. We sailed up to Bimini from Dollar Harbour, a favorite little quiet anchorage of ours, to pick up Daya at the airport, had lunch, did a few errands and motored back to Dollar Harbour, in the western Bahamas at the edge of the Gulf Stream, which would be our last crossing before Florida.

It was a bit windy and rough at our anchorage, but I took Daya snorkeling. Although she had snorkeled several times off the Yucatan, she had never seen a shark. This was not a problem where we were, plus Wayne and I while snorkeling a few days before had found a nice pinnacle out a ways with diverse fish, some colorful sponges, sea fans, and a little hard coral, which she thoroughly enjoyed. I found more conch, but Daya wasn't interested in them, as many aren't when they see the actual body of the conch before it's cleaned. Years earlier when Wayne had broken his arm on one of our Bahamas' cruises, I had to clean the conch, and I couldn't eat it for a while afterward. I found a few nurse sharks for Daya, which delighted her, although she peered at them through her snorkel mask while keeping behind me.

Bahamas: Nurse sharks at rest.

On July 16, 2010, we pulled up anchor for the last time. It wasn't the wind and salt spray making me cry. I had gotten all our courtesy flags ready and spent the time crossing the Gulf Stream sitting at the pilot-house table stringing them on a line: forty-one countries, although we were missing a few flags. It is a tradition for circumnavigators to fly all their courtesy flags of the countries they sailed to when they arrive at their last port. We did so as we entered Fort Lauderdale harbor. We slowly skimmed by a dock to pick up the broker who would be listing *Bali Ha'i III* for sale and had arranged

dockage for us in one of the canals, and was directing us through the labyrinth to get there. We passed under several drawbridges, and a few other yachts recognized the meaning of our flags and saluted us smartly. It was over.

Final Passage: The author organizing the courtesy flags.

Final Passage: Wayne hoisting the courtesy flags.

Final Passage: Taking *Bali Ha'i III* under a drawbridge in Ft. Lauderdale harbor.

16

A Wandering Song

There are no words to the song of the ocean, but the message is and always has been simple: not to forget where we came from. The melody is locked in the water that composes much of what we are. Most humans tend to ignore the song, but not all. You are one of the lucky ones who hold the melody in your heart. But be warned: it is a wandering song carried by the winds and the currents.
—Jimmy Buffett, *A Salty Piece of Land*

None of it is important or all of it is.
—John Steinbeck, *The Log from the Sea of Cortez*

The Spirit of the Journey

There are by various counts some seventy to eighty people, starting in 1895, who have sailed around the world alone—single-handed it's called. Most who have written about it often felt totally alone, isolated not only from the human world, but at odds with the sea too. In fact, this aloneness was often their biggest problem, not the storms, not the pirates, not the ruining of their provisions, not equipment failures. Although I wouldn't and couldn't do this alone, with Wayne's increasing emotional distance, I often felt alone in spirit. I looked at what some of these single-handers had written to see if they could help me with my reintroduction to life on land.

Many of these stories even in the simplest telling are riveting. The first was Joshua Slocum, who recounted his adventure in *Sailing Around the World Alone*, which he did in *Spray*, a derelict remnant of a yacht given to him that he rebuilt into a 39-foot 9-inch sloop. He was the first person to circumnavigate single-handedly, starting at age fifty-four in 1895. Three years and two months later he returned to the very spot where he had launched *Spray*. I remember reading how he had put tacks upright on his deck to prevent pirate boardings, a trick we might have used between Yemen and Somalia. But he spoke of his aloneness too:

[I]n the dismal fog I felt myself drifting into loneliness, an insect on a straw in the midst of the elements.... The ominous, the insignificant, the great, the small, the wonderful, the commonplace— all appeared before my mental vision in magical succession.... The loneliness of my state wore off when the gale was high and I found much work to do. When fine weather returned, then came the sense of solitude, which I could not shake off. I used my voice often, at first giving some order about the affairs of a ship, for I had been told that from disuse I should lose my speech. Again from my cabin I cried to an imaginary man at the helm, "How does she head, there?" and again, "Is she on her course?" But getting no reply, I was reminded the more palpably of my condition. My voice sounded hollow on the empty air, and I dropped the practice. However, it was not long before the thought came to me that when I was a lad I used to sing; why not try that now, where it would disturb no one? My musical talent had never bred envy in others, but out on the Atlantic, to realize what it meant, you should have heard me sing. You should have seen the porpoises leap when I pitched my voice for the waves and the sea and all that was in it. Old turtles, with large eyes, poked their heads up out of the sea as I sang. But the porpoises were, on the whole, vastly more appreciative than the turtles; they jumped a deal higher.

Then there was Bernard Moitessier and his 39-foot steel ketch, *Joshua*, named for Joshua Slocum. Already an accomplished French sailor and sea bum, of sorts, he entered the first single-handed-around-the-world race, the Golden Globe, sponsored by the London Sunday Times in 1968. Much more than any novel, the story of this race is full of plot and characters, adventure and tragedy, bravery and cowardice, lies and integrity, complexity and simplicity. Moitessier was one contestant who was reluctant to be a contestant in the first place. An extremely competent sailor, more at home at sea than on land, Moitessier was as scornful of the idea of a race as he was of the modern world: "It is a thousand times truer to have men guided by heart and instinct than the twisted gimmicks of money and politics." Of the sea, he wrote shortly after leaving Great Britain, "I feel passing through my whole being the breath of the high seas that once felt is never forgotten." Off South Africa, he crossed his outbound track, thus completing a solo circumnavigation and likely would have been the winner, but instead of returning, he kept going—more than halfway around again.

Leaving from Plymouth and returning to Plymouth now seems like leaving from nowhere to go nowhere.... [I] sailed around the world...but what does that mean, since the horizon is eternal? Round the world goes further than the ends of the earth, as far as life itself, perhaps further still.[1]

And so he kept going, forsaking adulation, money, his family, the modern world. Like so many before him, from the crew of the HMS *Bounty* to Herman Melville, he set sail for Polynesia.

≈≈≈

Most of the words defining someone who has had myriad travels are pejorative: nomad, vagabond, drifter, rolling stone. For those who remember the 1950s in the United States, the term *fellow traveler* was used to describe Communist sympathizers in the neurotic times of the Cold War, as if being a traveler was quite unacceptable. While fellow traveler meant to belong to a specific ideological group; contrarily, what does it mean to not belong?

Because of this voyage, I no longer felt as though I belonged to a country, although I expected to continue living in the United States. I will vote and be a responsible citizen; but in terms of belonging, I have a different allegiance as a result of my wandering around the world in a sailboat. There are, no doubt, many people on this planet who through travel, displacement, choice, or beliefs have this sense of nonbelonging. Perhaps we could all benefit by having dual citizenship: our home country and the world at large, taking more responsibility for all who inhabit it. Travel is, as Mark Twain said, "poisonous to prejudice, bigotry, and narrow-mindedness," but, of course, it is more than that. It takes us out of ourselves and brings us back again—full circle—a circumnavigation of self.

Sitting in the cockpit one evening, I said to Wayne, "You know, if I were five years younger, I'd say, let's do this again. Just turn around and head out again."

Wayne responded, "I'd have to be ten years younger."

We may not have been ready, but *Bali Ha'i III* was. She had brand-new sails that fit perfectly, everything was fixed, some even better than originally, like the sails. I could feel she wanted to be where she could perform best. It seemed a crime to keep her tied up to a dock waiting for the right person to want to search for their own adventures out there.

≈≈≈

I had worked on my Spanish, and had been more or less understood with a smile of encouragement; I massaged my French accent until it had been usually tolerated except by fastidious and haughty French persons; I had managed limited conversations in Tongan; and had struggled with tonal Thai, but never quite heard the different sound when I was corrected with a friendly laugh. At one time, I had occasionally dreamt in French, but I have never been able to discuss concepts, express the myriad emotions of love, or tell an ironic joke in any language other than my own—thus could I really be a citizen of the world? Perhaps one of my rediscoveries of this world was that there are deeper connections than just the spoken word.

My affiliations range from Abdullah in Aden; the Lucky School kids in Palmerston, Cook Islands; the Hamera family in Eritrea; the mama whale and her calf in Tonga; the bashful, timid little Blue Penguins scurrying from sea to burrow in New Zealand and Australia; and others of the human and wildlife kingdoms around the edges of this voyage. Does having affiliations lessen my sense of displacement or heighten it?

I used to have the classic 1970s Mother Earth poster of earth from space, which intrigued me. Underneath the large photo were the words: "Love Your Mother." I remembered all the water. Now when presented with such a picture, I see Chief Jimmie on a remote island in northern Vanuatu; the orphans in Phnom Penh; the grandmother who looked her life and welcomed me into her garden in the Maldives; and others around this world path I have created.

A circumnavigation is a journey with a defined end—where it began. But that ending is strictly for electronic and paper charts. The impenetrable spirit of the journey is retained forever. For me, the combined experiences, challenges, accomplishments create an immeasurable awareness, an additional sense of the world. This is not the sixth sense defined by humans as instinct or intuition. I think of the additional sense beyond sound, sight, taste, smell, and touch that sharks have. Called the ampullae of Lorenzini, these vesicles and pores sense the electrical charges given off by all living organisms, but at close range only. Sharks use them for the final laser-like attack on their prey.

Unlike sharks, prey is not what I use my circumnavigation ampullae for, but it is like a small electrical impulse allowing me to look at close range for what I can distill from this combination of information and experiences melded together from the oceans. These oceans made up of a multitude of drops take me to the core where everything fits, everything belongs. It's not like categorizing and compartmentalizing my life, which is only an academic exercise. My ampullae convert time and space. It's not just memories and ten years of images combined with feelings, a mélange neither incongruous nor disparate. It's a new way of being. It is this that makes me feel like a citizen of the world and of belonging everywhere and nowhere.

It Is Written

It is written:
Time is inextricably interconnected
with space,
and both are relative
to one caught in that definitive,
yet infinite, envelope.

Sailing through storms and calms,
from the Gulf of Honduras
to Golfo de los Mosquitos,
the Coral Sea to the Gulf of Carpentaria,
the Andaman Sea into the Indian Ocean;
across the Nazca tectonic plate
past the Pacific plate,
the Indo-Australian plate over the Somali plate;
with the south equatorial
to the south subtropical currents,
across and down the east Australia current,
going with, then fighting,
the equatorial countercurrent;
winds abeam, forward, aft, and all points in between,
from starboard, port, dead ahead.

It is all of a piece.

My spacetime becomes a trail
of bioluminescence,
a gravitational pull,
a hand-woven silken carpet—
patterned magically with luminous silver stars
across the midnight blue of sky and sea—
all woven through
my relative existence.

This is what is left for me: I could believe there was no land, no mountains, no rocks, no trees, no soil, only this water, this landscape of moving, shimmering water: this water, gems of turquoise when the sun shines through the end of a towering wave; this water, the colors of night, the deepest blue-black in the spectrum and a color still; this water, the purple-tinged blue just before dark over two-, three-, four-thousand foot depths; there is only this water that hints at eternity. I wanted it to last forever, but there is always a landfall as the end.

What I Have Learned

My goals early on were not only to learn to see, but to feel. And in feeling is belief, and in belief, hope. Is that the point of the cycle of giving when the giver receives the real gift? And what better gift than hope?

What I learned to feel—in the deepest personal spiritual sense—is that all life is interconnected. I had known this theoretically and academically, but now I understood it from a personal perspective as one of the truths of the human spirit. It was not just my relationship with the family on Toau; but with Princess, the orangutan mother I empathized with as her son Percy scampered about in southern Borneo; Antonio who loved his land and river in Guatemala; John in Suwarrow who taught me patience and the art of making a broom.

Lessons Learned

I learned that the Earth isn't round;
although it certainly isn't flat.
It's a soft, gentle curve beckoning us
on as far as the light goes.
I learned that the earth is there for us to find.

I learned that people smile
the same through parched, cracked lips;
land-mine scared faces;
the blackest skin;
more pain than we can imagine.
I learned that people smile when you smile at them.

I learned that children believe
what you tell them.
They believe in ghosts and spirits
and that you will somehow
do the right thing for them
even if you never have.

I learned that time
isn't absolute or even constant.
It is illusory, deceptive,
and plays games with space.
I wanted to learn how to make friends
with time.
Sometimes I did.

I learned that nothing exists
by itself.
Nothing. Not a drop of oceanic water,
not a person, not a fish,

not a forest, not a word.
Nothing.

I learned, too,
that lessons find us
wherever we may be,
and if we listen
we may discover
what we believe.

I learned that a circumnavigation
isn't about sailing around the world;
it's about floating within oneself,
a womb of spacetime
that never ends.

Hatred, bias, divisiveness, and prejudice are as much poisons as those that we use to pollute the soil, air, and water. In the diversity of our languages, skin colors, customs, and beliefs is found the human beauty of this planet. I learned, saw, felt, and continue to believe that there is a desperate need for stewardship by all of us for the cultures and environment of this special planet Earth. This is part of the place I now know. This is part of me, where I started and now have returned.

Time To Say Good-bye

From my early childhood, I have always loved the sea, as I have always loved the mountains. They were the places where I could lose personal pain. They were bigger than life itself, bigger than any world I could imagine;

they were my spiritual home. I wanted them both—together. One of my persistent thoughts on this voyage was to find a place with that: a Greek island, along the Thai shore, in the Balearics? But could I ever live with both mountains and sea at once? Could I breathe for long in such a place? It seemed as if it would be a satiation, a surfeit of beauty and inspiration, an exuberance of emotion. In all my years of travel, both before and during this voyage, I never quite found this perfect place, my *querencia*, so now I choose what I chose many years ago when I moved to the Rocky Mountains of Colorado with my young children. Now I return from the sea to my mountains with salty tears to remind me of what I am losing.

In my soul I feel the whisper of the feathered vagabond spirit of the albatross who flies around the southern ocean for thousands of miles and never sets foot on land, who belongs nowhere but within the space and time in which it flies. The memories of this voyage are as interwoven in my physical self as in my soul. They are with me for life. I cannot say good-bye.

*Bali Ha'i III a*lone in a remote anchorage.

Bibliography

Bayburtluoğlu, Cevdet. *Lycia.* Kaleiçi, Turkey: Suna & Inan Kiraç Research Institute on Mediterranean Civilizations, 2004.

Buffett, Jimmy. *A Salty Piece of Land.* New York: Back Bay Books/ Little, Brown and Company, 2004.

Bulloch, David K. *The Underwater Naturalist: A layman's guide to the vibrant world beneath the sea.* New York: Lyons & Burford, 1991.

Burn, A. R. *The Pelican History of Greece.* New York: Penguin Books, 1985 (orig. *A Traveller's History of Greece,* 1965).

Daniels, Patricia, and Stephen Hyslop. *Almanac of World History.* Washington, DC: National Geographic Society, 2003.

Darwin, Charles. *The Voyage of the Beagle: Journal of Researches into the Natural History and Geology of Countries Visited During the Voyage of the H.M.S. Beagle Around the World.* New York: The Modern Library, 2001 (orig. 1908).

Dulumunmun Harrison, Max. *My People's Dreaming.* Sydney: Finch Publishing, 2009.

Gelman, Rita Golden. *Tales of a Female Nomad: Living at Large in the World.* New York: Three Rivers Press, 2001.

Grahame, Kenneth. *The Wind in the Willows.* New York: Charles Scribner's Sons, 1954 (orig. 1905).

Graves, Robert. *The Greek Myths: 1.* New York: Penguin Books, 1980 (orig. 1955).

Hamilton, Edith. *Mythology: Timeless Tales of Gods and Heroes.* New York: Mentor Books, 1942 (orig. 1940).

Homer. *The Odyssey.* Trans. Robert Fagles. New York: Viking Penguin, 1996.

Lindbergh, Anne Morrow. *Gift from the Sea.* New York: Vintage Books/Random House, Inc., 1991 (orig. 1955).

Marx, Wesley. *The Frail Ocean.* Vancouver, Canada: Hartley and Marks, 1999.

McCullough, David. *The Path Between the Seas.* New York: Simon and Schuster, 1977.

Mitchell, Andrew. *The Fragile South Pacific: An Ecological Odyssey.* Austin, TX: University of Texas Press, 1989.

Moitessier, Bernard. *The Long Way.* Dobbs Ferry, NY: Sheridan House, 1995 (orig. *La Longue Route,* 1971).

Moss, W. Stanley. *Ill Met by Moonlight.* Philadelphia, PA: Paul Dry Books, 2010 (orig. 1950).

Noyce, Philip (director). *The Rabbit-Proof Fence.* DVD. Australia: 2002. Based on the book by Doris Pilkington Garimara.

Psychoundakis, George. *The Cretan Runner.* New York, NY: Penguin Books, reissue 2009.

Rogers, Lisa. "Riding Ancient Waves." *Humanities,* May/June, Volume 20/Number 3, 1999.

Safina, Carl. *Eye of the Albatross: Visions of Hope and Survival.* New York: Henry Holt and Company, 2002.

Santayana, George. *The Life of Reason.* Amherst, NY: Prometheus Books, 1998 (orig. 1905).

Te Rangi Hiroa (Sir Peter Henry Buck). *Vikings of the Sunrise.* Microsoft reader, 2007.

Wilkinson, Clive, ed. *Status of Coral Reefs of the World: 2004, vols. 1 and 2.* Townsville, Australia: Australian Institute of Marine Science, 2004.

Notes

*A*s I stated in Author's Notes, most of the historical and cultural information about the countries we visited is from many diverse sources ranging from placards and brochures at sites I visited to stories and legends from local people; from museums to publications by the country's historical, cultural, and tourist departments; and, of course, books from guide books to Homer's *The Odyssey*. It is not possible to cite them all, but when relating unusual, not commonly known stories, I have tried to provide a corroborating source—often from the Internet—even if that was not my original source. Do not include the final period when copying URLs to access websites.

Chapter 2

1. Yasmin Saikia, *Fragmented Memories: Struggling to be Tai-Ahom in India* (Durham, NC: Duke University Press, 2004).
2. Jared Diamond, *Collapse: How Societies Choose to Fail or Succeed* (New York: Viking, 2005).
3. Yasmin Saikia, *Fragmented Memories*.
4. www.unfpa.org/pds/trends.htm.
5. Robert S. Ridgely and John A. Gwynne, Jr., *A Guide to the Birds of Panama*, 2nd ed. (Princeton, NJ: Princeton University Press, 1989).
6. Peter Rudiak-Gould, *Surviving Paradise: A Year in the Marshall Islands* (New York: Union Square Press, 2009).
7. David McCullough, *The Path Between the Seas* (New York: Simon and Schuster, 1977). This is an excellent rendition of all this and more.

Chapter 3

1. Wayne J. Arendt, "Range Expansion of the Cattle Egret (*Bubulcus ibis*) in the Greater Caribbean Basin," *Colonial Waterbirds*, vol. 11, no. 2 (Waterbird Society, 1988): 252–262; www.avianweb.com/cattleegrets.html.
2. www.proserpineecotours.com.au/crocs.htm.
3. www.academia.edu/1228776/Rethinking_Polynesian_mobility_A_new_Polynesian_Triangle.
4. www.pbs.org/wayfinders/polynesian2.html.
5. www.hokulea.org/moolelo/.
6. Ibid.

Chapter 4

1. www.cookislands.org.uk/marsters.html; cookislands.org.uk/marsters-claim.html#.UcZQr5zhfKo.
2. www.samoa.co.uk/history.html.
3. U.S. General Accounting Office 2006 Report, *U.S. Insular Areas: Economic, Fiscal, and Financial Accountability Challenges* (GAO report number GAO-07-119, December 13, 2006).
4. www.gao.gov/products/GAO-10-347.
5. www.whc.unesco.org/en/list/715.
6. www.marinebio.org/species.asp?id=39.
7. Unfortunately all my whale pictures are videotape. Clinton Bauder, a professional photographer, was kind enough to allow me to use one of his photos, although this Humpback happens to be in Alaska, where I also had seen Humpbacks some years ago.
8. www.hwrf-uk.org/About-humpback-whales.html.

9. www.csiwhalesalive.org/newsletters/csi07303.html.
10. Wesley Marx, *The Frail Ocean* (Vancouver, Canada: Hartley and Marks, 1999).
11. Ibid.
12. For a highly recommended Gray whale watching experience in Mexico check out this website—it's much closer to the United States than Tonga—www.pachicosecotours.com.
13. *San Francisco Chronicle*, July 2, 2007.

Chapter 5

1. www.greatbarrierreef.org/great-barrier-reef-facts.php; geography.about.com/od/belizemaps/a/Belize-Barrier-Reef.htm.
2. www.csiwhalesalive.org/newsletters/csi07303.html; www.sci.waikato.ac.nz/evolution/geologicalHistory.shtml.
3. www.nzbirds.com/birds/haasteagle.html.
4. www.terranature.org/flightlessBirds.htm.
5. www.erranature.org/moa.htm.
6. www.teara.govt.nz/en/extinctions/page-4.
7. www.newzealandecology.org/nzje/free_issues/NZJEcol12_s_11.pdf.

Chapter 6

1. www.independent.co.uk/news/world/australasia/pacific-islanders-fatal-diet-blamed-on-kiwi-exports-655190.html.

Chapter 7

1. www.australiangeographic.com.au/journal/top-30-deadly-animals-in-australia.htm.
2. www.co-ops.nos.noaa.gov/restles1.html.
3. www.flyingdoctor.org.au/default.aspx.
4. www.humanrights.gov.au/timeline-history-separation-aboriginal-and-torres-strait-islander-children-their-families-text.
5. Morten Rasmussen, et al., "An Aboriginal Australian Genome Reveals Separate Human Dispersals into Asia," *Science* 7 ,vol.

334, no. 6052 (October 2011): 94–98; www.sciencemag.org/content/334/6052/94/suppl/DC1.
6. Inga Clendinnen, *Inside the Contact Zone: Part 1* (Australian Broadcasting Corporation's Radio National, Boyer Lectures, December 5, 1999).
7. Max Dulumunmun Harrison, *My People's Dreaming* (Sydney: Finch Publishing, 2009).
8. Ibid.

Chapter 8

1. For more information on this excellent klotok tour and more, see www.OrangutanGreenTours.com. This is run by Herry (pronounced Harry) Roustaman, a local person who has done much for his community. When you travel overseas, especially for adventures, ecotourism, or local color, it's really important to use local entrepreneurs, not U.S.-based travel companies who put little back into the local economy you're visiting. You can experience so much more using local people.
2. George Santayana, *The Life of Reason, vol. 1* (www.gutenberg.org/ebooks/15000; orig. New York: Charles Scribner's & Sons, 1905).
3. www.yale.edu/cgp/.
4. *The Flute Player* (Over the Moon Productions, Inc. 2003, Documentary, DVD); www.pbs.org/pov/thefluteplayer/credits.php.

Chapter 9

1. www.ajaratetanks.site11.com/kalawewa.htm.
2. For additional information on the Sri Lankan civil war and United States involvement see the following: www.gpo.gov/fdsys/pkg/CPRT-111SPRT53866/html/CPRT-111SPRT53866.htm; www.economist.com/node/398302, the online source for «Sirimavo Bandaranaike: Sirimavo Bandaranaike, a 'first' among women, died on October 10th, aged 84," *The Economist*, October 19, 2000; www.globalresearch.ca/top-level-talks-continue-on-us-led-military-intervention-in-sri-lanka; www.fas.org/sgp/crs/row/RL31707.pdf.

3. srilankacoffee.com/history1.html.

4. Ibid.

5. There is an interesting side note to Sri Lanka's coffee story. Today an expat and his Sri Lankan wife have reinstituted a sustainable, environmentally sound, fair traded, and, by all reports an excellent, coffee business, Hansa Ceylon Coffee, and there may be others following suit. For more information see srilankacoffee.com/.

6. www.triposo.com/loc/Yemen; www.bbc.co.uk/history/ancient/cultures/sheba_01.shtml.

7. www.fanack.com/countries/yemen/history/prehistory.

8. www.nationsonline.org/oneworld/History/Yemen-history.htm.

9. Ibid.

10. www.reuters.com/article/2012/02/21/us-yemen-idUSTRE81J0RQ20120221.

11. www.thebureauinvestigates.com/2013/01/03/yemen-reported-us-covert-actions-2013/.

12. www.yementimes.com/en/1686/culture/2497/You-better-not-be-chewing-qat-right-now!.htm.

13. Mohammed Mahmoud Al-Zoubairi, 1958, Quoted in *Qat in Yemen and in Yemeni Life* (translated from Arabic) (Sana'a, Yemen: Center for Yemeni Studies, 1982).

Chapter 10

1 www.eritrea.be/old/eritrea-history.htm.

2. www.africanhistory.about.com/od/eritrea/p/EritreaHist1.htm.

3. Ibid.

4. www.adroub.net/default.aspx?page=History%20Suakin%20in%201541.

5. Nefertari was the first and most beloved chief queen of Ramesses the Great (II). A PBS special and subsequent website stated, "Although Ramesses was primarily in love with himself, he was also devoted to Nefertari and wrote at length of his love and her beauty. He demonstrated this by building her a magnificent tomb, the finest in the Valley of the Queens." www.pbs.org/empires/egypt/newkingdom/nefertari.html.

6. www.history.com/topics/hatshepsut.

7. www.womenshistory.about.com/od/hatshepsut/a/How-Did-Hapshepsut-Die.htm.

8. www.ngm.nationalgeographic.com/print/2009/04/hatshepsut/brown-text.

Chapter 11

1. www.kypros.org/Cyprus/history.html. This website covers basic Cypriot history, but, as with so many places I have written about, most of my information came from visiting historic sites, museums, and talking to people there including archeologists and museum curators, thus I have not cited each paragraph; see also www.cypnet.co.uk/ncyprus/history/.

2. Ibid.

3. For more detailed information from various perspectives about the Cyprus situation see the following: www.rcenter.intercol.edu/Newsletter/In%20Depth/volume%206%20issue%204/article09.htm; www.kypros.org/Cyprus/history.html; www.hentucky.co.uk/archive/editorial/talkingpoints/talking_19742.htm; www.cypnet.co.uk/ncyprus/history/british/; www.mfa.gov.tr/cyprus-in-the-period-1571-1959.en.mfa.

4. George Santayana, *The Life of Reason*. This quote has frequently been attributed to Plato, but it doesn't appear to have been found in his writings.

5. www.naqshbandi.org/ottomans/protectors/protectors.htm; www.historyofwar.org/articles/weapons_janissaries.html: this is the site for J. Rickard's (10 October 2000), *Janissaries (Ottoman Empire)* article.

6. As was true for many sites I visited, my information about Ephesus came from being there and the Ephesus guidebook in English.

7. Like Ephesus, my information about Cappadocia comes from being there, the historic sites themselves, guidebooks, and local historians.

8. Cevdet Bayburtluoğlu, *Lycia (*Kaleiçi, Turkey: Suna & Inan Kiraç Research Institute on Mediterranean Civilizations, 2004).

9. Edith Hamilton, *Mythology* (New York: New York American Library, Inc., 1942).

10. A. R. Burn, *The Pelican History of Greece* (New York: Penguin Books, 1985, orig. 1965); Robert Graves, *The Greek Myths: 1* (New York: Penguin Books, 1980, orig. 1955).

11. George Psychoundakis, *The Cretan Runner* (New York, NY: Penguin Books, reissue 2009).

12. www.guardian.co.uk/news/2006/feb/21/guardianobituaries/secondworldwar; en.wikipedia.org/wiki/George_Psychoundakis.

13. Annina Valkana, *The Knights of Rhodes* (Attiki, Athens, Greece: Michael Toubis Editions, 2005).

Chapter 12

1. *Querncia* also defines in Spanish the place in a bullfight ring where the wounded bull goes to regain his strength. From that, it has apparently evolved to have this greater meaning, or, perhaps it is the other way around. Either way it is a word with an interesting etymology and a profound meaning.

2. www.sacred-destinations.com/greece/delos.

3. Homer, *The Odyssey*, trans. by Robert Fagles (New York: Viking Penguin, 1996).

4. Ibid.

5. Ibid.

6. www.history.com/this-day-in-history/the-battle-of-actium.

Chapter 13

1. Ibn Majah 1/224 and Tirmidhi 218.

2. Tirmidhi 5197.

3. Tradition alleges that this saying was inscribed on the Pillars of Hercules that flank the Straits of Gibraltar. The strong implication was that beyond was the dangerous unknown. The Pillars are Gibraltar on the north and probably Jebel Musa in Morocco to the south, although that one is not agreed on.

Chapter 15

1. www.oceanexplorer.noaa.gov/explorations/03trench/trench/trench.html.

2. *Saving the Ocean with Carl Safina*, Season 1, "Scourge of the Lionfish" (The Chedd-Angier Production Company, 2012; distributed by PBS Distribution, 2013; DVD).

Chapter 16

1. Bernard Moitessier, *The Long Way* (Dobbs Ferry, NY: Sheridan House, 1995; orig. *La Longue Route*, 1971).

Readers Guide

Note: Some questions were adapted from LitLovers, an online community.

1. Which countries or cultures did you find most interesting and why? Were you surprised at any of the author's revelations? What was surprising, intriguing, or difficult to understand about those other cultures?

2. Why do you think the author used poetry in addition to her text to express some experiences? Did it help you to understand or picture the situations?

3. What are some of the examples the author gave of her environmental concerns? Have you witnessed similar issues? Did she make you rethink any of these concerns? Did she provide adequate information about why she thinks what she does?

4. What main point(s) does the author make? Do you agree with her? What evidence or arguments does she use to support her position? Is the evidence convincing, definitive, or speculative? Does the author depend on personal opinion, observation, and assessment? Or is the evidence factual—based on science, historical documents, or quotations from credible experts?

5. Are any of the issues the author discusses relevant to your own life? Was there anything she wrote about that affected how you think?

6. What kind of language does the author use? Is it objective and dispassionate? Or passionate and earnest? Is it polemical, inflammatory, sarcastic? Does the language help or undercut the author's premises?

7. How controversial are the issues raised in the book? Who is aligned on which sides of those issues? Where do you fall in that line-up?

8. Talk about specific passages that struck you as significant—or interesting, profound, amusing, illuminating, disturbing, sad? What was memorable, and why did you find that memorable?

9. What have you learned after reading this book? Has it broadened your perspective about a difficult issue—personal or societal? Has it introduced you to something you didn't know before, but now might be interested in?

10. What do you think were the author's favorite places? What would have been your favorite places if you had been taking this voyage? Why?

11. Do you think the author was courageous or just curious about the world? Does curiosity sometimes require risk? What sort of risks would you take to explore an aspect of the world you're interested in?

12. Did you find the word *querencia* (heart place, place where you find your inner strength) interesting? Do you think you know where your *querencia* is?

CPSIA information can be obtained
at www.ICGtesting.com
Printed in the USA
FSOW03n1048130115
4441FS